The Ancient Schools of Gloucester

The Ancient Schools of Gloucester

A study of education from medieval times until 1800

DAVID EVANS

THE CHOIR PRESS

First published in the United Kingdom in 2022 by
The Choir Press

ISBN 978-1-78963-295-8

*To the students and teachers of the schools of the
City of Gloucester, past, present and future*

Contents

Contents

INTRODUCTION

A Thousand Years of History

Although a relatively small city, Gloucester is blessed to have among its educational establishments three ancient schools: the Crypt School, King's School and Sir Thomas Rich's School. Each of these traces its origins back to the 16th and 17th centuries and in some cases to medieval schools that preceded them. The creation of Gloucester's very first school is lost in the mists of time, but most probably occurred approximately a thousand years ago, perhaps in the years between 1020 and 1022. It is an event that deserves to be better known, but such is the shortage of hard evidence that to hold millennium-style commemorations would be fraught with difficulties akin to celebrating a birthday without having a birth certificate.

The earliest providers of education in our city were the cloister, almonry and song schools run by St Peter's Abbey, which is now Gloucester Cathedral, and the two grammar schools sponsored by the priories of St Oswald and Llanthony Secunda. Historians have some knowledge about how these schools were run and the individuals associated with them, but it is usually dependent on patchy references in documents that deal primarily with other issues, such as legal cases or leases on properties. Building around the few definitive facts that emerge, an overall picture can be created, but it is one with many gaps that can only be filled by making comparisons with other locations, assuming that Gloucester followed a similar pattern.

From Tudor times, when both the Crypt and the King's School were founded or re-founded, evidence becomes much more plentiful, although focused mainly on the lives and religious views of important headmasters. Every attempt has been made in this study to try to delve deeper into the way the schools operated, what the pupils learnt and how they felt about their education, but for this our references are tantalisingly sparse, especially in the case of elementary schools.

The difficulties in putting together a work of this kind have been acknowledged by many who have gone before. One of the very first people known to have been educated in Gloucester Abbey, Gerald of Wales, wrote this in his *Journey Through Wales* in 1191: 'Writing is a demanding task: first you decide what to leave out, and then you have to polish what you put in. What you finally commit to parchment must face the eagle eye of many readers, now and in the future, and at the same time run the risk of meeting hostile criticism'.

The inspiration for this book has come from a lifetime spent teaching in one of our ancient schools. A further inspiration has been Nicholas Orme's great study, *Medieval Schools from Roman Britain to Renaissance England*. This is the seminal work for anyone in search of the national picture against which the story of Gloucester's ancient schools is set, and it is Professor Orme's study that has provided the direct basis for the development of the medieval educational scene outlined in this book.

Schools in all ages tend to reflect the expectations of the society in which they exist, which means that for the period before 1800 we are required to set aside the assumptions that underpin our modern system of state-provided, free and compulsory education. We need to step outside the world we have today of highly organised schools with hundreds of pupils, expensive buildings and equipment, and a staff of specialist teachers with guaranteed salaries. All of these are relatively recent developments, the product of the last 200 years or so. To a much greater extent than now, life before the 19th century was ordered by the ever-present influence of the Church, society was much more small scale and gross inequalities lay at the heart of almost everything that happened. The state, which dominates modern education, had little or no interest in it before 1800. Education was utterly different from today because it developed in a very different social order.

Any judgements passed on the quality of the education provided by Gloucester's various schools have tried to take into account the startling differences that existed in expectations before 1800. For most of the period covered by this book, schools were little more than a group of children with a teacher meeting in any available room. Education was inevitably limited to a small minority and was the preserve of a male-dominated elite. Attendance at a school of any kind required a financial outlay that was beyond most families who operated at or near subsistence level; and Gloucester appears to have had no provision for female education outside the home until the 18th century.

By the end of the timescale of this book, things were just beginning to change and the range of schools available was growing and beginning to take on something of its modern appearance. Part of the increasingly varied provision included a number of privately run schools for girls, Sir Thomas Rich's Hospital catering for apprentice boys, a charity school and a plethora of Sunday schools, which extended basic education to some of the poorest children in the city. By 1800 the state was on the verge of making its first financial commitment towards mass education and in the decades that followed new schools were quickly established in every parish in and around the city. It is this that makes 1800 a suitable terminal point for any study into the origins of our most ancient schools.

Whilst thoroughly detailed books already exist outlining the histories of each of these individual establishments, I hope that this work will contribute a new insight by bringing the stories of the Crypt, King's, Sir Thomas Rich's and other now lost institutions together into a single chronological volume. Twenty-first-century Gloucester is fortunate to have a rich and stimulating educational provision offered by a variety of very different schools; and so it has been for many, many centuries, possibly even for a millennium.

CHAPTER ONE

Gloucester's First School:

Our Anglo-Saxon Inheritance

The monastic school at St Peter's Abbey

'The School of the Cathedral is of very ancient origin, being co-eval with the abbey.'[1] So wrote the antiquarian and topographical author Nicholas Carlisle in 1818. Over the course of the next century this assertion that education in Gloucester dated back to early medieval times produced a widespread belief that the city's first school was, in fact, established in the year 1072. When he opened new buildings for King's School on the Pitt Street site in 1929, the educational reformer and composer, Sir Henry Hadow, cited 1072 as the date of the school's foundation. 'Since 1072', he said, 'the school has taken part in the work of Gloucester and the history of the county.'[2]

The reference to 1072 is based on documentary evidence that demonstrates that the predecessor of Gloucester Cathedral, the Abbey of St Peter, at that date already had a tradition of taking in young boys and training them for careers in the church. The reference occurs in the *Historia Monasterii Sancti Petri Gloucestriae*. Usually known simply as the *Historia*, this was a document written in about 1400 by an unknown monk to record the history of St Peter's since its foundation by Prince Osric in 679. One of the original versions can still be seen in Gloucester Cathedral Library. When it mentions details of life inside St Peter's Abbey itself, we must presume that the *Historia* has a fair degree of accuracy. It almost certainly drew on a now lost year-by-year chronicle of events thought to have been begun as early as the 11th century by a Gloucester monk named Gregory of Caerwent.[3] Relating to the arrival of the

---

1   N. Carlisle, *A Concise Description of the Endowed Grammar Schools in England and Wales*, volume 1, London (1818), p. 449.
2   *The King's School Magazine*, No. 21, Christmas Term 1929, volume vi, p. 5.
3   M. Hare, 'The Chronicle of Gregory of Caerwent', *Glevensis*, volume 27 (1994), p. 42.

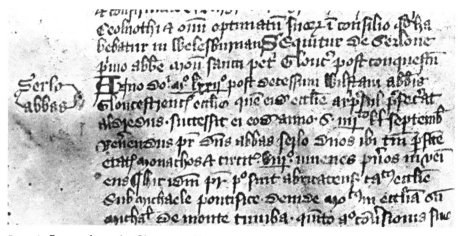

Figure 1: Extract from the Gloucester Historia, the medieval Latin document that refers to the arrival of Abbot Serlo in Gloucester in 1072, when he discovered 'eight little boys' receiving an education at St Peter's Abbey.

Norman Abbot Serlo, it states that 'in the year of Our Lord 1072, after the death of Wilstan abbot of the Gloucester Church whom Archbishop Aldred had put in charge, there succeeded to him the same year, to be exact on August 29th, the reverend father Lord Abbot Serlo, finding there only two monks of full age and about eight little boys'.[4]

There is no doubt that this extract records, albeit in passing, the existence of a monastery school here in Gloucester. To the modern reader eight boys may seem like a very small school, but it is important to appreciate that medieval education was not the same as that of our own day. We are familiar with schools taking in hundreds or even thousands of pupils, but this is a notion that emerged only in Victorian times, when great hope was placed in the scope offered by mass production. It would have been an idea alien to the medieval world, in which communities were much more small scale. The medieval view of a school was of an institution catering for a small number, maybe a handful, of young people, providing them with educational opportunities that could not be realised in the home.

---

[4] *Historia Monasterii Sancti Petri*, translated by William Barber (1988) and printed as Appendix XV in D. Welander, *The History, Art and Architecture of Gloucester Cathedral*, Alan Sutton (1991), p. 602.

The statement in the *Historia* does not, of course, refer to the actual foundation of Gloucester's first school. It gives no ground for suspecting that in 1072 education was in any way a new development within the abbey precincts, as it simply records a small school already in existence. The most well-known date in English history, 1066, has often been seen as a crucial watershed with the Norman Conquest bringing a radically different way of life to this country. This view has, however, been modified by recent historians, especially as far as social history is concerned.[5] The modern consensus is that in most respects the Normans who took control of England at the Battle of Hastings were less likely to be innovators than to build on existing practice. This means that it is probable that a school such as the one at Gloucester Abbey, which first appears in documents shortly after 1066, would already have been in existence in Anglo-Saxon times. The documentary evidence we have comes just six years after the Battle of Hastings, a short and chaotic period marked by rebellions when it is unlikely any radically new developments would have taken place in education.

Possible origins of the school in Anglo-Saxon times

Following the advent of Christianity in the early days of the Anglo-Saxons, monasteries and minster churches became the providers of education in England. They were by their very nature centres of literacy, since priests and monks were required to worship with books and to study religious texts. One of the very first references to the creation of schools in England is dated to the year 635 when, according to the Venerable Bede, King Sigbert of the East Angles 'founded a school for the education of boys. In this project he was assisted by Bishop Felix who had come to him from Kent and had provided him with teachers and masters from the school in Canterbury'.[6]

There were more than 200 monasteries in England by the year 800. One of these was St Peter's Abbey in Gloucester founded in 679 by Osric, a leader of the Hwicce, a Saxon-dominated group who became Christian

---

5   C. Daniell, *From Norman Conquest to Magna Carta*, Routledge (2003), p. 21.
6   Bede, *A History of the English Church and People*, edited by L. Sherley-Price, Penguin (1955), pp. 166–7.

about 660 and settled in the southern part of what eventually became the Kingdom of Mercia.[7] The exact location of this abbey, roughly on the site of Gloucester Cathedral, is unknown today. It may have been on the site of the cloisters, but more likely just to the south of the present Cathedral in the area recently landscaped with planting and seating.[8] Initially it functioned as a 'double foundation' and was led by Osric's sister, Kyneburga, as a single religious community shared by male monks and female nuns. The admission of nuns was dropped after 767 and St Peter's quietly transformed itself into a small minster church staffed entirely by male secular clergy.[9] The minster resembled the earlier monastery with a community based around a set pattern of regular religious worship, but the rules of monastic life were applied less strictly. The clergy, known as secular canons, used the church as a basis for evangelism and, unlike cloistered monks, several lived in their own homes outside the minster itself.[10]

No documentary evidence exists to confirm whether or not this minster had a school of any kind associated with it. The lack of hard evidence means that in our search for the possible origins of the school that developed at St Peter's, the very first school in Gloucester, we have to resort to assumptions based on comparisons with other similar settlements and on our awareness of local circumstances. We should not be surprised by this. Even in the best documented cities, such as Canterbury, we have tantalisingly few references to the various schools known to have been set up. It is almost impossible to trace the fortunes of a single school with any certainty at this time, leaving no alternative but to make informed speculation based on evidence from other similarly placed towns.

The case that pre-Conquest minsters, largely under the influence of St Dunstan, were responsible for the creation of a network of small schools was argued robustly by Arthur Leach, the most significant early 20th-century historian to survey the national educational scene.[11] He

---

[7] C. Heighway, *Anglo-Saxon Gloucestershire*, Alan Sutton (1987), pp. 35–8.

[8] T. Pain, *The Pre-Conquest History of St Peter's Abbey*, Gloucester Cathedral Guides (2018), p. 11.

[9] D. Welander, *The History, Art and Architecture of Gloucester Cathedral*, Alan Sutton (1991), pp. 6–8 & 10.

[10] C. Heighway, *Anglo-Saxon Gloucestershire*, p. 98.

[11] A. F. Leach, *The Schools of Medieval England*, Methuen (1915), pp. 79–80.

emphasised that the manner in which minster churches were endowed with precious objects, such as sacred books, naturally inclined them to become providers of education. Judging from the evidence of other minsters, this led him to suggest that formal education at Gloucester may have begun during the lifetime of the minster established in 767.

There is, however, no documentary proof for the existence of a minster school at St Peter's and a consideration of Gloucester's specific local circumstances actually casts doubt on the likelihood of such a school. For most of its existence, the minster of St Peter's was neither the principal nor the most flourishing religious foundation in Gloucester. It seems to have suffered severely during the brief Viking occupation of Gloucester in the winter of 877 – 78.[12] Thereafter and throughout the 10th century St Peter's was overshadowed by a rival minster established close by under the patronage of the West Saxon rulers of England. This was the minster of St Oswald's founded just before the year 900 by King Alfred the Great's daughter, Aethelflaed, the 'Lady of the Mercians', and her husband, Aethelred. It was part of the important garrison town (or 'burh'), which they created at Gloucester to help protect Mercia from future Danish attacks.[13] Looking at the ruin that exists today, it is hard to imagine the splendour and importance that St Oswald's originally had. Its apse was built in the latest Carolingian style and it had an interior so richly decorated with brightly coloured carved ornamentation that one contemporary described it as the 'golden minster'.[14] Its significance was underlined in 909 when Aethelflaed gave it the relics of St Oswald of Northumbria, king and martyr, which she transferred from Bardney in Danish-held Lincolnshire. It is likely that her intention was to elevate St Oswald's to become the religious capital of Mercia. Aethelred was buried in the crypt at St Oswald's on his death in 911, as was Aethelflaed when she died in 918.[15] St Oswald's remained the foremost religious centre in Gloucester for a hundred years or more, continuing to benefit from royal

---

[12] C. Heighway, S. Hamilton et alii, *Gloucester Cathedral: Faith, Art and Architecture*, Scala (2011), pp. 10–11.

[13] C. Heighway, *Anglo-Saxon Gloucestershire*, p. 43.

[14] C. Heighway, 'St Oswald's Priory – Gloucester's Oldest Church Building', *Glevensis*, volume 12 (1978), p. 47.

[15] C. Heighway and R. Bryant, 'The Golden Minster', CBA Research Report 117, Council for British Archaeology (1999), p. 11.

Figure 2: The ruins of St Oswald's Priory, Gloucester's most important religious building from the 10th century once known as the 'golden minster'.

Figure 3: Sculpture known as the 'Christos', which is one of the few remnants of the Anglo-Saxon Abbey of St Peter, probable location of Gloucester's first school.

patronage, keeping close links with the palace at Kingsholm and being known as 'the royal chapel of St Oswald'.[16] It is unlikely under such conditions that its less fortunate neighbour, the minster at St Peter's, would have had either the material resources or a sufficiently confident outward-looking mentality to found Gloucester's first school.

The Benedictine Reform Movement

Circumstances did not change for St Peter's until the 11th century following the accession in 1016 of the Viking king Cnut, whose homeland in Denmark had been Christianised two generations previously. Cnut began his reign as a Viking warrior, but he went on to become a founder of churches and a pious Christian king married to Aethelred the Unready's widow, Emma of Normandy.[17] He took a personal interest in education and, according to Herman the Archdeacon, an 11th-century historian of Bury St Edmunds, 'whenever he went to any famous monastery or borough, he sent there at his own expense boys to be taught for the clerical or monastic order'.[18] For reasons that are not entirely clear, Cnut removed royal patronage from St Oswald's in Gloucester, and began instead to favour the old minster of St Peter. This process resulted in the transformation of St Peter's from a minster staffed by secular priests into a fully functioning monastery with a community of black-robed monks basing their liturgical practice on the Benedictine Rule and blessed by patronage from the new house that ruled England. The exact date when this shift in royal patronage took place is not reliably recorded, but it was probably about the year 1022.[19] The change is recorded in the *Historia*: 'Wulfstan, the Bishop of Worcester, canonically and under the Benedictine Rule summoned the clergy who formerly had governed and guarded the Church of St Peter with the protection of God and the Apostles Peter and Paul and consecrated Edric as abbot and guardian of that monastery'.[20]

---

[16] H. Medland, 'St Oswald's Priory Gloucester', *Transactions of the Bristol and Gloucestershire Archaeological Society* (1888), volume 13, p. 118.

[17] M. K. Lawson, *Cnut: England's Viking King*, Tempus (2004), p. 121.

[18] A. F. Leach, *The Schools of Medieval England*, p. 91.

[19] C. Heighway and R. Bryant, 'The Golden Minster', p. 42.

[20] *Historia Monasterii Sancti Petri*, translated by William Barber, p. 600.

Whilst the existence of a school within the old minster cannot be ruled out, it is most likely that the Benedictines who arrived at this time were responsible for bringing formal education to Gloucester.[21] Other parts of the country saw the impact of the Benedictines long before Gloucester as the revival of this type of monasticism had begun in Wessex in the 930s under kings Athelstan and Edgar and the pioneering figure of St Dunstan.[22] The Benedictines saw education, good teaching and book resources as essential elements of a fervent spiritual life.[23] About 970 a church council at Winchester approved a code of religious observances for monasteries called the 'Harmonisation of the Rule', which included directions for the care and duties of monastic children. They were required to attend at least three of the eight daily monastic services. They went to bed like the monks in the early evening and had to rise at midnight for the service of matins or nocturns. They were to be looked after by a guardian and never left alone with an adult monk, even the guardian, presumably for what today we would call safeguarding reasons.[24] The Benedictine schools established across southern England followed a curriculum that began with the teaching of the alphabet in both English and Latin, followed by reading texts based on the Lord's Prayer and the Psalms. The study of Latin grammar came next, with two popular English grammarians writing specifically for schools, Aelfric of Eynsham and his pupil Aelfric Beata.[25] The more senior pupils then progressed to reading the works of Christian authors such as Donatus and Classical Roman writers such as Virgil and Cato.[26]

Benedictine monasticism arrived in Gloucester quite late. Of all the minsters and monasteries in Gloucestershire, St Peter's was in fact the last to be reformed along Benedictine lines.[27] Even after 1022 there was opposition to the presence of the Benedictines, since local landowners regarded the business practices of the new monks as a threat to their property and privileges. A text written in Tudor times entitled *The Rhyming History of the Abbey of St Peter* claims that seven of the monks

---

[21]   C.Heighway, *Anglo-Saxon Gloucestershire*, p. 47.

[22]   G. Hindley, *A Brief History of the Anglo-Saxons*, Constable & Robinson (2006), p. 280.

[23]   J. Lawson & H. Silver, *A Social History of Education in England*, Methuen (1973), p. 13.

[24]   N. Orme, *Medieval Schools from Roman Britain to Renaissance England*, Yale University Press (2006), pp. 36-37.

[25]   A. Mould, *The English Chorister: A History*, London (2007), p. 13.

[26]   S. G. Hodgson, *Climbing Ladders: Childhood and Monastic Formation in England*, Lady Margaret Hall D.Phil. Thesis, Oxford (2019), p. 70.

[27]   C. Heighway, *Anglo-Saxon Gloucestershire*, p. 101.

were murdered on the road to Churcham in 1033 by a landowner named Ulfine de Rue.[28] Nonetheless, despite initial setbacks, the fortunes of the abbey did improve significantly under the Benedictines in the years leading up to the Norman Conquest. In the absence of evidence to the contrary, it may well be that part of the expansion that occurred at St Peter's at this time included the creation of the abbey's first school. King Edward the Confessor convened no fewer than nine councils to meet at Gloucester during his reign from 1042 until 1066. Several of these were held at Christmas and incorporated a prestigious ritual known as 'crown-wearing'.[29] This was a ceremony borrowed from the Carolingian kings of Germany, which involved a procession from the royal palace at Kingsholm to St Peter's Abbey, where part of the coronation would be re-enacted.[30]

We shall never know exactly when or where Gloucester's first school was created. As was the case in many other parts of the country, the event was not recorded in written sources. Schooling may have been a feature of life in old St Peter's Minster, although this had few resources and was never able to flourish because of its proximity to its more successful rival at St Oswald's. It is more likely that education arrived in the form of a small school set up by the first Benedictines sometime after the monastery was reformed about the year 1022. Despite an uncertain start, this monastery was to survive in the last years of Anglo-Saxon England and later to flourish following the arrival of the Normans, who kept alive the memory of the 'eight little boys' they found being educated and passed this on via oral tradition until the document we now know as the *Historia* was written in about 1400.

The school that existed at Gloucester from the 11th century was a pioneer. Through the Middle Ages it would develop into a highly regarded cloister school and later into the almonry and song schools that may be considered as the direct predecessors of today's King's School, which occupies a similar site within the confines of St Peter's Abbey, now Gloucester Cathedral.

---

[28] D. Welander, *The History, Art and Architecture of Gloucester Cathedral*, p. 16.
[29] M. Hare, 'Kings, Crowns and Festivals: The Origin of Gloucester as a Royal Ceremonial Centre', *Transactions of the Bristol and Gloucestershire Archaeological Society*, CXV (1997), p. 43.
[30] C. Heighway, S. Hamilton et alii, *Gloucester Cathedral: Faith, Art and Architecture*, p. 11.

CHAPTER TWO

The Cloister School in St Peter's Abbey:

The Growth of Scholarship during the 12th and 13th Centuries

The Benedictine child-oblates

The Abbey of St Peter at Gloucester grew as a centre of learning in the years after the Norman Conquest, raising the fortunes of the small school it supported. It took in boys who were destined for monastic life and those who required a firm grounding in Latin for other roles in the church or administration.

William the Conqueror appointed Serlo, a monk from Mont St Michel, as the first Norman abbot of Gloucester in 1072. He was one of a number of church leaders brought over from Normandy to set about reforming the English church. At Gloucester specifically he was entrusted with the tasks of enforcing the Benedictine Rule more intensely, increasing the number of monks and improving the abbey's financial position. Once these aims had been met, Serlo was allowed to rebuild the Saxon abbey in the latest Norman or Romanesque style.[1] This rebuilding began in 1089 and, although Serlo himself died in 1104, most of the basic structure that makes up the Cathedral we know today had been completed by about 1130. As well as having the intellect to produce the master plan for this building, Serlo was a charismatic personality able to lead and inspire others. A 13th-century effigy on the south side of the quire is traditionally said to be a monument to Serlo; the recumbent figure may originally have covered his grave and shows his head supported by two angels.[2] Serlo is also

---

[1] C. Heighway, S. Hamilton et alii, *Gloucester Cathedral: Faith, Art and Architecture*, Scala (2011), pp. 12–14.

[2] D. Welander, *The History, Art and Architecture of Gloucester Cathedral*, Alan Sutton (1991), p. 25.

Figure 4: Thirteenth-century effigy thought to be of Abbot Serlo.

Figure 5: Gloucester's Benedictine monks, as depicted in a Cathedral stained-glass window.

commemorated at the King's School where, since the 1920s, one of the day houses has been named in his honour.

It was from the time of Abbot Serlo that Gloucester Abbey had the Benedictine Rule applied to it strictly. This Rule, which had been drawn up by St Benedict in Italy about the year 535, placed great importance on young people as one of the major sources of recruitment into the monasteries. It encouraged parents to offer their sons in childhood on the assumption that the boys concerned would grow up to become monks and remain so for the rest of their lives. These boys were to be placed in the charge of the cellarer of the monastery, under the abbot's supervision, until they reached fourteen or fifteen, which was regarded as the age of adulthood.[3] Appropriate food was to be given to them, overriding the requirement for fasting imposed on adult monks.[4] The Rule states that the young boys were also required to attend church and learn how to recite the daily services, psalms, antiphons, responds and lessons. In order to do this, the Rule envisaged that they would need education and rigorous training.

Following the Benedictine Rule, Gloucester Abbey educated a small number of boys each year throughout the 12th century. These boys were known as child-oblates.[5] They were usually presented to the abbey at the age of seven, which was regarded as the boundary between infancy and childhood, and received free board and lodging inside the monastery precincts. They attended most of the services held by the monks, although rather than being allowed to sing in the quire itself they were generally confined to a separate retro-choir, which at Gloucester was most likely to have been between the monks' stalls and the pulpitum screen at the east end of the nave. They practised plainsong chants, learnt to read psalms and canticles and were introduced to Latin grammar in a small 'cloister school', which was supervised by a trustworthy monk known as the 'guardian of the children'.[6]

Some of the details of the work of the oblates are conveyed in a set of decretals or explanations of canon law written by Lanfranc of Bec, who became Archbishop of Canterbury in 1070. Chants specifically reserved for

---

3   W. K. Lowther Clarke, *The Rule of Saint Benedict*, Pax – SPCK London (1931), p. 16.
4   Ibid, p. 19.
5   D. Welander, *The History, Art and Architecture of Gloucester Cathedral*, p. 77.
6   N. Orme, 'Education in Medieval Bristol and Gloucestershire', *Transactions of the Bristol and Gloucestershire Archaeological Society*, volume 112 (2004), p. 11.

the boys to sing included the hymn 'Inventor Rutili' and short responsories such as the 'Benedicamus Domino'.[7] In addition to singing, the boys were responsible for liturgical readings as well as carrying candles and books. They also acted as servers, assisting the monks in the abbey who had been ordained as priests and had to celebrate a private mass each day in one of the many side chapels off the ambulatory or in the crypt. Palm Sunday was one occasion in the year when the oblate children took a leading role, carrying palm branches in a procession and alternating with the adult monks in the singing of the processional hymn 'Gloria Laus'. At this point they were not in any sense choristers with their own specialised music to sing; the expectation was simply for them to accompany the adult monks and sing what the adults sang.[8]

Oblates were drawn from a variety of social backgrounds and had mixed motives. Perhaps the largest group were younger sons of noble families, boys whose position at birth made it unlikely that they would personally inherit substantial landed estates. Monastic life could be quite appealing for them as it provided a secure existence in the company of others from a similar background keen on pursuing intellectual and spiritual interests. Others taken on as oblates might come from more modest backgrounds, so for these boys the provision of free board, lodging and education operated in effect as a kind of scholarship system that enabled less well-endowed families to access schooling.[9] The majority of child-oblates in the early 12th century were clearly preparing to become monks, but they would have included within their number others who would eventually decide on a career outside the walls of the abbey, perhaps as a parish priest.

There was a special ceremony to mark the admission of a child-oblate, and this was described in another of Archbishop Lanfranc's works, a guide for monasteries known as the *Monastic Constitutions* written sometime between 1070 and 1089.[10] He explained that the first step for a child-oblate on entering the monastery was to have the crown of his head shaved to create a tonsure, which was one of the most easily recognised medieval symbols of religious devotion. The boy would then be accompanied by his parents into the monastery church at the time of Mass. After the Gospel

7   S. Boynton & E. Rice, *Young Choristers 650 – 1700*, Boydell Press Woodbridge (2008), p. 40.
8   D. Knowles, *The Religious Orders of England*, Cambridge (1955), volume II, p. 294.
9   N. Orme, *Education in the West of England 1066 – 1548*, University of Exeter (1976), p. 14.
10 D. Knowles, *The Monastic Constitutions of Lanfranc*, Oxford Medieval Texts (2002), p. 108.

reading in that service, the oblate took part in an offertory procession, carrying the bread and wine for the Eucharist and offering it to the celebrant priest. The parents went with their son to the altar and wrapped his hands in the altar cloth as a sign that he was being offered as a gift to the church. They made promises of stability, conversion and obedience, which were witnessed and written down, confirming that they would not remove the boy from the monastery. The abbot untied the boy's cloak and said to him in Latin: 'May the Lord strip you of the old man'. Then, giving the boy a monk's cowl, the abbot proclaimed: 'May the Lord clothe you with the new man'.[11]

Figure 6: Thirteenth-century depiction of a boy being received into a monastery.

Documentary evidence from Gloucester confirms several aspects of this admission ceremony as it operated in St Peter's Abbey, making clear that boys who became oblates and attended the cloister school were required to have the

---

[11]   S. Friar, *Sutton Companion to Cathedrals and Abbeys*, Stroud (2007), p. 268.

tonsure shaved on their heads, like adult monks. We hear, for example, in 1345 of the Bishop of Hereford confirming on one of his priests, John Pine, the tonsure that he had originally received when he was a boy at Gloucester.[12] It is because of the fact that the child-oblates wore the tonsure that schoolboys in this period were often referred to as clerks or clerklings.

As well as the initiation ceremony, the *Monastic Constitutions* of Lanfranc also reveal details about the living arrangements of the oblates and the strict discipline under which they operated.[13] The boys were brought up amongst the adult monks, sleeping alongside them in the dormitory and working alongside them in the cloister. They were roused from sleep early in the morning by the prior as soon as there was sufficient light for them to begin reading in the cloisters. During their study, they were to sit separate from each other, not being allowed to speak, touch one another or move from their places without permission. If they broke the rules, their punishment would be flogging, but in a room that was separate from the adult monks.[14] Regarded as a particularly serious offence worthy of whipping was the failure to own up if mistakes were made when singing psalms.[15] This is considered to be the origin of the custom upheld in modern choir practices of the confessional raising of a hand if a wrong note is sounded.

The first-known pupil to have attended the cloister school at St Peter's was Walter de Lacy. He was a child-oblate who came from a wealthy and powerful Norman family.[16] An inscription on the wall of the Chapter House reveals that one of his ancestors, a benefactor of the abbey who fought at the Battle of Hastings, had been buried on the site of the Chapter House in 1085. It is likely that Walter was one of the original eight boys mentioned in the *Historia* as already being in the abbey at the time of Abbot Serlo's arrival.[17] The *Historia* states that 'his parents offered him to God and St Peter at the very tender age of about seven years because of

---

12   J. H. Parry (ed), *Reg Trillek Hereford*, Canterbury and York Society (1912) cited in N. Orme, *Medieval Schools from Roman Britain to Renaissance England*, Yale University Press (2006), p. 135.

13   S. G. Hodgson, *Climbing Ladders: Childhood and Monastic Formation in England*, Lady Margaret Hall D.Phil. Thesis, Oxford (2019), p. 92.

14   A. F. Leach, *The Schools of Medieval England*, Methuen (1915), pp. 100–1.

15   A. Mould, *The English Chorister: A History*, London (2007), p. 17.

16   D. Welander, *The History, Art and Architecture of Gloucester Cathedral*, p. 76.

17   See Chapter One.

their devotion to religion and the monastic way of life'.[18] Walter de Lacy went on to spend his whole life within the confines of Gloucester Abbey, rising eventually to become its Abbot from 1131 until 1139. It was during Walter de Lacy's abbacy that the burial of Robert, Duke of Normandy, took place in 1134.

Figure 7: The nave of Gloucester Cathedral, which before 1541 was the Benedictine Abbey of St Peter.

Study and scholarship in Gloucester Abbey

Throughout the 12th and 13th centuries the size of the monastic school at St Peter's remained very small by later standards. Judging from evidence recorded in other similar communities, it has been estimated that there would usually have been no more than three or four oblates at any one time at Gloucester, although occasionally numbers may have risen to a maximum of ten.[19] That said, it is likely that the cloister school began to grow somewhat in size as its reputation spread during this period.

---

[18]   *Historia Monasterii Sancti Petri Gloucestriae*, translated by William Barber and printed in Welander, *The History, Art and Architecture of Gloucester Cathedral*, p. 606.
[19]   W. Page, *The Victoria History of the Counties of England: Gloucestershire*, volume 2, London (1907), p. 337.

Referring to the general growth in educational facilities attached to large churches right across the country at this time, some historians have spoken of a 12th-century renaissance, 'an intellectual revolution which marks an era in the history of learning and education'.[20] Church leaders were keen to encourage greater educational provision and to commission as many teachers as possible. The Third Lateran Council of 1179 required every cathedral to provide a schoolmaster, instructing that 'in order that the poor, who cannot be assisted by their parents' means, may not be deprived of the opportunity of reading and proficiency, in every Cathedral Church a competent benefice shall be bestowed upon a master who shall teach the clerks of the same church and poor scholars freely'.[21] This obligation was repeated by the Fourth Lateran Council of 1215, which extended the same requirement to all large churches of any kind.[22]

Against this background, Gloucester Abbey became increasingly well known for its learning and book production. The *Historia* describes how the second Norman abbot, Abbot Peter (1104 – 13), 'surrounded the abbey with a splendid stone wall and enriched the cloister with an abundance of books'.[23] At the same time a formal system came into being to encourage private reading, meditation and study among the monks. At the beginning of Lent the whole community gathered in the Chapter House for a ceremony at which books were issued for the year.[24] When their name was called out, the monks stepped forward, returned the book they had been using the previous year and received a new text on which to meditate for the next twelve months. It may seem restrictive that the same book had to be retained for the whole year, but this underlines the fact that these were not books to be read for information but rather texts designed to support meditation as part of the discipline of Lectio Divina, in which monks aimed for communion with God. The majority of the works would have been Bibles, psalters and the writings of church fathers, but some dealt with a wider array of subjects such as history, philosophy or medicine.[25]

The south walk of the cloister functioned as a scriptorium with

20   A. L. Poole, *From Domesday Book to Magna Carta*, Oxford (1951), p. 232.
21   D. W. Sylvester, *Educational Documents 800 – 1816*, Methuen (1970), p. 14.
22   J. Lawson & H. Silver, *A Social History of Education in England*, Methuen (1973), pp. 20–1.
23   *Historia Monasterii Sancti Petri Gloucestriae*, translated by William Barber and printed in Welander, *The History, Art and Architecture of Gloucester Cathedral*, p. 604.
24   J. Kerr, *Life in the Medieval Cloister*, Continuum London (2009), p. 180.
25   Ibid, p. 182.

twenty-two carrels, or study booths, at which manuscripts and books would painstakingly have been copied by a team of monks seated at individual desks.[26] By 1125 the abbey library was being maintained by a monk specially designated as librarian, with the responsibility of creating a catalogue of the books that were held at St Peter's.[27] Despite a serious fire in 1122, book production continued to expand after Gilbert Foliot became abbot in 1139. He allocated a regular income for the provision of ink and parchment to increase the number of volumes in the library.[28] One individual who raised the reputation of St Peter's Abbey as a place of learning and scholarship was Reginald Foliot, Gilbert Foliot's nephew, who went on to be Abbot of Evesham until his death in 1149. Another of the Gloucester monks, Benedict, was known for the account he wrote about 1130 of the life of St Dubricius.[29]

The status of Gloucester Abbey was enhanced even further by the links it forged with the new university at Oxford. In the 13th century Benedictines gradually embraced the importance of some of their order being educated to university level, and it was the monks of Gloucester who took a lead in this. In 1283 they established Gloucester College in Oxford as a place of study for thirteen monks, using a site (now absorbed into Worcester College) granted to them by Sir John Giffard of Brimpsfield.[30] The foundation document expressed the hope that the monks 'are now disposed to put aside ignorance, the mother of error, and to walk in the light of truth that they may become proficient in learning to the augmentation of their merits'.[31] William de Brok, a monk of St Peter's Abbey, became the first Benedictine to gain a doctorate of divinity at Oxford in 1298, an occasion celebrated with great rejoicing in his order. Five abbots and many priors, monks, clerks and gentlemen attended the festivities that marked it.[32] The *Historia* records how his examination in Oxford took the form of a public debate with another Gloucester monk,

26 C. Heighway, S. Hamilton et alii, *Gloucester Cathedral: Faith, Art and Architecture*, p. 40.

27 R. B. Patterson, *The Original Acta of St Peter's Abbey Gloucester*, Bristol and Gloucestershire Archaeological Society (1998), p. xxiv.

28 D. Welander, *The History, Art and Architecture of Gloucester Cathedral*, p. 129.

29 W. Page, *The Victoria History of the Counties of England: Gloucestershire*, volume 2, p. 54.

30 G. W. Counsel, *The History and Description of the City of Gloucester*, Gloucester (1829), p. 83.

31 A. F. Leach, *Educational Charters and Documents*, Cambridge (1911), p. 199.

32 A. B Emden, *A Biographical Register of the University of Oxford*, (Oxford 1957 – 9), volume 1, cited in N. Orme, *Medieval Schools from Roman Britain to Renaissance England*, p. 268.

Figure 8: Gloucester College, established at Oxford in 1283.

Laurence de Honsom, in the presence of Gloucester's abbot John de Gamages and many other ecclesiastical dignitaries. It records that William de Brok's 'admission was completed to the honour of this house and of the whole order'.[33] William's influence at Gloucester remained strong as he is recorded as prior in 1301.[34] Near the eastern cloister entrance to the nave there still exists today part of a grave slab which forms a section of the bench set into the wall. As it bears the initials 'WB', there is the possibility that it may have once marked the site of William de Brok's grave.

Figure 9: Possible gravestone of William de Brok, first Gloucester monk to receive an Oxford doctorate.

Another medieval scholar who may have been associated with St Peter's was Andrew

---

33 *Historia Monasterii Sancti Petri*, translated by William Barber (1988) and printed as Appendix XV in D. Welander, *The History, Art and Architecture of Gloucester Cathedral*, p. 620.

34 Ibid, p. 621.

Horne.[35] In the 1320s he was one of the authors of a legal treatise known as the 'Mirror of Justice' and was also responsible for a now lost chronicle of the history of Gloucester.[36] The presence of such men must have provided a real intellectual stimulus to the community at Gloucester Abbey and linked the monks with the new learning that began to emerge from Oxford. It was against this background of increasing scholarship that the monastic cloister school continued to develop.

The decline of the oblate system

The terms on which most of the boys came to the cloister school began to change from the mid-12th century. This was because the recruitment of child-oblates gradually ceased as the 12th century proceeded, leaving the majority of children attending the monastic school less likely to become monks and usually seeking a general education to pursue other careers, although most of these remained church-related.[37]

Several factors were responsible for the decline of the oblate system. The most important was one of the papal decrees issued at the Fourth Lateran Council of 1215 that put an official ban on the use of oblates as a method of recruitment.[38] Another factor was that monasteries increasingly had access to a pool of young men educated in the growing number of free-standing grammar schools that came into existence outside the monasteries at this time. One of these new schools was established in Gloucester by the canons of St Oswald's around the year 1100.[39] The existence of these new types of school made monasteries like St Peter's less dependent on child-oblates. Instead, they began to take in youngsters in their late teens known as 'postulants'; these were young men who had been educated elsewhere and then expressed a vocation for joining a religious order.[40] This had the attraction that rather than start from scratch with young boys, the abbey could now seek volunteers who had already reached a sound standard of education and literacy in Latin. When he visited Gloucester Abbey in 1301,

---

[35] T. D. Fosbrooke, *An Original History of the City of Gloucester*, London (1819), reprinted by Alan Sutton (1986), p. 151.
[36] G. Crabb, *A History of English Law*, London (1829), p. 214.
[37] N. Orme, *Medieval Schools from Roman Britain to Renaissance England*, pp. 256–7.
[38] J. Burton, *Monastic and Religious Orders in Britain 1000 – 1300*, Cambridge (1994), p. 174.
[39] See Chapter Three.
[40] J. Lawson, *Medieval Education and the Reformation*, Routledge & Kegan Paul (1967), p. 53.

Archbishop Winchelsey ordered that prior knowledge in reading and singing should be expected of all those entering the cloister school.[41]

Another reason for abandoning the practice of child oblation was to improve discipline in the monastery. The recruitment of more highly motivated teenagers reduced the problems associated with young, and sometimes highly spirited, trainee monks who were discontented but forced to stay in the monastery simply because their parents had offered them to it many years earlier. In 1301 Abbot John de Gamages provided Gloucester Abbey with new statutes designed to promote better discipline within the community. These dealt with a variety of matters ranging from the diet of the monks to the way Mass was celebrated, but there was a particular focus on improving relationships in the cloisters. It was enacted, for example, that a particular monk be charged with the task of supervising reading-time in the cloisters and reporting any who did not attend. When it came to the school, the statutes sought to raise the authority of the monks who had special responsibility for teaching: 'As to the discipline of the boys, one master must reside continuously with them in the cloister. No one must give them playthings, except through the masters, or invite them to private meetings. No youth is to be promoted to service except by the Chapter on the recommendation of the masters to be given without partiality'.[42]

The decline of child-oblation meant that the core body of pupils at the cloister school in Gloucester now came to consist of 'lay boys', who were not necessarily seeking a permanent monastic life, although that may have been one of their options. These boys were drawn from well-connected families right across the country. Those from the most privileged backgrounds would have lived in the private household of the abbot himself.[43] Others would have been given lodgings in some suitable location in the outer monastic precincts, perhaps near the infirmary.

One example of a boy who attended the cloister school at Gloucester but went on to a career as a secular clerk rather than a cloistered monk was Gerald of Wales. Gerald began his education with his uncle, David

---

41   W. H. Hart, *Historia et Cartularium Monasterii*, Rolls Series (1863), volume 1, cited in N. Orme, *Medieval Schools from Roman Britain to Renaissance England*, p. 267.

42   W. St Clair Baddeley, 'Early Deeds Relating to St Peter's Abbey Gloucester', *Transactions of the Bristol and Gloucestershire Archaeological Society* (1914), volume 37, p. 221.

43   N. Orme, *Medieval Schools from Roman Britain to Renaissance England*, p. 285.

Fitzgerald (Bishop of St David's), and then probably at the age of nine or ten was sent on to Gloucester.[44] Arriving about the year 1160 during the abbacy of Hameline, it was in Gloucester Abbey that Gerald developed his mastery of Latin, his extensive knowledge of Classical and later authors, and through the study of logic and rhetoric the ability to argue clearly and persuasively. He went on to the University of Paris, but the foundation had already been laid at Gloucester for the long career he was to have as a churchman, royal administrator and recruiting agent for the Third Crusade. Gerald rose to become Archdeacon of Brecon, a personal friend of King Henry II and a prolific writer, who based several books on his travels around both Wales and Ireland. Despite the heights he achieved, he retained memories – good and bad – of his roots in Gloucester. One of the passages Gerald wrote looked back with some contempt at the wealth and worldliness of some of the churchmen he encountered at Gloucester, especially the canons of Llanthony Secunda, whom he compared unfavourably with the saintly and frugal inmates of their mother house at Llanthony in the Black Mountains.[45] His continued links with Gloucester are also reflected in his hagiographic work, the *Life of St Remigius of Lincoln*, in which he records that one of the western towers of Gloucester Abbey dramatically collapsed while Bishop Roger of Worcester was celebrating Mass there, most likely in 1164.[46] Gerald may possibly have been an eyewitness to the event.

Most historians also believe that another pupil of the same era at St Peter's Abbey was Walter Map (1140 – 1209).[47] He was another key figure at the court of Henry II, who headed diplomatic missions for the king and rose to become precentor at both Lincoln and Hereford Cathedral. The evidence for his association with Gloucester's cloister school lies in his lifelong friendship with Gerald of Wales and the similarities in their careers.[48] Both attended Paris university and both became leading churchmen, writers and confidants of the king.[49] Walter Map was the

---

[44] C. Kightly, *A Mirror of Medieval Wales: Gerald of Wales and His Journey of 1188*, Cadw 1988, p. 9.

[45] L. Thorpe, *Gerald of Wales: The Journey Through Wales and the Description of Wales*, p. 10.

[46] M. Hare, 'The Chronicle of Gregory of Caerwent', *Glevensis*, volume 27 (1994), p. 42.

[47] R. B. Patterson, *The Original Acta of St Peter's Abbey Gloucester*, p. xxv.

[48] J. B. Smith, *Walter Map and the Matter of Britain*, University of Pennsylvania Press (2017), p. 2.

[49] M. Staunton, *The Historians of Angevin England*, Oxford University Press (2017), p. 135.

author of *Trifles of Courtiers*, a collection of satirical anecdotes and trivia famous for providing the earliest stories of vampires in England. One of his anecdotes was headed 'Anecdote of Gregory, a monk of Gloucester'. Another was attributed to Abbot Gilbert Foliot, whom he probably first met as a young man at Gloucester. The link with Foliot remained a strong one throughout Walter's career. On returning from Paris, he served with the household of Gilbert Foliot, who was by then Bishop of Hereford; and in 1163, when Foliot became Bishop of London, Walter seems to have followed him there and become a canon at St Paul's.

Figure 10: North walk of the cloisters, probable location of Gloucester Abbey's 12th and 13th-century school.

Figure 11: Statue by Henry Poole in Cardiff City Hall of Gerald of Wales, who studied at the Gloucester cloister school in the 1160s.

23

The cloister school and its teachers

The cloisters at Gloucester are today best known for their lavish fan vaulting, which was begun during the 1350s. This fan vaulting was described by John Leland, the Tudor traveller and antiquary, as 'a right goodly and sumptuous piece of work'.[50] The basic layout of the cloisters, however, including their walls and stone ledges, is much older and dates from the period of the Norman builders who worked at the time of Abbot Serlo.[51]

It was in the north walk of the cloisters, or at least its eastern half between the lavatorium and the Dark Cloister entrance, that the cloister school at Gloucester probably met in the 12th and 13th centuries. One of the main pieces of evidence for this comes from the scratchings that are still visible on the stone bench in this part of the cloister. They are thought to be board games carved by bored schoolboys, just like pupils of later generations may have gouged out graffiti on their desks. Two in particular have been identified as counter games called Nine Men's Morris and Fox and Geese.[52] It is likely that the north walk was partitioned off by draughtproof wooden or leather screens to provide a self-contained environment with some warmth and privacy for the boys who were studying there.[53]

No other special facilities would have been necessary for the cloister school; stone seats or wooden benches were the only actual requirement. The few pictorial sources that exist from these times show pupils holding books on their laps and sitting around the master on simple benches, which were called 'forms'.[54] As boys of the same age were naturally inclined to sit next to each other, the word 'form' eventually began to take on its modern meaning of a group of pupils of a similar age who are taught together. For writing the boys would have used tablets of wood, which were polished or waxed; they did not have desks as they simply rested the tablets on their knees.[55] Lessons were of necessity flexible and entailed long

[50] Cited in D. Welander, *The History, Art and Architecture of Gloucester Cathedral*, p. 231.
[51] C. Heighway, S. Hamilton et alii, *Gloucester Cathedral: Faith, Art and Architecture*, p. 20.
[52] D. Welander, *The History, Art and Architecture of Gloucester Cathedral*, p. 232.
[53] W. H. St John Hope, *Notes on the Benedictine Abbey of St Peter Gloucester* in *Records of Gloucester Cathedral 1885 – 7*, volume III, p. 113.
[54] N. Orme, *Medieval Schools from Roman Britain to Renaissance England*, Yale University Press (2006), p. 139.
[55] Ibid, p. 134.

Figure 12: Fourteenth-century manuscript showing boys seated on their bench or form in a monastery school.

Figure 13: The Fox and Geese board game carved on a stone bench in the cloisters.

periods of self-study, as they had to fit around the times of the daily monastic services. The life of the boys, like the monks in general, would have been regulated by the summoning bell that hung in an alcove at the western end of the north walk beyond the lavatorium.[56] It would have been rung to notify the community of the time for services, meals and all other activities.

The original teachers at the cloister school would have been monks, for whom teaching was only a small part of their daily work. Taking the title 'guardian of the children', their duties involved little more than the supervision and disciplining of the boys.[57] As the 12th century wore on, this became less the case as the claims of worship became more exacting for most monks and less compatible with teaching. As a result, a new class began to emerge of monks who specialised as professional teachers.[58]

We know only a few of the names of the teachers who worked in Gloucester's cloister school, but they were crucial to its success. With the move towards more specialist teaching, the fortunes of a school revolved

56   D. Welander, *The History, Art and Architecture of Gloucester Cathedral*, p. 319.
57   J. Barnes, *The Life of the Monks in St Peter's Abbey Gloucester*, Gloucester Cathedral Guides (2019), p. 23.
58   C. Dainton, 'Medieval Schools of England', *History Today*, volume XXIX (1979), p. 490.

to a large degree around the skills and scholarly attributes of its main teacher. A genuine scholar could attract pupils from near and far, and it seems that Gloucester did well in this respect.[59] One of the first monks to specialise in teaching at St Peter's in the mid-12th century was Osbern of Gloucester, also known as Osbern of Pinnock, suggesting that he was probably brought up in that village. He was a grammarian of European importance, the author of an etymological dictionary called *Liber Derivationum* (*Book of Derivations*), which listed Latin words according to their stems or word families and provided information about the origins of the words and their relationships with other words.[60] He had begun his book whilst he was teaching grammar elsewhere in the country, but he completed it when he had become a monk at Gloucester Abbey.[61] His work circulated throughout Europe and was one of the sources used by the Italian scholar Hugutio of Pisa, who created an even more widely used dictionary. The Tudor antiquary and traveller, John Leland, regarded Osbern as 'the most elegant Latinist and commentator of the age in which he lived'.[62] As well as his distinction in Latin grammar, Osbern added several works of divinity to the monastic library. According to Thomas Fosbrooke writing in 1819, his *Panormia* was one of the few books to survive the Reformation.[63]

Possibly the most well-known teacher at Gloucester Abbey in the 12th century was Haimo, who more than 600 years later was still remembered by one Gloucestershire antiquarian as 'the most learned man of his time'.[64] It was under Haimo that Gerald of Wales studied about the year 1160. Lewis Thorpe, who edited Gerald's works, believed that 'he approved of the instruction which he received at St Peter's and he later described his teacher there as that most learned scholar Master Haimo'.[65] 'Long ago', wrote Gerald in his autobiographical works written in the 1190s, 'when I

---

[59]   D. Welander, *The History, Art and Architecture of Gloucester Cathedral*, p. 87.

[60]   R. M. Thomson, 'England and the 12th-Century Renaissance', *Past and Present,* number 101 (1983), p. 12.

[61]   T. Hunt, *Teaching and Learning Latin in 13th-Century England*, Cambridge (1991), volume I, p. 373.

[62]   S. Y. Griffith, *New Historical Description of Cheltenham*, Longman London (1826), p. 171.

[63]   D. Welander, *The History, Art and Architecture of Gloucester Cathedral*, p. 88.

[64]   S. Rudder, *A New History of Gloucestershire*, Cirencester (1779), republished by Alan Sutton in 2006, p. 127.

[65]   L. Thorpe, *Gerald of Wales: The Journey Through Wales and the Description of Wales*, Penguin (1978), p. 10.

was in the years of boyhood and the days of my green youth, I studied in the Abbey of St Peter at Gloucester under that most learned scholar Master Haimo during the abbacy of Hameline the Frenchman'. [66]

With staff such as Osbern and Haimo, and with all the resources of an increasingly wealthy Benedictine abbey and its links with Oxford, the school that met in the north walk of the cloisters at Gloucester had the ability to draw in boys from the most aristocratic of families in southern and central England as well as Wales. Despite catering for small numbers, it made a crucial contribution to the development of education and good learning in the 12th and 13th centuries.

---

[66] S. Brewer, *Giraldus Cambrensis Opera*, volume IV, translated in J. Gillingham *The Autobiography of Gerald of Wales*, Boydell Press (2005), p. 79.

CHAPTER THREE

Our Two Grammar Schools of St Oswald's and Llanthony:

Education at the Heart of Medieval Gloucester

The school at St Oswald's

The cloister school inside the confines of St Peter's Abbey was not the only school to exist in Gloucester during the 12th and 13th centuries. Two free-standing grammar schools emerged, which were fierce rivals of each other. The first of these was sponsored by St Oswald's Priory; the second and ultimately more successful was the creation of Llanthony Priory.

Many major towns in England developed their own free-standing grammar schools during the course of the 12th century.[1] Gloucester was no exception. Schools of this kind followed a curriculum very similar to that of a cloister school, dominated by Latin, but without the emphasis on singing and monastic discipline. Unlike the cloister school, which catered principally for those who expected to go on to become monks, the grammar schools were open to a wider cross section of boys and existed to meet the general needs of their town.

Gloucester's first free-standing grammar school open to the general public was created about the year 1100 by the canons of St Oswald's Priory. Although we know very little about its location, its pupils or its teachers, the existence of this school is well-documented in legal records. The first reference to it comes in a copy of an undated charter of King Henry I confirming a grant made by Ralph de Saint-Samson, who was Bishop of Worcester from 1096 until 1112. This was before the creation of the diocese of Gloucester, a time when Gloucestershire was part of Worcester diocese.

---

[1] N. Orme, *Medieval Schools from Roman Britain to Renaissance England*, Yale University Press (2006), pp. 192–3.

The charter states: 'I have confirmed to the church of St Oswald at Gloucester, my chapel, the school for all Gloucester, which the Bishops of Worcester, Samson and the rest, gave to the aforesaid church'.[2] This charter is one of the earliest charters to establish clear patronage rights over a school anywhere in England.[3]

The school would have been run by the canons of St Oswald's, which at that point was a small minster, past its heyday, but one with an illustrious history.[4] St Oswald's saw itself as a rival to St Peter's which, although once a minster itself, had long since become a cloistered monastic community following the Benedictine Rule. Professor Orme has suggested that the decision Samson made to found the new school at St Oswald's may have reflected local unease at the intensification of monasticism at St Peter's under Abbot Serlo, which caused the cloister school to become less receptive to boys who had no anticipation of a monastic life.[5] St Oswald's was staffed by six secular canons, who were not constrained by the rigidity of monastic vows and therefore had no scruples about opening their school to the general population.

Throughout the Middle Ages all education was carefully controlled by the bishop of each diocese or his chancellor, without whose licence no one could open a school or teach.[6] The purpose of the charter issued by Samson for St Oswald's was to establish in law that the patronage of the new school resided firmly with the Bishop of Worcester. By using the phrase 'school for all Gloucester', Samson was implying that his patronage rights extended over the whole town, establishing in law the important principle that the provision of education outside the precincts of St Peter's lay with the canons of St Oswald's under the patronage they received from their diocesan bishop.[7] He was also seeking to establish a monopoly over education, preventing others from setting up rival educational establishments in order to preserve his school's financial viability, which depended on fee-paying pupils not being syphoned off by other institutions.[8]

---

2   A. F. Leach, *Educational Charters and Documents*, Cambridge (1911), p. 77.
3   N. Orme, *Medieval Schools from Roman Britain to Renaissance England*, p. 48.
4   See above in Chapter One for the past history of St Oswald's Minster.
5   N. Orme, *Education in the West of England 1066 – 1548*, University of Exeter (1976), p. 58.
6   A. L. Poole, *From Domesday Book to Magna Carta*, Oxford (1951), p. 232.
7   A. Platts and G. H. Hainton, *Education in Gloucestershire: A Short History*, Gloucestershire County Council (1953), p. 7.
8   J. Lawson & H. Silver, *A Social History of Education in England*, Methuen (1973), p. 21.

The role of patron, in this case the Bishop of Worcester, was defined formally at the Third Lateran Council of 1179 and was jealously guarded. 'The right to keep a school', observed one mid-20th-century historian, 'was then a privilege as exclusive, and sometimes almost as lucrative, as the landlord's right to keep a mill or an oven'.[9] A patron's role was to provide a school with the buildings, books and other resources it needed. He also had the important function of providing a degree of continuity for a school as, although schoolmasters were usually appointed locally, it was the patron who took on the responsibility for licensing them. This meant that, when a schoolmaster retired or died, the patron had the overall duty to see to it that the vacancy was filled so that education would not be disrupted. The patron's power also extended to stopping other schools from opening in the same town, something necessary to protect the licensed master from rival teachers who might threaten his income by enticing away fee-paying pupils.[10]

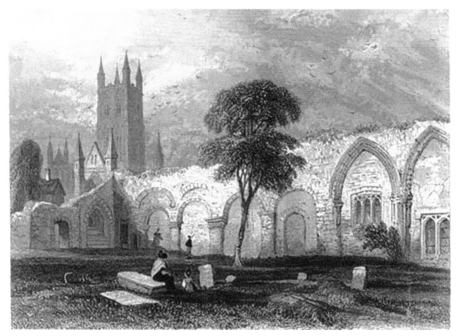

Figure 14: St Oswald's Priory as illustrated by the 19th-century architect, Benjamin Baud (1836).

9   G. G. Coulton, *Europe's Apprenticeship*, Nelson (1940), p. 123.
10   N. Orme, *Medieval Schools from Roman Britain to Renaissance England*, p. 195.

About the year 1153 St Oswald's, in common with many other minsters, transformed itself into an Augustinian priory.[11] First arriving in England in 1108, the Augustinians were not called monks, but regular canons ('regular' because they followed a Rule) and they observed a way of life that came somewhere between that of the monks and the parish clergy.[12] Erasmus later referred to them as a middle kind of creature, an amphibious sort of animal like the beaver.[13] Allowed to move more freely among the general population of Gloucester than the cloistered monks of St Peter's, the Augustinian canons naturally involved themselves in matters of social concern. They were bound by a threefold rule of poverty, chastity and obedience and they lived a communal life based around the priory's cloister and dormitory but, unlike monks, they lived in their own vicarages and moved about freely in the world. They were therefore especially suited to playing a prominent part in the provision of education and cherished the kind of school they inherited at St Oswald's.[14]

The decision to install Augustinian canons at St. Oswald's was made in 1152 – 53 by Henry Murdac, Archbishop of York (1147 – 53). As a result of a grant made by William Rufus in 1094, St Oswald's became part of an area called the 'jurisdiction of Churchdown'.[15] This consisted of six parishes to the north of Gloucester that withdrew from the jurisdiction of Worcester diocese and became a peculiar under the direct control of the Archbishop of York.[16] This complex situation came about because for a long period before the Norman Conquest the sees of Worcester and York had been held jointly.[17] St Oswald's remained under the jurisdiction of York right up until its dissolution in 1536, and this was to have important consequences for the way in which the canons there defended their monopoly rights over the 'school for all Gloucester'.

---

11   H. Medland, 'St Oswald's Priory Gloucester', *Transactions of the Bristol and Gloucestershire Archaeological Society* (1888), volume 13, p. 124.

12   G. Waters, *King Richard's Gloucester: Life in a Mediaeval Town*, Alan Sutton (1983), p. 48.

13   J. G. Nichols, *Pilgrimages to St Mary of Walsingham by Desiderius Erasmus*, Westminster (1849), p. 12.

14   W. Page, *The Victoria History of the Counties of England: Gloucestershire*, volume 2, London (1907), p. 315.

15   Ibid, p. 14.

16   C. Heighway and R. Bryant, 'The Golden Minster', CBA Research Report 117, Council for British Archaeology (1999), p. 16.

17   W. Page, *The Victoria History of the Counties of England: Gloucestershire*, volume 2, p. 84.

The Llanthony Priory school

The growing influence of the Archbishop of York over St Oswald's may have been responsible for a challenge launched against its school in the second half of the 12th century by the rival Augustinian priory of Llanthony Secunda. This priory was founded in the southern suburbs of Gloucester in 1136 by Robert de Braci initially as a subsidiary to Llanthony Prima, its parent house, the ruins of which can still be seen in Gwent.[18]

The Llanthony Secunda canons very quickly claimed the right to set up a school of their own in Gloucester, presumably complaining that the patronage rights over education in Gloucester that legally belonged to the Bishops of Worcester were being compromised by the dependency St Oswald's now had on York. The result was a grant made by Roger, who was Bishop of Worcester between 1163 and 1179, giving Llanthony the right to set up 'one school' in the town.[19] This was a direct challenge to St Oswald's, but the phrase 'one school' may imply that it was initially intended only as a partial encroachment on the general right that St. Oswald's had to be Gloucester's main educational provider. It may be that for a time there were two schools, each under the control of one of the Augustinian houses, but at some point the older school run by St. Oswald's closed, perhaps for as long as a whole century.

By the late 12th century it appears that the school established by Llanthony had become the most successful school in Gloucester outside the precincts of St Peter's Abbey. The school was a grammar school that existed for the benefit of the people of Gloucester and, unlike St Peter's cloister school, in no sense was it a monastic school of any kind. All that was expected of the priory was to provide the building, appoint the schoolmaster under the oversight of the Bishop of Worcester and perhaps remove him if circumstances warranted it.[20]

We do not know exactly where in Gloucester the school established by Llanthony Priory was situated during the first decades of its existence. It is unlikely that it was ever inside the priory itself. A tradition that still circulated among antiquarians of the 18th and 19th centuries was that it

---

[18]   I. Holt, *A Brief History of the Five Priories of Gloucester*, Gloucester Civic Trust Guide (2018), p. 5.

[19]   N. Orme, *Education in the West of England 1066 – 1548*, pp. 58–9.

[20]   W. Page, *The Victoria History of the Counties of England: Gloucestershire*, volume 2, p. 315.

Figure 15: Llanthony Priory as illustrated by the 19th-century architectural draughtsman, John Coney (1825).

may have been based inside the walls of the Eastgate.[21] A more likely suggestion is that it met in Southgate Street in the priory church of St Owen. This is based on the fact that shortly after his accession in 1154 Henry II gave Gloucester Castle to the canons of Llanthony and in his grant acknowledged once more their right to maintain 'one school' in the town. St Owen's Church was linked to the castle.[22] Although Henry's original charter does not survive, confirmations issued by Richard I in 1198 and by King John the following year remain in existence.[23] They refer to 'the gift of King Henry our father, the chapel in Gloucester castle and a school in the same town'.

One of the first masters of the Llanthony Priory school was named in a document of 1203 as 'Master Roger rector of the school of Gloucester'.[24]

21   T. Rudge, *The History and Antiquities of Gloucester*, J. Wood Gloucester (1811), p. 156 and G. W. Counsel, *The History and Description of the City of Gloucester*, Gloucester (1829), p. 63.
22   B. Lowe, *Commonwealth and the English Reformation: Protestantism and the Politics of Religious Change in the Gloucester Vale*, Routledge St Andrew's Studies in Reformation History (2010), p. 59.
23   A. F. Leach, *Educational Charters and Documents*, Cambridge (1911), pp. 95–7.
24   T. D. Fosbrooke, *An Original History of the City of Gloucester*, London (1819), reprinted by Alan Sutton (1986), p. 151.

Later schoolmasters mentioned in the reign of Richard II (1377 – 99) were Walter Sigrith, John Hamelyn and Edward Cleche.[25] They would not have been canons of Llanthony, but part of the class of specialised teachers that grew up at this time. The two main qualities looked for when appointing a schoolmaster were sufficient knowledge of grammar and an honest reputation but, as time went by, there was an additional expectation that a master should be university-educated. When the canons appointed John Hamelyn in 1396, the contract provided for him to leave the school for a year to attend university before taking up his appointment. The salary that these masters could earn was fairly modest as most schools at this date were required to be financially self-supporting. Especially if they could take in a few boarders willing to pay extra, a master with a class of seventy or eighty pupils could make about £10 a year, although he did not get to keep all the fees. The Llanthony schoolmaster had to pay 24s a year for the rent of the schoolroom.[26]

Schooling cost money, although every effort was made to keep fees as low as possible. In the 13th century 4d per term was a typical fee to attend a grammar school, but prices rose with inflation after the Black Death. By the 15th century fees for those learning reading or song may have remained at 4d per term, but 8d became a more common sum in the grammar schools.[27] The receipt of fees was the only source of income for a schoolmaster; he was not paid a set salary. The need to charge fees meant that throughout the Middle Ages, most schoolboys were the sons of the gentry, merchants, substantial townsmen and rural yeomen with the means from which to commit to regular payments.[28] It is likely, however, that a few fortunate individuals from more modest backgrounds received subsidies similar to modern scholarships. Some of the older boys may have had their fees subsidised in return for working as parish clerks in nearby churches such as St Mary de Lode or St Nicholas. Parish clerks in the 1200s were often teenagers known as 'holy water-bearers'.[29] They rang the church bells for services or to mark deaths, served at the altar during Mass and dispensed the holy water used in religious rites.

---

[25] N. Orme, *Education in the West of England 1066 – 1548*, pp. 60–1.
[26] Ibid, p. 14.
[27] N. Orme, *Medieval Schools from Roman Britain to Renaissance England*, p. 132.
[28] J. Lawson & H. Silver, *A Social History of Education in England*, p. 48.
[29] N. Orme, *Medieval Schools from Roman Britain to Renaissance England*, p. 205.

At some point the Llanthony Priory grammar school established itself in a rectangular building situated across two tenement plots in Longsmith Street (which for a time was known as School House Lane).[30] The school was on the right-hand side of Longsmith Street on the corner of Bull Lane, the site now occupied by a large multi-storey car park.[31] Like the cloister school in St Peter's, the grammar school on the Longsmith Street site took in boys when they were seven years old, although all ages were taught together in the same schoolroom.[32] According to medieval theories based on writings of the 7th-century scholar Isidore of Seville, an individual was considered an infant until the age of seven and a child between the ages of seven and fourteen.[33]

Figure 16: Modern car park in Longsmith Street built on the site of the Llanthony Priory school.

We can make informed assumptions about what the schoolroom in Longsmith Street probably looked like. It would have been oblong in shape; the ideal size of a medieval classroom seems to have been about 70

---

[30] J. Rhodes (ed), *A Calendar of the Registers of the Priory of Llanthony by Gloucester*, Bristol and Gloucestershire Archaeological Society (2002), p. 60.

[31] W. Page, *The Victoria History of the Counties of England: Gloucestershire*, volume 2, p. 320.

[32] C. Dainton, *Medieval Schools of England*, p. 494.

[33] H. Leyser, *Medieval Women*, Weidenfeld & Nicolson (1995), p. 133.

feet long and 25 feet wide, providing sufficient space to house up to eighty boys.[34] It was probably lit by a range of small windows, placed fairly high above ground level to let light in to the room but not allow a view out. Benches were situated along the walls, so that the pupils sat with their backs to the walls looking into the room, resting books on their knees. Seating the pupils around the walls with nothing to hinder their view was thought to help with focus and discipline. There was no separation into different classes, but boys sat with others of similar aptitude on groups of benches known as forms.

The layout of the school was based on the pattern of a great hall in a medieval manor house.[35] In the manor the lord of the manor presided, the household sat round the room and there was an usher to keep control of the door. Heads of households never left their seats; people came to them as they were ordered. The same was true of the grammar schoolmaster. All early pictures of medieval schools depict the master dominating the room from a large chair.[36] He tended not to walk up and down; he stayed where he was, giving lessons and issuing commands from his chair, then calling up groups of boys for testing. Boys came to the master, not he to them, just as the lord of a household sat and was approached by his retainers.

Unlike the cloister school at St Peter's, the boys who attended the Longsmith Street school were not training to become monks. They were divided into three groups. The lowest level, usually the younger boys, would be taught the ability to read Latin convincingly to a standard sufficient to sing in a church choir. The next level of pupil would be able to read Latin with some understanding, as was necessary for church leaders or scribes engaging in accurate copying. The final level brought with it the skill of composing Latin and using it to appreciate the works of scholars circulating around the Christian world.[37]

Many medieval grammar schools had to rely on the services of just one master, but the importance of the school at Gloucester is shown by the fact that, at least from the early 1400s, it was large enough to support a second teacher. This probably meant that the school catered for up to eighty pupils. The second teacher was known as the usher. Usually a young man, his main

---

34 N. Orme, *Medieval Schools from Roman Britain to Renaissance England*, pp. 138–41.
35 N. Orme, *Education in the West of England 1066 – 1548*, p. 58.
36 N. Orme, *Medieval Schools from Roman Britain to Renaissance England*, p. 139.
37 H. M. Jewell, *Education in Early Modern England*, Macmillan (1998), p. 15.

task was to supervise the younger boys, leaving the master free to take charge of the older ones.[38] He sat on a small seat at the far end of the room, as another of the usher's duties was to keep control of the door, intercepting those who arrived late and controlling those who wished to go out. Some ushers were fortunate enough eventually to run their own schools. The most well-known usher from the Longsmith Street school was Richard Darcy, usher in the 1410s; he went on to Winchester College as headmaster in 1418.[39]

With the school dependent on just two men, its success was really determined by the personal skills they possessed and the working relationship they were able to form between them. Darcy's promotion to Winchester suggests that the grammar school in Gloucester enjoyed a strong reputation during his time there at the start of the 15th century. Whilst we have no information about its fortunes at other points, there is no doubt that this school became the main provider of education in Gloucester, far surpassing in number those who attended the older cloister school at St Peter's. It was schools like the Longsmith Street school that played a key role in the gradual increase in literacy that occurred across the country in the later Middle Ages.

Legal disputes between Llanthony and St Oswald's priories

Throughout the time of its existence the Llanthony Priory grammar school in Longsmith Street faced a number of serious legal challenges from St Oswald's. Both priories had charters that they could use to support the case that they alone should control education in the town, and at different times they made appeals for backing from the Bishop of Worcester and eventually even the king.[40]

The first dispute occurred at the end of the 13th century. St Oswald's reopened its school in 1286 [41] and, on the basis of Bishop Samson's original grant of 'the school for all Gloucester', the canons there revived their claim to be the sole provider of education in the town outside the precincts of St Peter's.

The dispute became an acrimonious one with the two rival houses both gaining support from the ecclesiastical hierarchy. Godfrey Giffard, Bishop

---

38   C. Dainton, *Medieval Schools of England*, p. 494.
39   A. F. Leach, *The Schools of Medieval England*, Methuen (1915), p. 238.
40   N. Orme, *Medieval Schools from Roman Britain to Renaissance England*, p. 200.
41   N. Orme, *Education in the West of England 1066 – 1548*, p. 59.

of Worcester, gave his support to Llanthony. He wrote to the Archdeacon of Gloucester in 1286 making it clear that he believed that the right to educate the boys of Gloucester belonged to Llanthony alone. He stated that 'the school in the borough of Gloucester, to which scholars flock for the sake of learning, some from our diocese and others from diverse parts, clearly belongs, as we have been informed by the evidence of trustworthy witnesses and as clearly appears by inspection of the muniments and charters which they have concerning the same school, to the religious men the prior and convent of Llanthony'.[42] He said that no one was to teach in Gloucester except for the master appointed by Llanthony and that any other schools that existed should be closed down.[43] He concluded with 'an inhibition against anyone calling himself a scholar keeping any school for the sake of teaching in the said borough, except that one the teaching of which has been granted to a fit master by the collation of the prior and convent of Llanthony, who have been and are notoriously in possession or quasi-possession of the right of collation to such a school from time whereof the memory of man runneth not to the contrary. Other schools, if there are any there, to which anyone has been collated to the prejudice of the said religious, should be wholly suspended'.[44]

Since St. Oswald's lay outside the Bishop of Worcester's legal jurisdiction, his orders would have had little direct effect, despite his request for them to be read out by the parish clergy of Gloucester in their churches on three successive Sundays. In 1289 John Romeyn, Archbishop of York, wrote to Giffard complaining that he had oppressed the canons of St Oswald's by eroding their rights over education in Gloucester, rights which he said went back to 'ancient times'.[45]

The canons of Llanthony seem to have emerged from this first spat with the upper hand. Their school continued to expand and the charter it had from Henry II was confirmed by both Edward II and Edward III.[46] The St Oswald's school by contrast floundered and may even have closed once again for a time.[47]

---

42   A. F. Leach, *The Schools of Medieval England*, Methuen (1915), p. 126.
43   N. Orme, *Education in the West of England 1066 – 1548*, p. 59.
44   W. Page, *The Victoria History of the Counties of England: Gloucestershire*, volume 2, p. 316.
45   N. Orme, *Education in the West of England 1066 – 1548*, p. 60.
46   Ibid, p. 60.
47   A. H. Thompson, 'The Jurisdiction of the Archbishops of York in Gloucestershire', *Transactions of the Bristol and Gloucestershire Archaeological Society* (1921), volume 43 p. 142.

A second challenge, even more serious than the first, was mounted by St Oswald's when Thomas Duke became prior towards the end of the 14th century. About 1380 he secured the services of Thomas More, a schoolmaster from Hereford, and employed him successfully to re-launch the school at St Oswald's.[48] Llanthony Priory immediately sought episcopal support, which resulted in the Bishop of Worcester, Henry Wakefield, confirming Giffard's ordinance of 1286 and commanding the beneficed clergy of Gloucester to publish it once again.[49] Two years later in 1382 John Nelme, a clerk from Gloucester, was summoned before the consistory court at Worcester Cathedral to explain why he was teaching grammar to boys 'to the prejudice of the general school in the town which belongs to Llanthony'. In 1384 when William Courtenay, the Archbishop of Canterbury, conducted a metropolitan visitation of Worcester diocese, he commanded the clergy of Gloucestershire to warn all who encroached on the liberties of Llanthony that they would be required to appear before him to explain the reasons for their actions.[50] The canons of St Oswald's appealed to the Crown in 1388. After authorising a royal inspection, Richard II confirmed the charter from the time of Henry I, which had made the original grant of patronage rights to St Oswald's and appeared to have given its canons control over education in Gloucester.

The dispute rumbled on with serious consequences for more than a decade. In 1396, armed with yet another confirmation of Giffard's ordinance from the latest Bishop of Worcester, Robert Tideman, Llanthony Priory made its own appeal to the Crown. The Canons of Llanthony summoned Thomas Duke, the prior of St Oswald's, and Thomas More, master of its school, to appear before the Justices of the Common Pleas at Westminster, where they attempted to sue them for a sum of up to £40, representing fees lost through boys attending the school at St Oswald's rather than the one at Llanthony. The court seems not to have given a judgement, perhaps reflecting the fact that neither of the rivals could dislodge the other by any legal process as both possessed charters that could justify their claims.[51]

---

48 A. Platts and G. H. Hainton, *Education in Gloucestershire: A Short History*, p. 7.
49 N. Orme, *Education in the West of England 1066 – 1548*, p. 60.
50 Ibid, p. 61.
51 Ibid, p. 62.

The two rival Augustinian houses appeared to agree on a compromise in 1400, claiming that they were doing so for the sake of the scholars of Gloucester. The agreement was in reality a triumph for Llanthony as it saw St Oswald's surrendering most of its claims. In return, the Llanthony school agreed to teach eight boys sent from St Oswald's without charge and to provide St Oswald's with an annual sum of 13s 4d and fifteen cocks in Lent, the season when schoolmasters were entitled to receive spoils from Shrove Tuesday cockfights.

The compromise of 1400 did not, however, prevent further battles between the two priories. In 1410 John Hamelyn, the master of the Llanthony school, and his usher, Richard Darcy, brought a case before one of the royal courts, the Court of Common Pleas, in order to claim for damages resulting from the competition they continued to face from St Oswald's.[52] The case resulted in a judgement still known today as the 'Gloucester Schools Case'. The judges on the Court of Common Pleas ended by dismissing the case and giving the opinion that competition and choice in education were good things 'which cannot be punished by our law'. They may have based their judgement on the fact that there was a rising demand for education in the years following the Black Death, which are often regarded as an age of ambition and social advancement.[53] A higher standard of living was being enjoyed in the 15th century as the nation's resources were being shared among fewer people.

In turning down the case, the judges of the Common Pleas declined to take on the responsibility of adjudicating between rival patrons and laid down the principle that teaching was a spiritual matter rather than one that the secular courts needed to concern themselves with.[54] At the same time, to the detriment of Hamelyn and Darcy, the court ruled that in any case one schoolmaster could not sue another for establishing a rival school unless there was clear evidence of the second schoolmaster actively preventing children from attending the first school. Just as one miller could not sue another for starting a mill near his own, even though it reduced his trade, the court argued that one schoolmaster could not sue another for a similar action.[55] In taking this stance the judges of the

---

[52] J. Baker, *Sources of English Legal History: Private Law to 1750*, Oxford (1986), p. 671.
[53] F. Du Boulay, *An Age of Ambition*, Thomas Nelson (1970), pp. 117–18.
[54] A. F. Leach, *The Schools of Medieval England*, pp. 127 & 238.
[55] J. Baker, *Sources of English Legal History: Private Law to 1750*, Oxford (1986), p. 672.

Common Pleas intimated that Llanthony Priory's monopoly was illegal.

Whilst this may potentially have led to a major threat to the Llanthony school, the passage of time resulted in the significance of the case becoming merely theoretical. In practice, from 1410 onwards, economic and financial circumstances left St Oswald's in sharp decline and no longer in any position to mount a serious challenge against Llanthony's dominance. St Oswald's was badly affected by the Black Death. Even more significantly, it suffered from a prolonged period of maladministration. In 1486 Thomas Rotherham, the Archbishop of York, found the priory slack in its observance of the Augustinian rule and heavily in debt.[56] When the Reformation began, the community at St Oswald's had dwindled to just seven canons and eight servants.[57] The church was said to be ruinous and it was one of the first priories in the country to be dissolved by Henry VIII in 1536.[58]

The Llanthony grammar school in the 15th century

Llanthony Secunda prospered with the demise of its rival in the 15th century; it became a well-endowed house with lands in Ireland and many manors in its possession and was possibly the richest Augustinian house in the whole of England.[59] Richard II and Henry VII are known to have stayed at the priory. Edward IV granted the Gloucester Llanthony all the possessions of the older community in Gwent.[60] Henry Dene, prior at the end of the 15th century, became a counsellor to Henry VII and rose to become Archbishop of Canterbury in 1501.[61]

With its confidence buoyed, Llanthony carried on defending its right to be the sole provider of grammar school education in Gloucester and the school in Longsmith Street continued right up to the eve of the Reformation.[62] The 'Rental of All the Houses in Gloucester' compiled in 1455 by Robert Cole, one of the Llanthony canons, tells us that in

---

[56]   G. Waters, *King Richard's Gloucester: Life in a Mediaeval Town*, p. 49.
[57]   C. Heighway, *Gloucester: A History and Guide*, Alan Sutton (1985), p. 98.
[58]   W. Page, *The Victoria History of the Counties of England: Gloucestershire*, volume 2, p. 25.
[59]   J. Rhodes (ed), *A Calendar of the Registers of the Priory of Llanthony by Gloucester*, p. xiv.
[60]   J. N. Langston, 'Priors of Llanthony by Gloucester', *Transactions of the Bristol and Gloucestershire Archaeological Society* (1942), volume 63, p. 123.
[61]   M. Bayley, *St Mary de Crypt Gloucester*, Leyhill (1995), p. 3.
[62]   N. Orme, *Medieval Schools from Roman Britain to Renaissance England*, p. 200.

Longsmith Street 'the prior of Llanthony holds in fee there a curtilage with a tenement, wherein a school is held, with appurtenances'.[63] William Breter and John Goode[64] are referred to as its masters in 1430 and in 1441 respectively. Thomas Browning was appointed as master in 1502. Under the terms of his appointment, he received a salary of four marks per year paid quarterly, a house in Severn Street, food and drink including a loaf and ale every night, and a gentleman's gown each year.[65]

It is often said that the basis of the medieval curriculum lay in the 'trivium' of grammar, rhetoric and logic established by Aristotle and others in the Classical World. [66] In any practical sense, however, life in the Longsmith Street grammar school, as in every other type of medieval school, was dominated by Latin. The boys were required to speak to each other in Latin throughout the day. This made the kind of Latin they used very much a living language, the universal vehicle of speech and writing that opened access to the world of learning.[67] The Bible they had was the Latin Vulgate, and Greek philosophy and Arabic science were available only through Latin translations. Latin was the language of lecture rooms and text books. Latin was also the language of trade and administration and the language in which all business and legal records were maintained. An education in Latin was therefore key for most careers, not just those in the church, but also in the law, in government administration or at universities.

Figure 17: Woodcut of c.1490 showing a grammar schoolmaster, birch in hand and surrounded by his pupils reading their books.

---

63   G. Waters, *King Richard's Gloucester: Life in a Mediaeval Town*, p. 48.
64   N. Orme, *Education in the West of England 1066 – 1548*, p. 64.
65   J. Rhodes (ed), *A Calendar of the Registers of the Priory of Llanthony by Gloucester*, p. 59.
66   J. Lawson, *Medieval Education and the Reformation*, Routledge & Kegan Paul (1967), p. 9.
67   A. L. Poole, *From Domesday Book to Magna Carta*, p. 232.

Alongside spoken Latin, the school provided a rigorous study of grammar, which meant the detailed study of Latin words and phrases. Boys learnt how words were inflected and spent a long time memorising their meanings. The importance attached to this is reflected in the fact that the Longsmith Street school itself was called a 'grammar school' and its master was sometimes referred to as a 'grammarian'. Parsing was a common exercise; the master chose a word in a text and asked the pupils to identify it as a noun or verb and to name the paradigm it was displaying. Another of the main activities was the 'making of Latins', translating sentences or short prose passages from English into Latin in order to demonstrate how the language worked. A more advanced task, which aimed to develop a wider vocabulary and a deeper understanding of syntax, was composing a 'Latin' on a theme without being given any English to start with.[68] In an attempt to interest the pupils, the themes of a 'Latin' were often taken from amusing proverbs, everyday life or ceremonies in the church calendar. One example that has survived is: 'The nearer the church, the further from God'.[69]

Books had a major role in the 15th-century grammar school. The most basic Latin textbook was the *Ars Minor* of the Classical scholar Donatus, a book that originated in the 4th century and was updated at various points in the Middle Ages. It explained the different parts of speech, set out the inflexions of common nouns and verbs and conveyed the elementary rules of syntax.[70] Alphabetical word lists and dictionaries that provided information on the etymologies of words were also available. These might include the *Liber Derivationum* written in Gloucester Abbey by Osbern or the *Synonyma* and the *Equivoca*, which were attributed to an English grammarian known as John of Garland. Books of this type would have been used mainly by the master or usher, who would have read out passages over and over again until their pupils had learnt them by heart. Nonetheless, late medieval woodcuts and manuscript illustrations do exist that show books proudly being shared between boys and masters.[71] For Latin verse they would have accessed the *Grecismus* of Evrard of Béthune, an early 13th-century French scholar, or the

---

[68] N. Orme, *Medieval Schools from Roman Britain to Renaissance England*, p. 112.
[69] N. Orme, 'Education in Medieval Bristol and Gloucestershire', *Transactions of the Bristol and Gloucestershire Archaeological Society*, volume 112 (2004), p. 21.
[70] N. Orme, *Education in the West of England 1066 – 1548*, p. 22.
[71] M. Seaborne, *The English School: its Architecture and Organisation 1370 – 1870*, Routledge & Kegan Paul (1971), p. 1.

Doctrinale (*Teaching Manual*) of Alexander of Ville-Dieu, which was written in hexameter verse in the hope that the grammar it contained would be remembered more easily.[72]

Where boys at a school such as the grammar school in Longsmith Street learnt to write and to perfect their written skills is a point of considerable obscurity. As writing formed a very limited aspect of the curriculum, it appears that most had to attend out-of-school classes run by scriveners, who were writing professionals making their living from copying business and judicial records.[73]

Rather than involving lengthy written work, a lot of learning in the grammar school took place through memorisation, especially consigning to memory texts that were written in rhyming couplets or verse. Another common method of learning involved the use of questions and answers; masters would ask a question and train the pupil to give the appropriate response.[74] Classwork involved plenty of oral interchange. Pupils sitting on their own benches were usually able to progress at their own speed. The master would call them out to his seat, give them a task to do or a text to learn, and then examine them on the subject until it was taken to heart. At a time when corporal punishment was common throughout society, beating acted as an additional incentive for those who were slow or reluctant to learn. When a man qualified as a master of grammar at university, he was given a birch as a symbol of his new profession. Pictures of medieval schools invariably show the master grasping his birch, a bundle of twigs that could be used to administer beatings, although the degree of harshness with which it was used is impossible to assess.[75]

The oldest boys in the grammar school aged sixteen to eighteen moved on to the final stage of the curriculum, which included the study of logic (the science of reasoning), rhetoric (the art of effective public speaking), literary texts and the principles of literary criticism. Key texts from Classical times – the works of Cato, Virgil, Juvenal, Horace and Ovid – were widely available. One anthology, known as the *Sex Auctores* (*Six Authors*), which contained selected poems by Cato and other Romans, seems to have been particularly valued.[76] Other poems read in school

---

72   J. Lawson & H. Silver, *A Social History of Education in England*, p. 48.
73   J. Lawson, *Medieval Education and the Reformation*, p. 26.
74   N. Orme, *Medieval Schools from Roman Britain to Renaissance England*, pp. 147–8.
75   D. W. Sylvester, *Educational Documents 800 – 1816*, Methuen (1970), p. 34.
76   N. Orme, *Medieval Schools from Roman Britain to Renaissance England*, pp. 97–8.

tended to focus on wisdom, morality and worship. One of the most popular texts was the *Liber Parabolarum* (*Book of Parallels*) ascribed to Alain de Lille,[77] a French poet who died in 1203.

The medieval calendar already followed a well-established practice of dividing the year into quarters or terms: Michaelmas, Christmas, Easter and Midsummer.[78] The grammar schools adapted these terms for their teaching, although Midsummer was generally lost through the custom of taking a long vacation, thereby creating the outline of the three-term year with which we are familiar today.

Non-academic activities, including drama and sport, had no formal part in the medieval curriculum, but they were encouraged by schools as part of religious festivals and holidays. Among these, two occasions stood out for the boys who attended the Llanthony Priory school in Longsmith Street. The first came early in Advent with the feast of St Nicholas, which was marked by the ceremony of the Boy Bishop.[79] There is a specific reference to this in the agreement of 1400 reached by Llanthony and St Oswald's, which stated that each of the grammar schools retained the right to choose its own Boy Bishop.[80] In some respects this was a solemn festival designed to make boys think about the nature of authority and the rules on which their communities were based. Each year the boys chose one of their number to become a Boy Bishop. At a service of Vespers on the eve of St Nicholas, as the choir chanted one of the verses from the Magnificat, 'He shall put down the mighty from their seat', the boy selected was given a bishop's robe, a mitre and a crozier. He then ascended into the pulpit, where he preached a sermon that he had prepared with the help of the schoolmaster.[81] As the duties of a 'Boy Bishop' lasted for three weeks until Holy Innocents' Day, he also became involved with a range of festivities, sometimes called the 'Feast of Fools', which included feasting, dancing and mummers' plays, some of which could take on a much more raucous tone.[82] It was through the plays associated with these ceremonies that medieval grammar schoolboys received their first training in the rudiments of drama.

---

77   N. Orme, *Education in the West of England 1066 – 1548*, p. 22.

78   N. Orme, *Medieval Schools from Roman Britain to Renaissance England*, p. 155.

79   C. Dainton, *Medieval Schools of England*, p. 495.

80   N. Orme, *Education in the West of England 1066 – 1548*, p. 62.

81   See next chapter for the ceremony of the Boy Bishop in St Peter's Song School at Gloucester.

82   N. Mackenzie, *The Medieval Boy Bishop*, Matador (2012), p. 88.

The other holiday most anticipated by the boys of the Llanthony Priory school came at the beginning of Lent and in particular on Shrove Tuesday, a day given over to sports of various kinds. This was an occasion for 'Shrovetide mob football', which involved an unlimited number of boys on opposing teams attempting to drag an inflated pig's bladder by any means

Figure 18: Shrovetide cockfighting, a popular sport at the Llanthony grammar school.

Figure 19: Fourteenth-century misericord carving in Gloucester Cathedral showing two boys possibly playing mob football.

possible to markers at each end of a street.[83] A glimpse of this sport in action can be seen on a mid-14th-century misericord carving in the quire of Gloucester Cathedral. This shows two competitive youths running vigorously towards each other bouncing a ball in mid-air.[84] The other medieval Shrovetide sport that was popular in Gloucester was cockfighting. The agreement of 1400 between Llanthony and St Oswald's states that both priories would share the birds, with the prior of St Oswald's being guaranteed at least fifteen cocks after the Shrove Tuesday cockfighting was over.[85] It is likely that the school would have trained its own cocks for this occasion, sharpening their beaks and attaching metal spurs to their legs. The origins of the custom in London were described by William fitz Stephen in a biography of Thomas Becket written in the 1180s. 'Every year on the day which is called the carnival', he wrote, 'all the boys in each school bring their master their game-cock, and the whole morning is devoted to the boys' play, they having a holiday to look on at the cock-fights in their schools. In the afternoon, the whole youth of the city then goes into the suburban level for a solemn game of ball'.[86]

The demise of the Llanthony Priory grammar school

As the 16th century dawned, in response to the growing sophistication of polyphonic music used in late medieval services,[87] it would appear that – like St Peter's Abbey – Llanthony began to run a small music school inside the priory alongside the public grammar school in Longsmith Street. When he was appointed master in 1502, Thomas Browning was allowed to supplement his pay by teaching other 'singing boys' in the priory and receiving their fees, provided they did no harm while staying there.[88] William Peryeman of Westbury-on-Severn is recorded as one who took advantage of this arrangement in 1513 when he joined the priory school for

---

83   F. P. Magoun, 'Football in Medieval England and in Middle-English Literature', *The American Historical Review*, volume 35 (1929), p. 34.

84   D. Welander, *The History, Art and Architecture of Gloucester Cathedral*, Alan Sutton (1991), p. 551.

85   N. Orme, *Medieval Children*, Yale University Press (2003), p. 185.

86   A. F. Leach, *Educational Charters and Documents*, p. 85.

87   These developments in music are explained in Chapter Four.

88   J. Rhodes (ed), *A Calendar of the Registers of the Priory of Llanthony by Gloucester*, pp. 59–61.

three years. He was 'to be taught and informed at playing organs by the space of one year and then in grammar the other two years'.[89]

Throughout this period Llanthony Priory continued to defend its claim to have the sole legal right to provide education outside St Peter's Abbey. In 1513 a decree was proclaimed in all the parish churches of Gloucester 'against anyone calling himself a scholar keeping any school for learning or sending anyone not of mature age to such schools, except those schools or school the teaching of which has been freely granted by the prior and convent of Llanthony to a fit master'.[90]

John Hogges of Coventry, appointed in 1533, was the last master at the Llanthony school before the Reformation.[91] As well as his duties in Longsmith Street, he was required to provide musical instruction for four boys in the priory, two as tenors and two as trebles. He was to teach them 'the science of music, that is to say singing and playing at organs, to keep Our Lady mass and anthem daily, and to further well and truly keep all other masses and anthems, evensongs and matins'.[92]

The Longsmith Street school was by this date on the point of closure. It did not survive the upheavals of the Reformation, but seems to have closed about 1534 – 35 in the wake of a particularly sad scandal about the welfare of some of its pupils. Allegations of intimate relations between the prior of Llanthony, Richard Hart, and some of the schoolboys are referred to in a letter preserved in the state papers of 1535.[93] According to the correspondent, the affairs were reported by a schoolmaster, probably John Hogges. The prior retaliated by having his critic placed in the stocks for three days and nights and driving him out of Gloucester.[94] After the Dissolution, Hogges reappeared as organist and master of the choristers at Hereford Cathedral.

It has been suggested that the scandal may have been fictitious, being deliberately invented as part of an attempt to blacken the reputation of the religious orders just as the Valor Ecclesiasticus enquiry was about to begin

---

[89]   Ibid, p. 114.

[90]   W. Page, *The Victoria History of the Counties of England: Gloucestershire*, volume 2, p. 319.

[91]   N. Orme, 'Education in Medieval Bristol and Gloucestershire', p. 25.

[92]   J. Rhodes (ed), *A Calendar of the Registers of the Priory of Llanthony by Gloucester*, p. 195.

[93]   B. Lowe, *Commonwealth and the English Reformation: Protestantism and the Politics of Religious Change in the Gloucester Vale*, p. 61.

[94]   J. N. Langston, 'Priors of Llanthony by Gloucester', *Transactions of the Bristol and Gloucestershire Archaeological Society* (1942), volume 63, p. 137.

the process of monastic dissolution. Alternatively, behaviour of this kind may have been commonplace and, whereas it might have been swept under the carpet in previous generations, in the 1530s the schoolmaster concerned may have decided to report it precisely because he thought that his allegations might be taken seriously in view of the rising tide of anticlericalism. We do not know, but what is certain is that later that same year, 1535, when another rental survey was undertaken in Gloucester, this time by David Mathew, the Longsmith Street schoolroom was referred to as 'the old school house which lies vacant'.[95]

On that pitiful note, just ahead of the sweeping changes that were about to be initiated by King Henry VIII, the 400-year association between Llanthony Priory and grammar school education in Gloucester came to an abrupt end.

---

[95] R. Furney, 'Manuscript of the History of the City of Gloucester' (1743), Gloucestershire Record Office D327/1, p. 98.

CHAPTER FOUR

The Almonry and Song Schools of St Peter's Abbey:

Serving the Medieval Benedictine Community

The creation of the almonry school

During the 14th century the leaders of St Peter's Abbey recommitted themselves to the importance of education and personal study habits. Pope Clement V issued a decree from the Council of Vienne in 1311 that encouraged Benedictine monks to continue their own formal education in order to build on the skills and knowledge they had acquired before entry to the order.[1] It stated that every monastery with sufficient resources should maintain a master to instruct the brethren in grammar and logic. In 1336 a later Pope, Benedict XII, issued a new constitution for the Benedictines known as 'Summi Magistri'. This laid down that all monks should be educated in grammar, logic and philosophy and that monasteries with more than twenty monks should be prepared to send at least one of them to university.[2] It was during this period that the cloister school established at Gloucester in the 11th century began to be run as an almonry school.[3]

The almonry was the part of the abbey that oversaw the distribution of charity to the poor. It was from this building that food left over from the monks' meals was distributed; it also acted as a hostel for paupers and pilgrims who were visiting the abbey. Boys from modest backgrounds who were being admitted for schooling were now taken into the almonry, where

---

[1] N. Orme, *Medieval Schools from Roman Britain to Renaissance England*, Yale University Press (2006), p. 270.

[2] D. Knowles, *The Religious Orders in England*, Cambridge (1955), volume II, p. 295.

[3] N. Orme, 'Education in Medieval Bristol and Gloucestershire', *Transactions of the Bristol and Gloucestershire Archaeological Society*, volume 112 (2004), p. 11.

they were given board and lodging as part of the abbey's charitable mission. The almonry boys received their own daily ration of bread and had the first call on other food left over from meals in the abbey before it was distributed to the poor who begged at the abbey gate. In return they took on a share of duties, which included washing the feet of the poor and serving at the altar.[4] It became common in the 14th century for monks to be ordained as priests, which brought a requirement to celebrate a private mass each day at one of the various side altars that sprang up in the nave, transepts and other areas of the abbey. This meant that altar boys were increasingly in demand as acolytes or servers.[5]

The buildings next to St Mary's Gate in the lower part of College Green served as the almonry at Gloucester. Outside this gate, the main thoroughfare between the abbey and the town, the poor assembled each day to receive alms. The almonry boys' lodging was probably on the site just to the north of St Mary's Gate now occupied by Community House, which contains

Figure 20: St Mary's Gate, close to which was the lodging house for boys attending the almonry school at St Peter's Abbey.

4   A. Mould, *The English Chorister: A History*, London (2007), p. 39.
5   S. Boynton & E. Rice, *Young Choristers 650 – 1700*, Boydell Press Woodbridge (2008), p. 44.

medieval work in its basement.[6] Access was through a (now blocked) door on the west side of the 14th-century arched gateway that leads into Miller's Green. By having the boys living in this building on the edge of the abbey, the authorities were emphasising the fact that they were no longer perceived as junior monks but as secular boys who were being given a general education and were free to leave the community when they wished.[7]

The link with the almonry should not lead us to believe that all the boys who came to the new school were necessarily poor. As time went on, boys from less destitute backgrounds came to join them. Monks, for example, might ask for places for their relatives and even the most privileged landowning families eventually became keen on taking advantage of the offer of free board, lodging and education. Some of them even set up endowments to fund the almonry schools.[8] What began entirely as a charity therefore gradually became more complicated and, as competition for places intensified, the almonry would have been able to select the most talented from those who applied.

The average size of a late medieval almonry school was between twelve and twenty boys, although the number varied from place to place.[9] Thirteen was regarded as an ideal number – representing Christ and his twelve Apostles – and Gloucester was one of the abbeys that tried hard to stick to this fixed complement.[10] A grant of 1515 that appointed a new master to the school at Gloucester mentions a figure of at least thirteen; it refers to 'the youthful brethren of the monastery sent to him by the abbot and the thirteen boys of the clerks' chamber'.[11]

There is documentary evidence of the existence of the almonry schoolroom at Gloucester in 1378.[12] This was the year that Richard II held his Parliament in Gloucester for twenty-eight days during November and December, taking over pretty well the entire monastery and much of the rest of the town. The abbey's own record of events, the *Historia*, comments that

---

[6] D. Welander, *The History, Art and Architecture of Gloucester Cathedral*, Alan Sutton (1991), p. 312.

[7] N. Orme, *Medieval Schools from Roman Britain to Renaissance England*, p. 278.

[8] A. F. Leach, *The Schools of Medieval England*, Methuen (1915), p. 217.

[9] D. Knowles, *The Religious Orders of England*, volume II, p. 295.

[10] A. F. Leach, *Educational Charters and Documents*, Cambridge (1911), p. xxxii.

[11] W. Page, *The Victoria History of the Counties of England: Gloucestershire*, volume 2, London (1907), p. 343.

[12] Ibid, p. 337.

'to be sure, all places in the monastery being thus open to Parliament, they were thronged so that they looked to beholders more like a market fair than a house of religion. The green of the cloister was so flattened by wrestling and ball games that it was hopeless to expect any grass to be left there'. It records that the monks were required to take their meals in the schoolroom. 'When the king and his whole family were lodged in the abbey, which was so full everywhere with them and the Parliament, for some days the community ate impartially according to the circumstances in the dormitory and afterwards, which was more convenient, in the schoolroom, both on meat-days and fish-days, as long as the Parliament lasted'.[13]

We are not sure of the exact location of this almonry schoolroom. The most likely possibility is that it was in the 13th-century stone-built undercroft that forms the ground floor of the Parliament Room (the timber-framed upper storey of which was constructed later in the 15th century). A document of 1541, when this building became part of the deanery, referred to it as an empty, ruinous range extending to the inner gate and known as 'the old workhouse and old school house'.[14] This would have been a convenient location close to the almonry lodgings and related buildings, which were centred around St Mary's Gate.

The move of the school to this location from the cloisters may have taken place in the 1370s or 1380s. It was at this time that the Norman cloisters were ambitiously redesigned with their famous fan vaulting, the earliest full-scale structural fan vault to be found anywhere in England.[15] The *Historia* explains that the north walk of the cloisters, the site of the early medieval cloister school, had its fan vaulting inserted 'in fine style at great expense' over a period of several decades when Walter Froucester was abbot between 1381 and 1412.[16] The scale of this refurbishment and the noise of the hammering and chiselling it entailed would have been incompatible with the existence of a fully functioning school in the cloister and its requirements for silent study.[17]

---

[13]   *Historia Monasterii Sancti Petri Gloucestriae*, translated by William Barber and printed in Welander, *The History, Art and Architecture of Gloucester Cathedral*, pp. 634-635.

[14]   D. Welander, *The History, Art and Architecture of Gloucester Cathedral*, p. 309.

[15]   C. Heighway, S. Hamilton et alii, *Gloucester Cathedral: Faith, Art and Architecture*, Scala (2011), p. 39.

[16]   *Historia Monasterii Sancti Petri Gloucestriae*, translated by William Barber and printed in Welander, *The History, Art and Architecture of Gloucester Cathedral*, p. 636.

[17]   J. Kerr, *Life in the Medieval Cloister*, Continuum London (2009), p. 81.

Figure 21: The Parliament Room, built over a 13th-century undercroft which may have housed Gloucester's almonry school.

Figure 22: Memorial brass from Headbourne Worthy (Hampshire) showing a 15th-century schoolboy in the distinctive gown of a medieval scholar.

The almonry school at work

Like their predecessors in the cloister school, almonry boys were recruited from the age of about seven and were usually supported for at least four years in the school. Geoffrey Chaucer, writing in the 1380s, had an angelic seven-year-old schoolboy as the central character in his *Prioress's Tale*. Although he was only seven, the boy was sufficiently competent to sing with confidence both the 'Ave Maria' and the 'Alma Redemptoris' in Latin.

> This little child, his little lesson learning,
> Sat at his primer in the school, and there,
> While boys were taught the antiphons, kept turning,
> And heard the 'Alma Redemptoris' fair,
> And drew as near as ever he did dare,
> Marking the words, remembering every note,
> Until the first verse he could sing by rote.[18]

Although they lacked a uniform in the modern sense and were no longer required to have a shaven tonsure, the boys of the almonry school would have been easy to recognise. They usually wore a simple long gown lined with lambskin, which stretched to the ankles and covered their underclothes. The best illustration of one of these gowns comes from a brass in the church of Headbourne Worthy, Hampshire, in memory of a 15th-century schoolboy, John Kent, who died in 1434. It forms part of an extensive study made by the King's School's 19th-century usher, Herbert Haines, who was a national authority on monumental brasses; he says that the purpose of the gown was to make the boys resemble a wealthy leisured adult, indicating that they were neither clergy nor manual labourers.[19]

Details of the structure of the school day in Gloucester Abbey's almonry school almost certainly followed the national pattern. Most schools opened at 6 a.m., even in winter. The pupils worked until 8 a.m. or 9 a.m., when prayers were said and a psalm and the 'Ave Maria' were sung in the schoolroom. Breakfast was taken immediately after this. Studies resumed at 10 a.m. and continued until about noon, at which point dinner was taken. Afternoon school usually lasted about four hours, either from 1 p.m. to 5

---

[18] G. Chaucer, *The Canterbury Tales*, London (1988) edition, p. 174.
[19] H. Haines, *A Manual for the Study of Monumental Brasses*, Oxford (1848), p. 38.

p.m. or 2 p.m. to 6 p.m., depending on the length of the lunchbreak.[20] It is likely that the boys were allowed to eat their meals in the monks' refectory, the site of which now lies in the garden of Little Cloister House.

The curriculum followed in Gloucester's almonry school would have centred around reading and song. The younger boys spent most of their time learning the alphabet and then using it to practise the pronunciation and reading of Latin words. Children learnt the alphabet either from wall displays or from a hand-held board. It was recited as a kind of devotion, beginning with the sign of the cross and ending with 'Amen'.[21] Reading began with the Pater Noster (the Lord's Prayer), the Ave Maria, the Apostles' Creed and graces for mealtimes, which were written in prayer books called primers. Pupils then proceeded to read plainsong chants, hymnals, antiphonals and psalters. These existed in large numbers and often contained big clear letters easily recognisable by children. The oldest boys at the almonry school then followed the same curriculum as that of a grammar school based around Latin. The best pupils could be expected to reach standards similar to those of the grammar school itself and had access to books in the abbey library.

Although most schoolmasters remained priests, by this date the teaching profession was a well-established one for laymen too. These were individuals who in an earlier age might have become clerics, but instead now chose a life as a schoolmaster, one of the advantages being that they could marry and have a family rather than be required to follow a celibate lifestyle.[22] The master who ran the almonry school was usually a university graduate recruited from outside the monastic community. He would have been of the same social status as his colleagues employed in a grammar school and would have received much the same salary. Wages were generally in the region of £6 per year, plus board and lodging, fuel and a gown.[23]

John Tucke was master of the Gloucester almonry school from 1515 until 1540.[24] A native of Burford and then a boarder at Winchester College, he arrived in Gloucester after graduating from New College, Oxford, and

---

[20]   N. Orme, *Medieval Schools from Roman Britain to Renaissance England*, p. 144.
[21]   Ibid, pp. 57-58.
[22]   J. A. F. Thomson, *The Transformation of Medieval England*, Longman (1983), p. 347.
[23]   N. Orme, *Medieval Schools from Roman Britain to Renaissance England*, p. 187.
[24]   N. Orme, 'Education in Medieval Bristol and Gloucestershire', p. 25.

following a stint as a young teacher at Higham Ferrers in Northamptonshire.[25] The job description he had in Gloucester Abbey was a demanding threefold one. His principal task was to teach grammar to the thirteen boys of the almonry. He was also charged with helping novice monks with their on-going education and lecturing to other adult monks when required.[26] His third set of responsibilities were in the abbey's song school, where he was required to teach plainsong and descant to five or six boys 'who were apt in learning to sing'.[27] For these tasks, his stipend was £6, plus a chamber, food and drink, fuel and a gown.[28] His gown was to be 'of the best cloth such as the gentlemen of our house receive', two cartloads of fuel were to be delivered to his house, and each day he was to receive a large helping of both the first and the second courses provided for the monks, supplemented by his own loaf and a flagon of abbey ale.[29] At least after 1527 Tucke lived with his wife, Anne, and his two children in a house called Newland, which may have been situated on London Road just outside Gloucester's outer north gate close to the site of the modern Gloucester Royal Hospital.[30]

The song school

Alongside the almonry school, St Peter's Abbey at Gloucester also maintained a separate song school. This concentrated on teaching boys plainsong chants, music and the ability to read Latin texts, although not necessarily the finer points of grammar.

We do not have an exact date for the creation of the song school at Gloucester, but it most likely occurred at some point during the second half of the 15th century. At this time there was a trend towards more elaborate polyphonic settings for the mass liturgies used in the larger abbeys, especially in the Lady Chapel, which unlike the quire was open to

---

[25] R. Woodley, *John Tucke: A Case Study in Early Tudor Music Theory*, Oxford University Press (1993), p. 2.
[26] N. Orme, *Education in the West of England 1066 – 1548*, University of Exeter (1976), p. 207.
[27] R. Woodley, *John Tucke: A Case Study in Early Tudor Music Theory*, p. 22.
[28] A. F. Leach, *The Schools of Medieval England*, Methuen (1915), p. 226.
[29] W. Page, *The Victoria History of the Counties of England: Gloucestershire*, volume 2, pp. 342–3.
[30] R. Woodley, *John Tucke: A Case Study in Early Tudor Music Theory*, p. 25.

townsfolk and the lay associates of the abbey.[31] Whereas early medieval monks sang Gregorian plainsong, the new anthems of the 15th century in praise of the Virgin Mary, called 'Marian antiphons', required a full range of voices, treble, alto, tenor and bass.[32] This meant that for the first time boys were required to make a distinctive contribution of their own to church music by singing separate parts rather than simply imitating the adult monks. The result was that boys and adult male singers who were not monks were brought into the Lady Chapel to sing together. [33]

Whereas instruction in music and chant had always been a feature of monastic schools, from the late 15th century the song school was hived off as a small and specialised institution in its own right. Polyphony involved the singing of highly demanding music, involving five, six or seven parts from high treble to low bass.[34] This in turn made the teaching more complicated and required a specialist teacher with the appropriate skills. Polyphonic singing also necessitated more rehearsal time to master the repertoire. It was no longer possible to teach such demanding skills whilst at the same time educating other boys who were engaged in reading and simple plainsong.[35] It has been estimated that at least a third of the time of the singing boys now went on their training and performances, leaving them less time for the study of grammar and other aspects of the curriculum.

It was in the 15th century that the Lady Chapel at St Peter's Abbey was enlarged and rebuilt, most of the work probably being undertaken in the 1470s.[36] This made it one of the largest Lady Chapels in the country.[37] It was intended to be a centre for the worship of the Virgin, employing the latest polyphonic music. Above the fan-vaulted chantry chapels that still exist on the north and south sides of the Lady Chapel are two singing galleries. They are accessed by small staircases set into the angles of the wall and would have been used by the boys of the song school and lay singing men who accompanied the monks chanting in the chapel below. [38] In the

---

[31] A. Mould, *The English Chorister: A History*, p. 39.
[32] C. Heighway et alii, *Gloucester Cathedral: Faith, Art and Architecture*, p. 45.
[33] J. G. Clark, *The Culture of Medieval English Monasticism*, Boydell Press (2007), p. 39.
[34] A. Mould, *The English Chorister: A History*, p. 37.
[35] N. Orme, *Medieval Schools from Roman Britain to Renaissance England*, pp. 66 & 282.
[36] C. Heighway et alii, *Gloucester Cathedral: Faith, Art and Architecture*, p. 43.
[37] D. Welander, *The History, Art and Architecture of Gloucester Cathedral*, p. 262.
[38] Ibid, p. 271.

Figure 23: Gloucester's Lady Chapel, built in the 1470s with the requirements of polyphonic singing in mind.

front of the galleries there still remain the medieval stone shelves on which books and music could be rested. The two choirs, one on the south side and one on the north, could sing, calling and responding to each other 'antiphonally' across the chapel.

The Gloucester song school clearly continued to work very closely with the almonry school; in many practical respects the two might actually be

Figure 24: The singing gallery on the north side of the Lady Chapel, which was used by the boys of the late 15th-century song school.

considered as separate departments of the same school. Some of the song school boys probably lived in the almonry lodgings.[39] They almost certainly shared some of their lessons with the almonry boys, but they would not have had access to as much grammar.

The grant of 1515 by which Abbot Parker appointed John Tucke as master of the almonry school made it clear that he was also required to teach the 'children of the chapel'.[40] He was to teach grammar to all thirteen boys in the almonry, but he also had the care of another five or six boys selected to specialise in plainsong and the increasingly complex demands of the new polyphonic singing. He was to 'teach and inform five or six of the boys, apt and ready to learn, in plainsong, divided or broken song and descant, sufficiently and diligently, and shall devotedly with the same boys keep the mass of the Blessed Virgin Mary and the antiphon belonging to it daily, and on Saturday mass of the name of Jesus with antiphon belonging to it, and on feast days shall be present at both Vespers and High Mass and

---

[39] A. Platts and G. H. Hainton, *Education in Gloucestershire: A Short History*, Gloucestershire County Council (1953), p. 7.

[40] F. W. Goodwin, *The King's School: Revised Notes upon its Foundation*, Gloucester (1922), p. 2.

at other times assigned by the precentor, solemnly singing and playing the organ'.[41]

A musical notebook compiled by Tucke for most of his career forms part of the archives held at the British Library in London. In it he describes himself as 'Master John Tucke, Bachelor of Arts and schoolmaster of both schools in Gloucester', the almonry and the song schools.[42] The book contains a wealth of entries on musical theory and passages that suggest that Tucke was an active composer. Illustrated with the square notation on four-line staves that were typical of this period, it devotes great attention to issues relating to the mensural notation used in vocal polyphonic music, including the use of coloration to mark notes in red, black and other colours to indicate different durational values. It also contains a list of terminological definitions, notes on compositional practices and even some medicinal recipes. The notebook, maintained in his own handwriting, was intended mainly for Tucke's own personal study, but it was also used as an aide-memoire in his teaching. The book, which has been described as 'the most wide-ranging theoretical treatment of mensural usage in England at this time', is one of the earliest teaching aids to have survived anywhere in the country and presents us with a unique insight into how music was taught in Gloucester Abbey on the eve of the Reformation.[43]

One colourful tradition associated with the Gloucester song school involved the election of a 'Boy Bishop' each year. This was a custom whereby a senior chorister was dressed in full bishop's regalia with a mitre and crozier as part of the festivities held on 6th December to celebrate the feast of St Nicholas, the patron saint of children. We do not know how far this was accompanied by the bawdy aspects of the celebrations reported elsewhere,[44] but despite various attempts to ban them the Boy Bishop rituals lingered on in the Gloucester song school until at least 1558, when a boy named John Stubs was elected.[45] The text of a sermon he was given to preach still survives, one of only three Boy Bishop sermons to remain in existence across the whole country.[46] Its theme, based on a reading from

---

[41] R. Woodley, *John Tucke: A Case Study in Early Tudor Music Theory*, p. 134.
[42] Ibid, p. 60.
[43] Ibid, p. 110.
[44] See Chapter Three.
[45] H. Maynard Smith, *Pre-Reformation England*, Palgrave Macmillan (1963), p. 139.
[46] W. W. Wooden, *Children's Literature of the English Renaissance*, Kentucky (1986), p. 31.

Matthew's Gospel, was 'Except you will be converted and made like little children, you shall not enter into the Kingdom of Heaven'.[47] Whilst much of what he said would have been written by an adult, the authentic voice of a schoolboy breaks through in several comments he included on the behaviour of his friends and the way punishments were administered in the song school. Stubs criticised the attitude of some of the children he saw being 'so evil-mannered for the most part and so viciously corrupted in their manners'.[48] He defended the use of corporal punishment on young boys, expressing his shock at the lack of reverence shown by a few of the choristers: 'how boyishly they behave themselves in the church, how rashly they come into the Quire without any reverence, never kneel nor countenance to say any prayer or Pater Noster, but rudely squat down on their tails and jostle with their fellows for a place'.[49] At the same time, however, his sermon criticised inconsistent teachers who beat boys for simple grammatical errors or singing out of tune, whilst neglecting more serious breaches of discipline such as offensive jokes or blasphemy.[50]

As the great changes associated with the Reformation approached, there was therefore already a long history of education of various kinds associated with Gloucester Abbey. The Valor Ecclesiasticus of 1535, a nationwide survey of the Church's financial situation ordered by Henry VIII, recorded that the abbey paid '£13 to poor scholars of the almonry in food and clothes; and £5 to three men and five boys of the Lady Chapel'.[51] Five years later when the abbey was in the process of being dissolved, Henry VIII's Court of Augmentations listed ten choristers who were about to transfer to the new Cathedral. A further five singing men – named as Thomas Veale, John Truman, Edward Swallow, John Ambrose and James Grith – made up the choir.[52]

In comparison with the numbers being educated in the grammar school run by the canons of Llanthony Priory, the scale of the educational provision by St Peter's Abbey was clearly quite modest. The numbers that were being educated in its two schools were relatively small. This has led

---

[47] C. Litzenberger, *The English Reformation and the Laity: Gloucestershire 1540-1580*, Cambridge (1997), p. 102.

[48] J. G. Nichols, *Two Sermons Preached by the Boy Bishop*, The Camden Society (1875), p. 23.

[49] Ibid, p. 24.

[50] Ibid, p. 28.

[51] W. Page, *The Victoria History of the Counties of England: Gloucestershire*, volume 2, p. 343.

[52] R. Woodley, *John Tucke: A Case Study in Early Tudor Music Theory*, p. 139.

Figure 25: Two pages from the musical notebook of John Tucke, master of the almonry and song schools at St Peter's Abbey; these pages illustrate a chant known as the 'Arsis and Thesis', which features an increasing strength in the chant followed by a fading.

one recent historian, surveying the provision of education across Gloucestershire as a whole at the end of the Middle Ages, to deplore 'the rather poor effort expended by the monks of St Peter's'.[53]

Most contemporaries would not have been so critical. Compared with previous generations, they perceived themselves to be living through an era of rising educational opportunity. It was this that led the author of *Piers Plowman*, William Langland, to complain that 'nowadays every cobbler's son and beggar's brat goes to school'.[54] The creation of both an almonry and a song school at Gloucester, financed largely out of the charitable resources of St Peter's, was an integral part of this process.

---

[53] B. Lowe, *Commonwealth and the English Reformation: Protestantism and the Politics of Religious Change in the Gloucester Vale*, Routledge St Andrew's Studies in Reformation History (2010), p. 60.

[54] J. W. Adamson, *A Short History of Education*, Cambridge (1922), p. 76.

CHAPTER FIVE

The Chantry Schools of Gloucester:

Our First 'Free' Schools

The development of chantries

During the 14th and 15th centuries another type of school began to make its appearance in medieval England, the endowed school set up by a wealthy individual benefactor. The majority of the endowed schools, including those at Gloucester, were small chantry schools attached to parish churches.[1]

The Black Death of 1348 – 49 and subsequent plagues, which may have killed a third or more of England's inhabitants, provided the main stimulus for this development. It seems that the reduction in population made it difficult for some grammar schoolmasters to attract sufficient pupils to make a living entirely from their fees. Wealthy benefactors were therefore asked to step in by endowing schools with property or annuities, so that the schoolmaster would receive a guaranteed income without being totally reliant on what his pupils paid. One way in which they responded was by founding chantries in the churches with which they were associated.

The main purpose of a chantry was to maintain services of intercession for the dead. Most people at this time believed that after death they were unlikely to enter heaven immediately, but their souls would be sent instead to a place halfway between heaven and hell. This was called Purgatory and belief in it increasingly featured in the teaching of the Church after the Council of Lyons in 1274. Purgatory was an unpleasant place, where it was thought the soul would be tortured potentially for a long period.[2] The exact length of time spent there would depend on the nature of the individual person's sins, on how frequently they had done good works or been on pilgrimages, and also crucially on the prayers being said for them by the

---

1   W. Page, *The Victoria History of the Counties of England: Gloucestershire*, volume 2, London (1907), p. 27.
2   R. Strong, *A History of the English Country Church*, London (2007), p. 39.

living, and the masses conducted on their behalf.[3] During the 14th century, those who could afford to, sectioned off parts of their parish churches and built special chapels there known as chantries, leaving money in their wills to employ a priest to celebrate votive masses and say prayers for the souls of the departed on a daily basis.

As the Middle Ages proceeded, the churches of Gloucester came to support a plethora of specially dedicated altars and chantry chapels. As early as 1274 William of Cheltenham left property in his will to the Church of St Mary de Crypt to support a priest who would celebrate mass for his soul and that of his wife, Alditha.[4] Richard Manchester made arrangements in his will of 1454 for the creation of another chantry in the church, stating 'that all his silver is to be sold by his executors, who are to fund with the proceeds of the sale an honest chaplain to continually celebrate at the altar of St John in the said Church of St Mary for the testator's soul and for the souls of Margery and Joan, his late wives, and of all his relations and benefactors for so long as the money will last . . . and that such chaplain should say on every Thursday in his mass the prayer "Deus cui proprium minor" for the soul of the testator and for the other souls above mentioned'.[5] Yet a third chantry dedicated to St Catherine was established in St Mary de Crypt by Garet van Eck in 1506.[6] St John Northgate, then known as the Church of St John the Baptist, supported a whole range of chantries dedicated to St Mary, St Anne, the Holy Trinity and the Holy Rood.[7] In St Mary de Lode Church a chantry of St Mary existed in 1331 and by 1420 another chantry had been established by the guild of the Holy Trinity.[8]

Important though their task was, even the most dutiful of chantry priests would have struggled to make the saying of prayers for the departed a full-time occupation. Some of the chantry bequests therefore included

[3]   S. Friar, *The Sutton Companion to Cathedrals and Abbeys*, Stroud (2007), p. 60.
[4]   N. M. Herbert, *The Victoria History of the Counties of England: Gloucestershire*, volume 4, London (1988), p. 300.
[5]   Unpublished papers by F. S. Hockaday, Lydney, 'Hockaday Abstracts', volume 216, Gloucestershire Record Office, D3439/1/216.
[6]   N. M. Herbert, *The Victoria History of the Counties of England: Gloucestershire*, volume 4, p. 301.
[7]   S. Rudder, *A New History of Gloucestershire*, Cirencester (1779), republished by Alan Sutton in 2006, p. 183.
[8]   N. M. Herbert, *The Victoria History of the Counties of England: Gloucestershire*, volume 4, p. 304.

Figure 26: Chantry Chapel of Thomas Seebroke which survives inside Gloucester Cathedral.

provision for the setting up of a small school, in which the priest would teach. The earliest scheme of this kind in Gloucestershire was the grammar school founded by Lady Katharine, widow of Lord Berkeley, at Wotton-under-Edge in 1384.[9] As well as teaching grammar, the schoolmaster appointed was required to celebrate masses for the soul of the foundress.

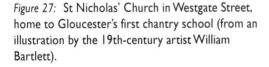

Figure 27: St Nicholas' Church in Westgate Street, home to Gloucester's first chantry school (from an illustration by the 19th-century artist William Bartlett).

---

[9]   N. Orme, *Education in the West of England 1066 – 1548*, University of Exeter (1976), p. 16.

The chantry school of St Nicholas in Gloucester

Within Gloucester itself the first chantry school to be established was attached to St Nicholas' Church in Westgate Street. A bequest in the will of Thomas Gloucester in 1446 made provision for the chantry he set up there to include a chaplain required 'to instruct all persons coming thither and so desiring in the faculty of grammar gratis and without reward'.[10] In return for imposing no fees for his teaching, the priest was to have a salary of 20 marks a year paid from rents on properties in Gloucester and London.[11] Thomas certainly had the financial resources to provide sufficient endowment for this purpose; he had been cofferer of the king's household, an office that gave him the responsibility of paying the wages of all servants working in the royal entourage.[12]

Beyond the reference in Thomas's will, we have no further knowledge of any aspect of the St Nicholas chantry school. The reasons are not recorded, but it would seem that the school was not a long-lived one. Perhaps its existence was snuffed out by a legal challenge from the canons of Llanthony Priory in just the same way as they put endless energy into pressurising the school that had existed at St Oswald's.[13]

The majority of chantry schools functioned as elementary schools, and we must assume that this was likely to have been the case at St Nicholas. Unlike in the grammar schools, teaching would have been mainly in English and focused on reading and writing. As part of the education they received, the pupils were expected to pray for the soul of the donor and his relatives.[14] The aim was to give them confidence with the alphabet and enable them to take part in the mass by memorising the Latin versions of the Lord's Prayer, the Salutation of the Virgin, the Apostles' Creed and other key prayers.

For an ordained schoolmaster willing to take on responsibility for regular masses and prayers alongside education, there were considerable attractions

---

[10] G. Walters, *King Richard's Gloucester: Life in a Mediaeval Town*, Alan Sutton (1983), p. 37.

[11] N. M. Herbert, *The Victoria History of the Counties of England: Gloucestershire*, volume 4, p. 309.

[12] B. Lowe, *Commonwealth and the English Reformation: Protestantism and the Politics of Religious Change in the Gloucester Vale*, Routledge St Andrew's Studies in Reformation History (2010), p. 59.

[13] See Chapter Three.

[14] H. M. Jewell, *Education in Early Modern England*, Macmillan (1998), p. 20.

in taking up employment at one of the chantry schools of the 14th and 15th centuries. As well as being endowed schools, the chantry schools were also often known as 'free schools', implying that they were not expected to charge fees.[15] If the original endowment was a generous one, it might be sufficient to provide a regular salary, which was generally expected to be between £6 and £10 a year along with a house or a chamber above the schoolroom.[16] The master at this kind of school might, in addition, supplement his income further by taking in several boarding pupils.

The absence of fees did not mean that the chantry schools were suddenly flooded by poor people. Most families in the lower ranks of society were never able to aspire to full-time education because harsh economic necessity meant that they simply could not afford to forfeit the wages a boy would otherwise earn in employment.[17] It continued to be the children of gentlemen and merchants, who attended the new chantry schools just as they were the ones who dominated the grammar schools. Increasingly, however, the sons of some shopkeepers and yeomen farmers were now found within their ranks, reflecting the rising social aspirations of the era that followed the Black Death. The chantry schools therefore played their part in widening horizons and beginning to broaden the spread of education. Although primarily envisaging apprenticeships, the Statute of Artificers of 1406 stated that 'every man or woman, of what estate or condition that they be, shall be free to set their son or daughter to take learning at any manner of school that pleaseth them within the realm'.[18]

Initial plans for a chantry school at St Mary de Crypt

The Crypt School in Gloucester cites 1539 as the year of its foundation, but its origins actually began a decade earlier in a chantry school that probably met inside the Church of St Mary de Crypt. The school was known initially as Christ School as St Mary de Crypt was at that time often referred to as Christ Church.[19] Its origins as a chantry seem to have been obscured by the

---

[15] N. Orme, *Medieval Schools from Roman Britain to Renaissance England*, Yale University Press (2006), p. 55.
[16] Ibid, p. 176.
[17] Ibid, p. 240.
[18] H. Leyser, *Medieval Women*, Weidenfeld & Nicholson (1995), p. 134.
[19] T. D. Fosbrooke, *An Original History of the City of Gloucester*, London (1819) republished by Alan Sutton (1986), p. 161.

passage of time, but they were generally well known as late as 1728. In a sermon preached in the Cathedral in that year Dr William Thomas, a well-known antiquary and Worcester cleric, referred to the early days of the Crypt School, stating that 'at the Reformation the chantry only was suppressed and the school continued'.[20]

This chantry school in St Mary de Crypt Church functioned for a whole decade before it was subsumed by the grammar school that replaced it. It was endowed in 1528 by John Cooke, a wealthy man who was born at Minsterworth in the mid-15th century and rose by dealing in the textile trade to become one of Gloucester's most prosperous mercers and a powerful burgess. He held the office of sheriff twice, in 1494 and 1498, and was mayor four times in 1501, 1507, 1512 and 1519.[21] His wife Joan, née Messenger, belonged to another of Gloucester's leading families. John died in 1528 and, having no children, left a will that made bequests for the upkeep of two local highways, the West Bridge and several of Gloucester's churches. He asked to be buried in the Church of St Mary de Crypt next to the altar of St John the Baptist, where his will arranged for a chantry priest to sing for his soul forever at a fee of £5 a year.[22] Today St Mary de Crypt Church boasts a well-preserved memorial brass to John and Joan Cooke. This once marked their original burial spot, but it was moved when the sanctuary floor was raised in 1845 and reset in its present location by the Old Cryptians' Club in 1923.[23]

John Cooke's will laid down specific arrangements for what he described as the 'school chantry'. It was to teach grammar every day and to do so without fees. The exact specifications in the will were 'to make and edify or cause to be made and edified in the parish of Christ in such place within the town as I have assigned and declared a school house and in the same shall as well establish and ordain a continual free school of grammar for the erudition of children and scholars there, and to ordain and establish the school master of the same school for the time being a priest daily to keep school and teach grammar freely within the said school'.[24] By specifying that the schoolmaster was to be a priest, it is clear that John Cooke had a

---

20 R. Austin, *The Crypt School Gloucester*, John Bellows Gloucester (1939), p. 61.
21 H. W. Allen, *The Crypt School: 475 Years*, Bristol (2014), p. 1.
22 The full text of John Cooke's will is printed in R. Austin, *The Crypt School Gloucester*, pp. 136–44.
23 M. Bayley, *St Mary de Crypt Gloucester*, Leyhill (1995), p. 4.
24 R. Austin, *The Crypt School Gloucester*, p. 25.

Figure 28: Details of John and Joan Cooke from their memorial brass, which is on display inside St Mary de Crypt Church.

chantry school in mind when he wrote his will. As well as teaching, the priest was expected to say a daily mass before the altar of St John the Baptist for the benefit of the soul of John Cooke, that of his wife and parents 'and for all Christians evermore'.[25] As he was sick in body at the time of writing his will, John left it to his wife, Joan, to work out further details of how the school was to be administered. He explained that every detail in the will had been discussed with his wife, who 'knows my full mind and purposes and intents, as I have at several times before my death shown to my said wife'.[26]

It is difficult to be specific about the exact location occupied by the chantry school inside the Church of St Mary de Crypt. The most likely site, however, was in the south transept of the church, where the remains of a medieval piscina can still be seen.[27] A piscina is a moulded recess in the wall of a church, which contained water used by a priest to wash his hands

---

[25] N. Orme, *Education in the West of England 1066 – 1548*, p. 138.
[26] C. Lepper, *The Crypt School Gloucester*, Alan Sutton (1989), p. 2.
[27] N. M. Herbert, *The Victoria History of the Counties of England: Gloucestershire*, volume 4, p. 301.

at the start of a mass and to clean the vessels at the end of the service. The existence of a piscina in a church therefore nearly always marks a spot on which a pre-Reformation altar or chantry chapel once stood.

Armed with great vision and energy, Joan Cooke began to put her husband's wider plans into effect the year after his death. In 1529 part of the churchyard belonging to the Church of St Mary de Crypt was set aside for the building of a 'schoolhouse for teaching young scholars the art of grammar'. The location of the plot was described as adjacent to the wall of the church and stretching along Southgate Street as far as the Mary Lane.[28] The details were set out in a grant drawn up by Richard Hart, Prior of Llanthony, and Robert Stynchcombe, Rector of St Mary de Crypt. The land was conveyed to a group of city burgesses who were advising Joan, including her brother, Thomas Messenger, Thomas Bell, William and Thomas Pury and Lewis Lysons. The nominal rent was a red rose payable at the feast of St John the Baptist.[29] Even in modern times a red rose is still handed to the Rector of St Mary de Crypt at the annual Crypt School Founders' Day in commemoration of these original terms.

Figure 29: St Mary de Crypt was home to several medieval chantries, including the chantry school set up by John Cooke's will of 1528.

We do not know how quickly the new schoolroom was built, but the general assumption is that it was not completed until 1539. To begin with at least, teaching probably took place inside the church, as was natural for a chantry school. Richard Fletcher was

---

28 R. Austin, *The Crypt School Gloucester*, p. 28.
29 N. Orme, *Education in the West of England 1066 – 1548*, p. 64.

Figure 30: Earliest drawing of St Mary de Crypt on a rental roll of 1455.

appointed as the first master, with Joan paying his salary of £10 out of her own funds for the first ten years.[30] Her main emphasis, however, was on securing long-term endowments for the future. In 1538 Joan and her advisers secured letters patent from Henry VIII that allowed them to buy up manors and other lands to the value of £50 a year that would provide permanent revenue to support the school and carry out other purposes specified in John Cooke's will, including the repair of Westgate Bridge and the provision of poor relief.[31] In the same year Hugh Latimer, Bishop of Worcester, wrote a letter on Joan's behalf to Thomas Cromwell, Henry VIII's chief minister. This opened the way for her to purchase the manor of Podsmead at a cost of £266 6s 8d; it had been one of the possessions of Llanthony Priory, which was in the process of being dissolved that year.[32]

---

30   N. Orme, 'Education in Medieval Bristol and Gloucestershire', *Transactions of the Bristol and Gloucestershire Archaeological Society*, volume 112 (2004), p. 25.

31   R. Austin, *The Crypt School Gloucester*, p. 29.

32   C. Lepper, *The Crypt School Gloucester*, p. 5.

Although legislation against chantries was not introduced until the reign of Edward VI, in the turmoil that accompanied the beginning of the Reformation it was already clear to those of a Protestant disposition that the day would soon come when chantries were dissolved in the same way as the monasteries. Already in the 1530s there was a bitter argument raging in Gloucester between Thomas Bell, one of the aldermen advising Joan Cooke, and Hugh Rawlings, a radical preacher based at Holy Trinity Church in Westgate Street. It was alleged in 1536 that Rawlings had associated with a radical preacher by the name of Benet, who claimed that 'even if the purgatory priests do pray with their tongues till they be worn to the stumps, their prayers shall not help the souls of the departed'.[33] Four years later a similar controversy hit St Mary de Crypt itself when a case was brought against Humphrey Grinshall for publicly denouncing the doctrine of Purgatory 'while reading on the Bible in English in Christ Church in Gloucester on the 18th day of April in the year of our Lord 1540'.[34]

Possibly with this in mind, Joan Cooke arranged for the oversight of her school to be entrusted to the mayor and burgesses of Gloucester. Rather than leaving the school linked to the saying of masses for the dead in a chantry, in 1539 she transferred the revenue made by the manor she had just purchased at Podsmead to the mayor and burgesses, asking them to fund the school and other charities for the relief of the poor, such as St Bartholomew's Hospital.[35] Most of the lands of this manor remained intact over the years and in 1939 would provide the site of the current Crypt School when it moved to the outskirts of Gloucester.

Similar developments occurred elsewhere in the country at this time as chantry schools were handed over to the secular authorities, resulting in town corporations stepping into the role of patrons of schools, just as ecclesiastical leaders had done in previous centuries. The schools benefited as the arrangement gave them a greater likelihood of surviving in the chaotic years of the Reformation.[36] In the case of Joan Cooke the decision was not a difficult one to make; she saw that chantries might be under

---

[33] K. G. Powell, 'The Beginnings of Protestantism in Gloucestershire', *Transactions of the Bristol and Gloucestershire Archaeological Society* (1971), volume 90, p. 149.

[34] Ibid, p. 147.

[35] W. Leighton, 'Endowed Charity in Bristol and Gloucestershire', *Transactions of the Bristol and Gloucestershire Archaeological Society* (1947), volume 67, p. 12.

[36] J. Simon, *Education and Society in Tudor England*, Cambridge University Press, p. 229.

threat in years to come and the choice of the town corporation to offer patronage was an obvious one as her husband had been a burgess and mayor.

So it was that the chantry school established in the Church of St Mary de Crypt adapted and survived the Reformation. The result was that John and Joan Cooke, although childless themselves, created a school for other people's children, enabling boys and eventually girls to benefit from their endeavours for over six centuries to come.[37] With the demise of Llanthony Priory's Longsmith Street school in 1535, this new school at the Crypt was uniquely poised to play a pivotal role in the future of Gloucester as it became a city. It would go on to provide a sound education for generations of young men in the 16th, 17th and 18th centuries before eventually expanding to become Gloucester's leading grammar school in the second half of the 19th century.

---

[37]   H. W. Allen, *The Crypt School: 475 Years*, p. 1.

CHAPTER SIX

The New Grammar School at the Crypt:

Joan Cooke's Legacy to the People of Gloucester

The status of the new Crypt School

Until the 1530s all the inhabitants of England owed allegiance to the Roman Catholic Church and the country was an organic part of a united Christendom ruled by the Pope. From childhood they were familiar with the use of Latin in services, the ritual of Mass, prayers for the dead and the invocation of saints, including the Virgin Mary. Then, within the space of thirty years or so, the Reformation transformed England into a Protestant country, following Henry VIII's decision to break with Rome.

The Reformation brought great disruption to education, especially in the short term. The early 20th-century historian who pioneered work in this field, Arthur Leach, wrote that 'schools were swept away either under Henry VIII or his son; or, if not swept away, plundered and damaged'.[1] Chantry schools were abandoned and the schools run by the religious orders ceased with the Dissolution of the Monasteries, which occurred between 1536 and 1540, leaving huge implications for educational provision. In Gloucester, however, the disruption that followed was mercifully short lived as alternative schools quickly came into existence both at the Cathedral that now replaced the Abbey of St Peter and at St Mary de Crypt. Rather than supporting Leach's damning verdict, the experience of our city chimes more closely with the conclusion reached by a later historian, Kenneth Charlton, that 'far from crippling schools, the Reformation put many of them on a far more solid foundation'.[2]

---

[1]   A. F. Leach, *English Schools at the Reformation*, London (1896), p. 6.
[2]   K. Charlton, *Education in Renaissance England*, Routledge & Kegan Paul (1965), p. 94.

The Crypt School in Southgate Street, which had begun its life in the previous decade as a chantry school,[3] now had its status quietly changed into that of a free grammar school in a process copied over the next decade by several other towns that acquired their own King Edward VI grammar schools. The new arrangements were listed in an agreement issued in January 1540 and known as the 'tripartite indenture' between Joan Cooke, the mayor and burgesses of Gloucester and the citizens of Worcester.[4] The change was clearly prompted by fears that the Reformation would make it difficult to find suitable priests to continue a chantry school in the future. The terms now set out were that the school should continue to teach grammar; a master was to be appointed 'to teach grammar to such children as might resort to the said free school now already built within the parish of Christ'.[5] For the first time, however, provision was now made for the possibility of the schoolmaster being a layman. The annual stipend was set at £10 if the next master was an honest and well-learned priest, but only £9 if a layman had to be appointed. It has been surmised from this that Joan Cooke was not entirely in sympathy with new Protestant ways and had a distrust both of married clergy and laymen taking on roles traditionally reserved for the clergy.[6] The schoolmaster was allocated living quarters in the chamber above the school, 'which is appointed for him and his scholars only, and not for his wife, family or strangers'.[7] With the dawn of the Reformation, Dame Joan and the burgesses of Gloucester were here clearly envisaging the possibility of a married priest or even a layman taking charge of the school. As it happened, the master appointed was another single priest, Thomas Yonge, who held the post from 1540 until 1543 or possibly 1547.[8] He is acknowledged as the first headmaster of the Crypt School proper.

The decision to change the school's status ensured that the Cooke family legacy to the city turned out to be an enduring one. It meant that the school was not threatened in any way by the Act passed at the beginning of

---

[3]   For details see Chapter Five.

[4]   The original deed is in Gloucestershire Record Office, D3270/4; the full text is printed in R. Austin, *The Crypt School Gloucester*, John Bellows Gloucester (1939), pp. 147–57.

[5]   W. Page, *The Victoria History of the Counties of England: Gloucestershire*, volume 2, London (1907), p. 344.

[6]   Ibid, p. 344.

[7]   C. Lepper, *The Crypt School Gloucester*, Alan Sutton (1989), p. 6.

[8]   N. Orme, *Education in the West of England 1066 – 1548*, University of Exeter (1976), p. 140.

Figure 31: John and Joan Cooke, founders of the Crypt School (painting by an unknown artist held at the school).

Edward VI's reign in 1547 that completed the dissolution of chantries all over the country.[9] The tripartite indenture also laid down the basis of the financial and management settlement that was to guarantee the school's survival by passing it over to municipal trusteeship. It was agreed that on Joan's death the mayor and burgesses of Gloucester would act as trustees, who were charged with the oversight of the school and would 'yearly and continually from thenceforth for ever find and provide an honest and well learned schoolmaster, being a priest if any such may conveniently be had, to teach grammar to all and singular such children and scholars as shall or

---

9   G. R. Elton, *The Tudor Constitution*, Cambridge (1965), p. 382.

will at any time come or resort to the said free school'.[10] The funding would be taken from the revenue of the manor of Podsmead and other lands in the hands of John Partridge, bailiff and receiver of rents for the city corporation.[11] This kind of settlement with a school run by a board of trustees and financed through the gift of lands became a standard model replicated across the country in this period.

In using the phrase 'the free school now already built within the parish of Christ', the tripartite indenture made it clear that the schoolroom had just recently been completed, hence the date of 1539 usually ascribed to it. That building, which continued to house the school right up to 1857, still stands in Southgate Street on the north side of St Mary de Crypt Church. It comprises two storeys. The lower room was used for teaching. The upper level, sometimes described as the chambers, which today is open plan, was partitioned to provide living accommodation for the use of the master and in the roof space above was his cockloft.

The building is handsome and well proportioned with its five bays of Tudor-arched mullioned windows, though it is likely to have been the work of local craftsmen rather than a professionally appointed architect.[12] Whilst the front of the building facing Southgate Street has been modernised and clad in stone and had its windows restored in the 1880s, the rear elevation with its rows of Tudor bricks and limestone buttresses looks almost exactly the same today as it did when first built in 1539. [13] The archway that spans the ancient thoroughfare of Marylone has the arms of King Henry VIII set above it together with shields featuring the Crypt School crest and the Tudor arms of Gloucester City.[14]

In order to ensure that the school functioned properly and was maintained in good repair, an annual visitation by members of the corporation was instituted. No less than twenty-one officials were involved: the mayor, recorder, two of the oldest aldermen, two sheriffs, the town clerk, four stewards, a sword bearer, four serjeants-at-mace and the five porters of the town gates. They were each given small payments for the

10   T. Rudge, *The History and Antiquities of Gloucester*, J. Wood Gloucester (1811), p. 127.
11   R. Austin, *The Crypt School Gloucester*, p. 31.
12   M. Seaborne, *The English School: Its Architecture and Organisation 1370–1870*, Routledge & Kegan Paul (1971), p. 35.
13   D. Verey & A. Brooks, *The Buildings of England: The Vale and Forest of Dean*, Yale University Press (2002), p. 491.
14   P. Moss, *Historic Gloucester*, Windrush Press (1993), p. 28.

responsibility they held.[15] In return they were expected 'to solemnly assemble themselves together once every year between Easter and Whitsuntide at the High Cross in the town of Gloucester and from thence go to view and survey the schoolhouse ... and such defaults of reparation or decay as they shall there find and see needful and right to be amended or repaired'. If at any time the Gloucester burgesses refused to honour their role in this agreement, then one final provision required the mayor, bailiffs and citizens of Worcester to do so.[16]

The importance of these trusteeship arrangements almost immediately proved invaluable in enabling the new school to survive and become established during the turbulent reigns of Edward VI and his sister, Mary. An unexpected threat appeared in the person of William Messenger, a Gloucester lawyer, future MP and mayor of the City who was a kinsman of John and Joan Cooke. He had been one of the executors of Joan Cooke's will, but was suspected of plotting to seize for his own use the manor at Podsmead and other lands which were essential for the school's financial security.[17] The Gloucester burgesses acted decisively in 1552 by taking him to court and successfully forced him to surrender any claims which might have threatened the future of the Crypt.

Figure 32: Part of Joan Cooke's Tripartite Deed of 1540 with the seal of the City of Worcester attached to it.

---

[15] T. Rudge, *The History and Antiquities of Gloucester*, p. 127.
[16] R. Austin, *The Crypt School Gloucester*, pp. 33–4.
[17] N. Carlisle, *A Concise Description of the Endowed Grammar Schools in England and Wales*, volume 1, London (1818), p. 453.

The first Crypt schoolboys

The Church of St Mary de Crypt, which the school adjoins, was known by a variety of names in Tudor times: Christ Church, St Mary de Christ and St Mary in the South all occur in documents alongside the now more familiar St Mary de Crypt.[18] The school shared these various titles and it was not until the mid-17th century that the use of the term 'Crypt School' became standardised.[19]

The arrangements made for the foundation of the school in 1539 – 40 were sufficiently generous to allow the sons of Gloucester burgesses and other local boys to attend without the payment of fees.[20] Unlike their predecessors at the medieval grammar school in Longsmith Street and unlike the new College School established at the Cathedral, most of those who attended the Crypt School were not required to pay directly for their education. The school could in this sense claim to be a genuinely 'free school', open to those who met the entry requirements based on a good command of written and spoken English and some knowledge of basic Latin. The boys who attended were drawn from a fair cross section of the upper and middling echelons of Gloucester society. They generally came from the families of merchants, traders, craftworkers and shopkeepers in the City, although some of the sons of professional people such as lawyers and yeomen farmers from the surrounding countryside could also be found among them.

The absence of fees did not, however, mean that a Crypt School education came without its costs in Tudor times. There would have been many incidental charges, some of which could be quite hefty.[21] Most grammar schools levied entrance fees of 1d or 2d a quarter known as 'entering pennies'. Some required the payment of a one-off admission fee of 12d as a condition of entering a pupil's name on the school register, particularly applicable to boys who came from outside the immediate local area. These impositions were supplemented by so-called 'voluntary' gifts to

---

18 N. M. Herbert, *The Victoria History of the Counties of England: Gloucestershire*, volume 4, London (1988), p. 300.

19 R. Austin, *The Crypt School Gloucester*, pp. 38–40.

20 J. Lawson, *Medieval Education and the Reformation*, Routledge & Kegan Paul (1967), p. 87.

21 D. Cressy, 'Educational Opportunity in Tudor and Stuart England', *History of Education Quarterly*, volume 16 (1976), p. 307.

the master at certain seasons.[22] Gifts of 6d or 1s were especially associated with Gloucester's Shrove Tuesday cockfighting festival which, though officially discredited, continued in this period.[23] Charges for books, writing accessories and wax candles also added up to a considerable sum. In the 1570s paper was reckoned to be 4d a quire, a bundle of pens and an inkhorn cost 4d, a grammar book 1s, and so on. Lessons in subjects such as arithmetic, calligraphy or foreign languages were also charged as extras. All this meant that attendance at the Crypt was inevitably far out of the reach of the sons of poor labourers who would neither be able to meet the costs nor afford to forgo the earning power brought in by their children to supplement the family budget. Attendance at the Crypt was not completely free; nor was the school open to all.

In the absence of a written admission register earlier than the 19th century, it is impossible to know precisely how many boys attended the

Figure 33: The elegant and largely unchanged brick-built Tudor schoolroom of St Mary de Crypt (1539).

---

22   J. Simon, *Education and Society in Tudor England*, Cambridge University Press, p. 370.
23   See Chapter Three.

Crypt at any one time, but based on the dimensions of the schoolroom, it seems that the school was designed for up to fifty or perhaps even sixty.[24] The furnishings it contained would have comprised a canopied pew and desk for the master, and a series of benches or forms for the boys. The school would have expected its intake already to be fluent in reading and to have a knowledge of the catechism, requiring the boys to have spent some time in an elementary or petty school beforehand.[25] Pupils generally joined the grammar school between the ages of seven and eleven and usually stayed for about six years. Some pupils remained at school until they went on to university at sixteen or seventeen, but most of the Crypt boys left around the age of thirteen when they tended to begin apprenticeships in trade.

Latin was the main subject studied at the Crypt, but no Greek was provided in the Tudor period. It was still the case that a thorough knowledge of Latin was a requirement for university or almost any profession. The main textbook in use was the grammar written by William Lily, the high master of St Paul's, which emerged as the prescribed King's Grammar after 1540.[26] It went through more than 300 editions and remained the standard grammar until transformed into the *Eton Latin Grammar* of 1758. John Stanbridge's *Vulgaria* was also used to help the boys master vocabulary and rules. It contained vocabulary lists arranged in hexameters so that they could be committed to memory more easily and it required boys to translate everyday sentences into Latin.[27] Through mastering composition, which was known as 'Making Latins', the boys went on to imitate Classical stylists, such as Cicero, Plutarch and Quintilian, and to write formal elegant Latin essays and verses in the style of 16th-century humanist thinkers.

In *As You Like It* Shakespeare paints a picture of 'the whining schoolboy with his satchel and shining morning face, creeping like a snail unwillingly to school'.[28] All boys were expected to carry in their satchels their own goose-quill pens, penknife, paper and even the wax candles that were used

---

24   R. Austin, *The Crypt School Gloucester*, John Bellows Gloucester (1939), p. 40; H. W. Allen, *The Crypt School: 475 Years*, Bristol (2014), p. 2.
25   H. M. Jewell, *Education in Early Modern England*, Macmillan (1998), p. 93; for details of the petty schools, see Chapter Eight.
26   J. Lawson & H. Silver, *A Social History of Education in England*, Methuen (1973), p. 101.
27   J. Simon, *Education and Society in Tudor England*, p. 89.
28   W. Shakespeare, *As You Like It*, Act II, Scene VII, lines 147–150.

to light the schoolroom in winter. Ink was made on the school premises from a mixture of gum arabic (a sticky substance produced by acacia trees), green vitriol (made from acid poured on old nails) and galls (small lumpy growths found on oak trees).[29] The most expensive equipment was paper, which was usually made abroad in Italy or France. Shakespeare's schoolboy would have had a 'shining morning face' as he would have been scrubbing it clean for fear of breaking rules that forbade anyone arriving in a dirty state.

The school day at the Crypt was a long one and would have begun at either 6 a.m. or 7 a.m., depending on the time of the year. The boys worked through until 11 a.m. with just one short break of about a quarter of an hour for a light breakfast, which might consist of bread, weak beer and a barley stew known as pottage. They had two hours free for dinner beginning at 11 a.m. and most boys would have gone home for this.

Figure 34: Window in Gloucester Cathedral showing a form of bandy-ball, which was played by Tudor schoolboys.

Lessons resumed at 1 p.m. and the boys worked through the afternoon, again with just a single short break, until either 5 p.m. or 6 p.m. The later starts and earlier finishes were allowed in the winter months.[30]

Physical games and sports took place outside of lessons, as in medieval times, and half-days were prescribed for such activities, probably on Wednesdays and Saturdays. Games were required to be 'of a gentlemanly appearance and free of all lowness'.[31] The older boys often engaged in running, wrestling and shooting with the longbow, while younger boys played with hoops and spinning tops.[32] In 2018, when the schoolroom was refurbished, archaeological excavations uncovered a

---

[29]   P. Chrisp, *A Tudor School*, Heinemann (1997), p. 9.
[30]   H. M. Jewell, *Education in Early Modern England*, p. 102.
[31]   W. A. L. Vincent, *The Grammar Schools: Their Continuing Tradition*, John Murray (1969), p. 59.
[32]   T. Kelly, *Children in Tudor England*, Stanley Thornes (1987), p. 18.

variety of objects beneath the floor. Among them were items, such as coins and a toy cannon, that had almost certainly been lost by past pupils. Cockfighting and mob football remained popular outdoor activities.[33] Boys also played bandy-ball, an early form of golf or hockey, one of the earliest-known depictions of which anywhere in the country can be seen on the Great East Window of Gloucester Cathedral.[34]

The masters of the Crypt School

Despite its elegant building and the careful legal documents that underpinned its foundation, the Crypt School was not as generously endowed as many other establishments elsewhere. This meant that the school got off only to a modest start. In particular, the salary of the master had been fixed at a medieval level (£10 per annum) and failed to take into account the inflation of the mid-Tudor period. In the reign of Edward VI, when a swathe of new grammar schools came into being across the country, the salary a master could command was generally £13 6s 8d plus a rent-free house.[35] The 1547 injunction to cathedrals lacking a grammar school recommended £13 6s 8d as the appropriate pay for a master and by Elizabeth's reign some were being paid £20 or even £25. Nor did the foundation at the Crypt initially contain any provision for an assistant master or usher.

The limitations of the salary on offer meant that the Crypt faced a real problem in attempting to retain any master in post for a sufficiently long period of time to provide the stability that the new school required. During the school's first seventy-two years there were at least twelve different masters, many serving for very short periods.[36] Most, but not all, were clergymen.

Following in the footsteps of the first headmaster, Thomas Yonge, came the second and third headmasters, John Disteley (1547 – 50) and Thomas Bowland (1550 – 51), both Oxford graduates. They were followed by a series of very short-lived masters. The salary of £10 specified by Joan

---

[33]   See Chapter Three.
[34]   D. Welander, *The Stained Glass of Gloucester Cathedral*, Frome (1985), p. 26.
[35]   N. Orme, *Medieval Schools from Roman Britain to Renaissance England*, Yale University Press (2006), p. 317.
[36]   C. Lepper, *The Crypt School Gloucester*, p. 12.

Cooke was a significant factor behind this instability, but the difficulties caused by the religious and political uncertainties of the period created further problems. One master, Nicholas Oldysworth, may have been dismissed because he sponsored the premature proclamation of Lady Jane Grey as queen in 1553.[37] His successor, Richard Hewis, who was recruited from Magdalen College School, stayed barely a year because of the upheavals that followed the accession of the Catholic Queen Mary I. Her attempts to overturn the changes made by her predecessors failed when Parliament warned that 'no interference with property now settled in other hands would be tolerated'.[38] In Gloucester, however, Hewis found himself in a city that was increasingly Puritan in outlook under its reforming bishop, John Hooper, who was eventually burnt at the stake outside the Church of St Mary de Lode. Taking advantage of the many ecclesiastical vacancies that existed across the country in this period of upheaval, he left in 1554 to become Rector of Rhoscrowther in Pembrokeshire, presumably preferring the Catholic traditions there. For the next three years there was no fixed appointment at the Crypt and the Gloucester corporation account book lists 'money paid to diverse persons teaching the grammar school'.[39]

Masters of the Crypt School in Tudor Times	
1539 – 1547: Thomas Yonge	1557 – 1577: Hugh Walker
1547 – 1550: John Disteley	1577 – 1578: Gregory Downall
1550 – 1551: Thomas Bowland	1579 – 1581: Edmonde Cugley
1551 – 1552: Nicholas Oldysworth	1581 – 1582: Alexander Bellshire
1553 – 1554: Richard Hewis	1583 – 1589: Henry Aisgill
	1589 – 1603: William Groves

No permanent master was found for the Crypt until the reign of Elizabeth I. Hugh Walker, appointed in 1557, stayed in post for a full twenty years, though his teaching was not generally held in high regard. The Elizabethan settlement of 1559 promoted stability by pursuing a 'middle way' through

[37] W. Page, *The Victoria History of the Counties of England: Gloucestershire*, volume 2, pp. 345–6.
[38] J. Simon, *Education and Society in Tudor England*, p. 302.
[39] R. Austin, *The Crypt School Gloucester*, p. 87.

the extremes of church politics and taking some of the venom out of the most bitter of religious controversies.[40] The injunctions Elizabeth I published in 1571 also encouraged stability by requiring all teachers to have a licence from their diocesan bishop, declaring that 'no man shall take upon him to teach but such as shall be allowed by the bishop and found meet as well for his learning and dexterity in teaching, as for sober and honest conversation, and also for right understanding God's true religion.'[41]

The Elizabethan Crypt School

We are able to gain an impression from the writings of two pupils of how the school operated in late Tudor times during its period of relative stability under Hugh Walker. One of these pupils was the poet John Taylor, who was at the school in the 1580s before he moved to Southwark, where he wrote a series of well-received witty rhymes to supplement his life as a Thames waterman. It is clear from his poetry that Latin had dominated his formal education and he had found the grammar required extremely challenging, commenting that he 'was mired and could no further get.'[42]

Much more detailed than Taylor's passing comment is a book entitled *Mount Tabor* written in 1639 by another pupil, Richard Willis. He studied at the Crypt

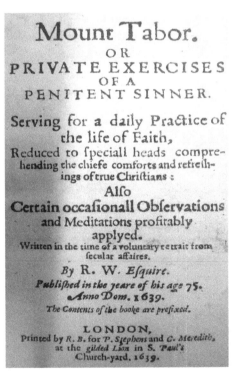

Figure 35: Richard Willis's book of 1639, in which he reminisced about his time at the Crypt School in the Elizabethan era.

---

40 S. Brigden, *New Worlds, Lost Worlds: The Rule of the Tudors*, Penguin (2001), p. 216.
41 N. Orme, *Medieval Schools from Roman Britain to Renaissance England*, p. 333.
42 'My Serious Cares and Considerations', J. Taylor, *All the Works of John Taylor the Water Poet* (1630), p. 57.

between 1571 and 1578 during the time that Hugh Walker was master. He went on eventually to become secretary to a series of government officials, including Lionel Cranfield who was Lord High Treasurer under James I. It is clear from his comments that he regarded the Crypt as a perfectly sound school and he was keen to acknowledge the debt he owed to its education. 'It was not my happiness to be bred up at the university', Richard Willis wrote, 'but all the learning I had was in the free grammar school called Christ's School in the City of Gloucester'.[43] In making this comment stressing his lack of university education, it may be surmised that Willis felt that his education might be deemed deficient, but the striking success of his career seems to prove otherwise.[44] His attendance at the Crypt had been his making.

Despite the good educational grounding he acquired, however, Willis evidently disapproved of Hugh Walker, whom he referred to as 'an ancient citizen of no great learning'.[45] He also criticised the monotonous and apparently futile way in which Latin was taught at the Crypt. Walker appeared content, he said, if he simply heard the correct answer to his questions regardless of how those answers had been arrived at; and in the process he allowed the oldest boys in the school to exercise great power over the younger pupils. 'Our schoolmaster's manner was to give us out several lessons in the evening and in the next morning to examine us thereupon, making all the boys in the first form to come from their seats and stand on the outsides of their desks, towards the middle of the school, and so the second form and the rest in order, while he himself walked up and down by them, hearing them construe their lesson one after another, and then giving one of the words to one, and another to another (as he thought fit) for parsing of it. When the two highest forms were dispatched, some of them whom we called prompters would come and sit in our seats of the lower forms, and so being at our elbows would put into our mouths answers to our master's questions, as he walked up and down by us; and so by our prompters' help, we made shift to escape correction; but we understood little to profit by it, having this circular motion, like the mill-horse that travels all day yet in the end finds himself not a yard further than when he began'.[46]

---

43 R. Willis, *Mount Tabor or Private Exercises of a Penitent Sinner*, London (1639), p. 97.
44 H. M. Jewell, *Education in Early Modern England*, p. 135.
45 R. Willis, *Mount Tabor or Private Exercises of a Penitent Sinner*, p. 101.
46 Ibid, pp. 101–2.

Richard Willis appears to have had little choice but to go along with this charade that prevented real learning, but he recalled that it eventually caused him great difficulties following a case of bullying. 'One of the eldest scholars and one of the highest form fell out with me upon occasion of some boy's play abroad. In his anger, to do me the greatest hurt he could (which then he thought to be to fall under the rod), he dealt with all the prompters so that none of them should help me and so (as he thought) I must necessarily be beaten. When I found myself in this strait, I gathered all my wits together (as we say) and listened the more carefully to my fellows that construed before me … And when I observed my adversary's displeasure to continue against me, so as I could have no help from my prompters, I doubled my diligence and attention to our master's construing our next lesson to us. Observing carefully how in construction one word followed and depended upon another opened the way to show me how one word was governed by another in the parsing. So I needed no prompter, but became able to be a prompter myself, and so the evil intended to me by my fellow scholar turned to my great good'.[47]

Figure 36: Interior of the Crypt schoolroom in its present function as a community hub and café.

---

[47]   Ibid, pp. 102–3.

Figure 37: Arms of King Henry VIII set above the Marylone Passage next to the schoolroom.

Whilst Willis's description was clearly intended to show his disapproval of Walker, it may also be seen as a wider criticism of Tudor teaching in general, which tended to be monotonously repetitive and unremittingly dependent on memorising information. The standard pattern was for boys to read the Latin rules they were required to know, repeat them, learn them and be tested on them endlessly with the same questions repeated over and over until everyone appeared to know the right answers by heart.[48]

Hugh Walker's retirement was followed by another series of short-lived headships between 1577 and 1589. During Henry Aisgill's time as master (1583 – 89), there was the first attempt to provide the Crypt with an assistant master or usher, paid just £4 a year, though this seems to have been simply a temporary arrangement.[49] It was not until the end of the Elizabethan Age that the school once more found stability with William Groves (1589 – 1603), a man of whom the Gloucester corporation account book records 'there is good liking generally had of him in the city'.[50] He was a committed Puritan, whose gifts for preaching resulted in him being offered the role of lecturer in the city in 1598. He also combined his

[48] P. Chrisp, *A Tudor School*, Heinemann (1997), p. 12.
[49] C. Ewan, 'The Crypt School Gloucester', *Gloucestershire Countryside*, Vol 7, No. 6 (1951), p. 377.
[50] R. Austin, *The Crypt School Gloucester*, John Bellows Gloucester (1939), p. 89.

responsibilities at the school with being rector of a succession of parishes, St Mary de Crypt itself, Hartpury and Elmore.

The picture of the Crypt School in the Tudor period therefore is one of intermittent success. It struggled to maintain stability in its leadership and aspects of its teaching appeared distinctly lacklustre. That said, in the context of its time the legacy of Joan Cooke was more than satisfactory at meeting the needs of the people of Gloucester and benefited the city by launching a large cross section of its young folk on their path to a rewarding career.

CHAPTER SEVEN

The Tudor Schools at Gloucester Cathedral:

Building on the Monastic Tradition

The foundation of the College School (King's)

The Reformation had a huge impact on the Abbey of St Peter in Gloucester, but as far as education was concerned the changes sought to build on the long monastic tradition established in medieval times.

The abbey, just like all the other monastic houses in the country, was dissolved immediately after its surrender to King Henry VIII's commissioners in January 1540. In its place in the following year the Cathedral Church of St Peter and the Holy and Undivided Trinity came into being at the head of the newly created diocese of Gloucester.[1] It was clear that in making these arrangements Henry intended to upgrade education by building on the Benedictine provision. A bill had already passed through Parliament in 1539 authorising the king to establish new bishoprics and cathedrals 'whereby God's word might be the better set forth and children brought up in good learning'.[2] Six 'new foundation' cathedrals were established on the sites of former abbeys. Gloucester was one of these, the others being Bristol, Oxford, Chester, Peterborough and Westminster. The charter that Gloucester received in 1541 expressed the hope that 'for the future the muniments of sacred eloquence may be purely administered, good morals be sincerely observed and the youth may be freely instituted in letters'.[3]

---

[1]   D. Welander, *The History, Art and Architecture of Gloucester Cathedral*, Alan Sutton (1991), p. 331.

[2]   N. Orme, *Medieval Schools from Roman Britain to Renaissance England*, Yale University Press (2006), pp. 303–4.

[3]   W. Page, *The Victoria History of the Counties of England: Gloucestershire*, volume 2, London (1907), p. 321.

Detailed arrangements for the new Cathedral school were outlined in statutes published in 1544.[4] Its main purpose was to teach grammar and, like the Crypt, it was initially conceived of as a free school open to all. Although the school is today known as the King's School, it was originally referred to as the College School; the term King's was not introduced until the end of the 17th century. The use of the name College School indicates that, like the medieval almonry school, it was intended as a collegiate body within the wider Cathedral foundation. The element of continuity with the former Benedictine abbey is striking. The schoolmasters lived in monastic properties and both they and the pupils they taught shared in the dining facilities provided by the old monastic kitchen. The Cathedral community that grew up at this time was called the 'College of Canons'. Cathedral services were often referred to as 'College Prayers' and the houses around the Cathedral Close as 'College Rents'.[5] Even today, the name College lives on in terms such as College Green and College Street.

The statutes gave the Dean as head of the Chapter the responsibility 'particularly to take care that the children be profitably instructed'.[6] This meant the appointment of two schoolmasters, and the process by which this was to proceed was outlined in chapter 25 of the statutes: 'We will and ordain that by the Dean, or in his absence by the Subdean and Chapter, one be chosen who is skilful in Greek and Latin, of good fame and a godly life, well-qualified for teaching, who may train up in piety and good learning those children who shall resort to our school to learn grammar. And let him have the first charge and be the chief schoolmaster. We also will that by the Dean, or in his absence by the Subdean, there be one other chosen of good repute and of a virtuous life well-skilled in the Latin tongue and who hath a good faculty in teaching, who shall instruct the youths under the headmaster in the first rudiments of grammar and shall therefore be called the undermaster or usher'. Both masters were to obey 'those rules and orders which the Dean and Chapter shall think fit to prescribe unto them'.

---

4   The full statutes first became available in print in R. Atkyns, *The Ancient and Present State of Glostershire*, Part 1,   London (1712), pp. 174–7. They are most easily consulted in Appendix 28 of S. Rudder, *A New History of Gloucestershire*, Cirencester (1779), republished by Alan Sutton in 2006, pp. xlii–xlix.
5   S. J. A. Evans, 'Cathedral Life at Gloucester in the Early 17th Century', *Transactions of the Bristol and Gloucestershire Archaeological Society* (1961), volume 80, p. 5.
6   A. Platts and G. H. Hainton, *Education in Gloucestershire: A Short History*, Gloucestershire County Council (1953), p. 9.

If either were found 'idle, negligent or unfit to teach', they could be removed from their posts after three warnings.[7]

In terms of the salary provided for the master and his assistant, the arrangements made at Gloucester were just about in line with those in other schools attached to the new cathedrals created at this time. The average stipend for a master in one of these was between £13 and £20.[8] The College School's headmaster was provided with an annual salary to the value of £13 0s 8d, which was made up of a stipend of £8 8s 8d, cloth to the value of £1 and an allowance for commons of £3 12s a year.[9] This reflected the importance that the school had within the new Cathedral college. The Dean received a salary of £27 a year plus allowances. The canons had a salary of £7 17s 8d and an extra allowance of 8d for each day they were in attendance at matins, providing a yearly entitlement of up to £20 1s in total. Minor canons, who were not members of the Cathedral Chapter, were provided with an annual income of £9 14s. The College School's headmaster therefore ranked in pay and position next to the canons and considerably above the minor canons.

The schoolroom and facilities

We do not know for sure where the College School met in the initial few years after its creation between 1541 and 1544, but very soon the Tudor school found a permanent home in the former monastic library, which had been built in the 14th century.[10] It is reached either from the north transept of the Cathedral or directly via a spiral staircase from the cloisters.

This schoolroom, which was a grand one with an impressive open collar tie beam roof, would be occupied by the school right through to the Victorian period. It was repaired and specially refurbished in 1587, being equipped with a range of wooden benches and tables to provide space for about fifty boys. This was made possible through a gift from Elizabeth Wiltshire, a member of a large family of clothiers based in Barton Street

---

[7]   Appendix 28 in S. Rudder, *A New History of Gloucestershire*, p. xlvi.
[8]   J. Lawson, *Medieval Education and the Reformation*, Routledge & Kegan Paul (1967), pp. 79–80.
[9]   W. Page, *The Victoria History of the Counties of England: Gloucestershire*, volume 2, pp. 322–3.
[10] D. Welander, *The History, Art and Architecture of Gloucester Cathedral*, p. 587.

Figure 38: The Cathedral Library, which from 1541 until 1849 was used as the College schoolroom.

Figure 39: The remaining wall of the monastic refectory in Little Cloister House garden, where College School pupils took their meals until 1612.

who had a considerable reputation for charitable work and made similar gifts to the Crypt School.[11] They evidently shared a belief common at this time among those engaged in trade that improved education was the best way to prevent poverty and meet the future requirements of commerce.[12] The Wiltshire patronage was, according to one writer, commemorated by a plaque in the schoolroom with thanks 'gratefully expressed in an inscription set up in the year 1587 that remained for many years afterwards'.[13]

The schoolroom was divided into two sections by a wooden screen, at the top of which was the inscription: 'What unto others you would do … Expect the same thing'. One end of the room housed the junior boys, the other the seniors.[14] Boys began in Lower School (possibly consisting of four forms), presided over by the usher, and then proceeded into Upper School for the final three forms. The transition was dependent on good progress measured against clear expectations and strict requirements. The forms were grouped according to the complexity of the work they were taught rather than strictly by age. These requirements were written down much later in 1686 when a dispute arose between a headmaster and his usher. The Dean and Chapter recommended on that occasion that 'the ancient customs shall constantly be observed, that is, that no child shall be removed out of the Lower School nor admitted "de novo" into the Upper School until he be so well grounded by the usher in the rudiments of the Latin tongue as that he shall be able to make for his exercise five or six lines of plain true Latin and shall understand the scanning and parsing of verses and the making of two verses from one night's exercises'.[15]

The College School was also keen to benefit from some of the facilities that had been created by the monks of the recently dissolved abbey. The monastic refectory and kitchens remained in use, albeit in an increasingly dilapidated state, as a 'common hall' for about another seventy years after the Dissolution. Single members of the clergy, others on the staff of the new

---

[11] T. D. Fosbrooke, *An Original History of the City of Gloucester*, London (1819), reprinted by Alan Sutton (1986), p. 115.

[12] W. A. L. Vincent, *The Grammar Schools: Their Continuing Tradition*, John Murray (1969), p. 6.

[13] S. Rudder, *A New History of Gloucestershire*, p. 170.

[14] D. Robertson, *The King's School Gloucester*, Phillimore (1974), p. 65.

[15] S. M. Eward, *Gloucester Cathedral Chapter Act Book 1616 – 1687*, The Bristol and Gloucestershire Archaeological Society Record Series, volume 21 (2007), p. 148.

Cathedral and members of the College School were provided with communal meals on site.[16] The statutes that created the Cathedral in 1544 stated: 'Those who live together and praise God together in the choir may also eat together and praise God together at table. We ordain and will that, as well as the minor canons and officers of the choir, teachers of the grammar scholars, and all other inferior officers in our church, and the children who learn to sing, shall feed together in the common hall'.[17] The school most probably also took in boarders from the outset, making use of former monastic properties to house boys who lived too far away to travel daily or lodging them with a local householder in the vicinity.[18]

These arrangements continued until about 1612 when a large section of the common hall or refectory had to be demolished. The last recorded cook, George Crew, died in 1611 and it seems he was not replaced.[19] Today,

Figure 40: The College schoolroom, as illustrated in the 18th century by Thomas Bonnor, showing the open collar tie roof, the wooden benches and tables and the screen that divided the room between Upper and Lower School.

---

16   D. Welander, *The History, Art and Architecture of Gloucester Cathedral*, p. 344.
17   S. J. A. Evans and S. M. Eward, 'The Common Kitchen', *Transactions of the Bristol and Gloucestershire Archaeological Society* (1972), volume 91, p. 169.
18   H. M. Jewell, *Education in Early Modern England*, Macmillan (1998), p. 93.
19   S. M. Eward, *No Fine But A Glass of Wine: Cathedral Life at Gloucester in Stuart Times*, Michael Russell (1985), p. 22.

all that remains of the common hall are the lower parts of its south wall, one of the Norman responds and a fragment of the springing of the undercroft vault.[20] They are visible in the rear garden of Little Cloister House.

A comparison with the arrangements made for the contemporaneous school at the Crypt indicates that the College School was intended to become Gloucester's foremost grammar school. As part of the Cathedral college, the school enjoyed a much less constrained site than the school in Southgate Street. The provision for modest boarding facilities and common dining attracted boys from a much wider catchment area. Whereas the Crypt School was patronised by the sons of local merchants, traders, craftworkers and shopkeepers, the College School set out to cater for the sons of gentry families across Gloucestershire as a whole and could also take in some from further afield. At £13 0s 8d the annual salary allocated for the College School headmaster was considerably higher than the sum of £10 allocated at the Crypt. Provision was also made for an usher, which allowed for more specialist teaching with boys divided into either Upper or Lower School according to aptitude and prior experience. The jewel in the College School's crown was, however, the requirement in the statutes of 1544 that its headmaster should be 'skilful in Greek and Latin'. This reference to the teaching of Greek is a new development in the history of education in Gloucester and reflected the growing interest in Greek scholarship that accompanied the various translations of the New Testament made during the Reformation. To have a master required to teach Greek was a great distinction for a school at this date.[21]

Whilst the College School may have stood out on the local scene, in comparison with other parts of the country it was rather meanly endowed by Henry VIII. Most of the new cathedral schools he created were given a number of endowed scholarships, which entitled the boys who received them to have board, lodging and clothing as well as education for free. The most generous arrangements were at Canterbury, where fifty scholarships of this type were made available, valid for four or five years each.[22] At Westminster there were forty such scholarships and at Peterborough

---

[20] D. Verey and A. Brooks, 'Gloucester: The Cathedral Church', extract from the *Buildings of England*, Yale (2002), p. 40.

[21] F. Watson, *The English Grammar Schools to 1660*, Cambridge (1908), p. 487.

[22] N. Orme, 'Education in Medieval Bristol and Gloucestershire', *Transactions of the Bristol and Gloucestershire Archaeological Society*, volume 112 (2004), p. 23.

twenty. Along with the new foundations at Bristol and Carlisle, Gloucester was treated much less favourably and received no endowed scholarships.[23] In particular no provision was made for the Cathedral authorities at Gloucester to take on financial responsibilities for the board and lodging of those studying at the school.[24]

The absence of a generous endowment meant that financial necessity required the school to levy fees from its very early years. Although the initial hope was for a free school open to all and although the term 'free school' was sometimes used in referring to the College School, the boys who attended had to be drawn from the limited social background of well-to-do families who could afford the payment of fees. Over the following centuries Henry VIII's failure to provide a full endowment was to have serious consequences for the College School, threatening its very existence towards the end of the 19th century. Even today the King's School has at its disposal relatively few of the financial resources enjoyed by some comparable public schools.

The College School curriculum

We can gain an insight into the way the College School would have been organised from a code entitled 'Reformation of Ecclesiastical Laws', which was produced by Archbishop Cranmer in 1553.[25] It attempted to lay down uniform standards in all cathedral schools. The school day was to begin and end with a recitation of the Creed, Lord's Prayer and Ten Commandments. On Sundays and feast days, the school was to meet for both morning and evening worship in the Cathedral. The boys were to be aged between eight and fourteen on their admission. They were to be examined twice a year, leading to the removal of those who were unfit for further instruction.

Only two text books were authorised for grammar teaching. One was an elementary grammar written largely in English and entitled *An Introduction of the Eight Parts of Speech*. It gave an outline account of basic Latin accidence, drawing on the earlier works of William Lily. Henry VIII's

---

23 D. Marcombe & C. S. Knighton, *Close Encounters: English Cathedrals and Society since 1540*, Nottingham (1991), p. 22.
24 A. F. Leach, *Educational Charters and Documents*, Cambridge (1911), p. xliii.
25 N. Orme, *Medieval Schools from Roman Britain to Renaissance England*, p. 330.

Figure 41: Copy of Hans Holbein's portrait of Henry VIII, which hangs in the main corridor at King's School.

proclamation prefacing this grammar required 'schoolmasters and teachers of grammar within this our realm and other dominions, as you intend to avoid our displeasure and have our favour, to teach and learn your scholars this English introduction here ensuing and the Latin grammar annexed to the same, and none other, which we have caused for your ease and your scholars' speedy preferment briefly and plainly to be compiled and set forth'.[26] The other book was a more advanced work in Latin called *Institutio Compendiaria totius Grammaticae*, published by Thomas Berthelet in 1540. It provided a detailed treatment of grammatical rules, syntax and prosody, again drawing on the earlier works of William Lily. Both works carried the king's authority and were intended as the standard texts to be imposed on all schools.[27]

Figure 42: The Gloucester Cathedral Endowment Deed, with Henry VIII seated on his throne.

---

26 J. Simon, *Education and Society in Tudor England*, Cambridge University Press, p. 191.
27 N. Orme, *Medieval Schools from Roman Britain to Renaissance England*, pp. 308–9.

Throughout Elizabeth I's reign her Privy Council continued the attempt to control many aspects of the curriculum in all schools, including cathedral schools. The royal injunctions of 1559 required all schoolmasters to have a licence from a bishop to teach, just as had been the case in the Middle Ages. They stated: 'No man shall take upon him to teach but such as shall be found meet for his learning and dexterity in teaching as for sober and honest conversation and also for right understanding of God's true religion'.[28] To ensure that these standards were upheld as far as possible, the qualifications, personal lives and religious outlook of schoolmasters were all assiduously examined at the time of regular bishops' visitations. From 1563 all schoolmasters in the land had to subscribe to the Thirty-Nine Articles and the Royal Supremacy. Elizabeth's canons of 1571 repeated the need for licensing, restricted teaching to the royally approved grammar texts and required schools to test each of their pupils' individual understanding of the sermons preached in their nearest church each Sunday.[29]

Any books used in the College School to supplement grammar text books had to comply with government edicts. A letter of 1582 asked bishops to ensure that all grammar schools used a new book written in Latin verse by Christopher Ocland. Its subject matter was a history of England up to 1558, followed by an outline of the main events of Elizabeth's reign. The letter described the book as 'worthy to be read of all men, especially in common schools, where divers heathen poets are ordinarily read and taught, from which the youth of the realm do rather receive infection in manners than advancement in virtue'.[30] Other books generally available to schools tended to be theological works from the Reformed centres on the Continent. Of particular importance were Castillion's *Dialogues Sacrés* (1543) and Cordier's *Colloquorum Scholasticorum* (1564), both of which were published in Geneva. The *Terentius Christianus* of Schonaeus was more innovative in that it provided schools with scripts to stage plays based on plots from the Roman playwright Terence but with suitably adapted biblical themes and speeches.[31]

---

28 J. Simon, *Education and Society in Tudor England*, Cambridge University Press, p. 299.
29 H.M. Jewell, *Education in Early Modern England*, pp. 25–7.
30 J. Simon, *Education and Society in Tudor England*, p. 324.
31 Ibid, p. 316.

The masters of the College School

Robert Aufield was the College School's first recorded master in 1558. Although he was almost certainly appointed earlier, there is no certainty that he was in office right at the foundation of the school.[32] He was an Eton scholar, who after graduating from King's College, Cambridge, returned to Eton, where he began his teaching career as usher and was remembered as 'eminent for his learning and piety'.[33] Beyond that, little is known of Aufield's approach to education. His life did, however, provide a sharp reminder of the dangerous religious antagonisms that divided Elizabethan England.[34] His two sons caused him great distress. Thomas, the elder, was born in 1552 at Gloucester, but became a Roman Catholic Jesuit priest and was denounced as a traitor by his younger brother. He was tortured in the Tower of London and executed at Tyburn in 1585, some would say as a Catholic martyr; the charge against him was that he had illegally imported books written by Cardinal William Allen, one of those involved in the planning of the Spanish Armada. At his trial, the Recorder, William Fleetwood, expressed surprise at Thomas's conviction because 'his father in King Henry's days, being an usher of Eton, of good religion had been brought up by many learned divines and others that served the Queen's temporal causes'.[35]

Masters of the College School in Tudor Times	Ushers mentioned in Tudor Times
1558? – 1575: Robert Aufield	1563: John Lightfoot
1576 – 1580: Tobias Sandford	1576: Francis Peerson
1580 – 1588: Thomas Wastell	1580: Henry Aisgill
1588 – 1598: Elias Wrench	1595: Francis Arnold
1598 – 1605: William Loe	

---

[32] W. Page, *The Victoria History of the Counties of England: Gloucestershire*, volume 2, p. 323.
[33] T. Harwood, *Alumni Etonenses: A Catalogue of the Provosts and Fellows of Eton College*, Birmingham (1797), p. 149.
[34] J. R. S. Whiting, *The King's School Gloucester*, Orchard & Ind (1990), p. 12.
[35] J. Strype, *Annals of the Reformation and Establishment of Religion*, volume 3, Oxford (1824), p. 451.

There was no statutory obligation laid down for the masters of the College School to be in holy orders, but so far as we can tell it is the case that every single headmaster right up until 1951 was a priest. All of Aufield's successors had a reputation for sound scholarship and the standards they set were crucial in building up the reputation of the school and attracting boys from some of the most prestigious gentry families of Gloucestershire. William Loe (1598 – 1605), for example, was referred to as 'much in esteem for Latin, Greek and human learning'.[36] Some combined the headmastership of the school with other positions in the Church. Thomas Wastell (1580 – 88) was curate at St Mary de Lode and Loe was Vicar of Churcham as well as headmaster. Most resigned the headship when they were promoted to more prestigious posts or when new careers beckoned. Tobias Sandford (1576 – 80) left the school to study medicine at Cambridge. Loe went on to become a chaplain to King James I, at whose court he influenced the writing of a poem by Joshua Sylvester that publicised the king's hatred of tobacco as 'a base and barbarous weed'.[37] After their resignation, both Elias Wrench (1588 – 98) and Loe also received the honour of becoming prebendaries of Gloucester Cathedral for the rest of their lives.

The assistant teacher or usher taught simpler lessons to the younger or less advanced pupils in the school. He also was without exception a cleric, John Lightfoot being the first one recorded in 1563. The teaching methods at his disposal would have been rather basic, relying mainly on drill and repetition to help boys develop skills in parsing, analysing syntax and building up Latin vocabulary.[38]

The usher was usually a young man, in or hardly out of his teens; he ranked below the minor canons of the Cathedral and on a par with the lay clerks who made up the Cathedral choir. His annual salary came to no more than £7 0s 8d, which was made up of a stipend of £2 19s 2d and other grants, such as cloth to the value of 13s 6d and an allowance for commons of £3 8s a year.[39] Ushers did not usually stay in post long but tended to regard their time in the school as a springboard from which to apply for a

---

36 A. Wood, *Athenae Oxonienses: the Fasti* (ed P. Bliss), London (1813), volume 3, p. 183.
37 S. Snyder, *The Divine Weeks and Works of Guillaume de Saluste*, translated by J. Sylvester, Oxford 1979, p. 31.
38 K. Charlton, *Education in Renaissance England*, Routledge & Kegan Paul (1965), p. 106.
39 W. Page, *The Victoria History of the Counties of England: Gloucestershire*, volume 2, p. 323.

headship or decent clerical living. The College School's second usher, Francis Peerson (1576 – 78), also held the post of Vicar of Holy Trinity Church in Gloucester. His successor, Henry Aisgill (1580 – 83) went on to become head of the Crypt School for six years between 1583 and 1589 and thereafter was Vicar of St Nicholas' Church in Gloucester and then of the village of Down Hatherley.[40]

The Song School

It is often said that the ultimate *raison d'être* of the King's School is the education of the Cathedral choristers. Whilst this may indeed have been partially true in recent centuries, it was not so in Tudor times. Alongside the College School, a separate Song School continued to exist within the Cathedral precincts more or less along the lines of its monastic predecessor. Any links between the two institutions came about simply because of their close proximity; a number of other cathedral statutes elsewhere in the country granted choristers preferential admission as scholars in the cathedral grammar school when their voices broke, but this was not the case at Gloucester.[41] The choristers were educated quite separately from the boys of the College School. The process of amalgamating the two institutions did not begin until the end of the 17th century and took a further 200 years thereafter to complete.[42]

The 1544 statutes issued for Gloucester outlined the arrangements for choristers to continue to be educated in their own Song School. They stated that: 'We decree and ordain that in our church aforesaid by the election and designation of the Dean there be eight choristers, youths who have good voices and are inclined to singing, who may serve, minister and sing in our choir. For the instruction of these youths and training them up as well in modest behaviour as in skilfulness of singing, we will that by the Dean, or in his absence by the Sub-Dean and Chapter, there shall be chosen one who is of a good life and reputation, skilful both in singing and in playing upon the organs, who shall diligently spend his time in instructing the boys in playing upon the organs and at proper times in

---

[40] J. N. Langston, 'Headmasters and Ushers of the King's (College) School, Gloucester', *Records of Gloucester Cathedral*, volume III, H. Osborne Gloucester (1928), pp. 156–7.

[41] W. Page, *The Victoria History of the Counties of England: Gloucestershire*, volume 2, p. 322.

[42] See Chapter Thirteen.

singing divine service'.[43] It is quite clear from the language used that this master of the choristers was completely separate from the headmaster and usher of the College School. Like them, he also was removable after three warnings. He was paid a salary of £5 7s a year, with 15s for cloth and £3 12s for commons, a total of £9 14s a year. This ranked the master of the choristers on a par with the minor canons of the Cathedral; he was senior to the College School usher but significantly below the headmaster.[44]

Boys who served as Cathedral choristers were required to sing services regularly on Sundays and most weekdays, for which they were paid an annual sum of £3 6s 8d each (half the salary of the adult lay clerks).[45] Although the Calvinist Bishop John Hooper prohibited polyphony, discouraged professional choirs and attempted to remove organs from churches, things became more settled under Queen Elizabeth I, who aimed to steer cathedrals into a middle way between Catholicism and extreme Protestantism. Injunction 49 in the Prayer Book she issued in 1559 stated:

Figure 43: Piece of graffiti incised on the book rest in one of the singing galleries above the Lady Chapel thought to have been made by a Tudor chorister; it may be the oldest surviving piece of artwork connected with a Gloucester school.

---

43 Appendix 28 in S. Rudder, *A New History of Gloucestershire*, p. xlvi.
44 W. Page, *The Victoria History of the Counties of England: Gloucestershire*, volume 2, pp. 322–3.
45 S. M. Eward, *Gloucester Cathedral Chapter Act Book 1616 – 1687*, p. xiv.

'in the beginning or in the end of common prayers, either at morning or evening, there may be sung a hymn or such like song to the praise of Almighty God in the best sort of melody and music that may be conveniently devised'.[46]

In comparison with their predecessors in the Song School maintained by the Benedictine abbey, the choristers of the Cathedral had their role extended. Their number was increased from five or six to eight and they had to learn a repertoire of new anthems, which were composed by church musicians such as Thomas Tallis and some of which were set to English rather than Latin words. Most importantly, they were now allowed to sing in the quire with the clergy and lay clerks. Previously the boys had sung almost exclusively in the Lady Chapel and hardly ever in the quire itself.[47] The Cathedral choristers differed from their medieval predecessors in one other important respect too. From about 1547 onwards choristers were not required to be tonsured as they were now considered to be ordinary schoolboys who happened to sing and no longer in any sense members of the lower orders of the clergy. Instead of having the crown of their head shaven, a 'short back and sides' haircut became the order of the day.[48]

Alongside their singing duties, the Gloucester choristers also received a practical education in musicianship underpinned by a knowledge of literacy, grammar and religious doctrine. For this they were under the care of the master of the choristers, who was also the Cathedral organist. The type of education they were offered had a much larger musical component than that in the College School, but in other respects it was more basic. It mainly involved the catechism and the teaching of Latin to the level at which the words of a hymn could be pronounced convincingly. Most of the choristers left the choir around the age of thirteen, the age when trade apprenticeships beckoned.

In many of the other Henrician cathedrals that were more generously endowed than Gloucester, the choristers received free places as boarders at the grammar school. The absence of funds for subsidised boarding provision did not make this possible at Gloucester. Whilst it is likely that some of the Gloucester choristers may have attended the College School, if they came from sufficiently affluent backgrounds, the majority did not do so.

---

[46] A. Mould, *The English Chorister: A History*, London (2007), p. 94.
[47] Ibid, p. 77.
[48] Ibid, p. 85.

One mystery that surrounds the reorganisation of the schooling at Gloucester in the 1540s is the fate of John Tucke, the much-respected master of the medieval almonry school and song school at St Peter's.[49] As he was nearly sixty years old at the time of the Dissolution, he would have been well-poised to take advantage of one of the pensions on offer and to retire.[50] However, a document drawn up by Henry VIII's commissioners in the Court of Augmentations listed him in 1540 as one of those to be kept on in the new Cathedral, referring to him as 'master of the children' and setting aside a stipend of £6 13s 4d a year, plus 2s a week for his meals.[51] This raises the intriguing possibility that, whilst making way for another man, possibly Robert Aufield, to head up the new College School, John Tucke may have stayed on as master of the choristers and organist at least for a time. We simply do not know.

The first definitely recorded post-Reformation master of the choristers was Richard Lichfield, who was appointed in 1562 and seems to have held the post for twenty years thereafter before his death in 1583, when he was buried in the Cathedral's south transept.[52]

---

49   See Chapter Four.
50   N. Orme, *Education in the West of England 1066 – 1548*, University of Exeter (1976), p. 28.
51   R. Woodley, *John Tucke: A Case Study in Early Tudor Music Theory*, Oxford University Press (1993), p. 36.
52   D. Welander, *The History, Art and Architecture of Gloucester Cathedral*, p. 344.

CHAPTER EIGHT

Elementary or Petty Schools:

The Growth of Basic Literacy and Reading Skills

Elementary schools for boys and girls

The grammar schools of medieval and Tudor Gloucester did not set out to educate boys from scratch; they looked to take in boys who had already been taught to read English and to write legibly.

Those who attended either the College School, the Song School or the Crypt School, just like their predecessors in the medieval grammar or almonry schools, therefore began their education at home in order to work on literacy skills that would meet the entrance requirements.[1] In all types of households, it was a mother's responsibility to teach her children basic manners and, if she could, reading skills. One of the most common depictions in medieval wall paintings and stained-glass windows showed St Anne, the patron saint of mothers, teaching her young daughter, the Virgin Mary, how to read a book.[2] Although no medieval example of this has survived in Gloucester, the Lady Chapel in the Cathedral does contain an early 20th-century window depicting the Virgin's home schooling in progress.[3]

Most young boys from wealthy families supplemented the teaching they received from their relatives with a short period of a year or two at a privately run petty school. These schools, which charged only a very basic fee, were also known as elementary schools, reading schools, ABC schools or 'abseyes'.[4] Their main function was to teach the alphabet, spelling and rudimentary English reading skills to young pupils, generally aged between

---

[1] K. Charlton, *Education in Renaissance England*, Routledge & Kegan Paul (1965), p. 98.
[2] H. Leyser, *Medieval Women*, Weidenfeld & Nicolson (1995), p. 135.
[3] D. Welander, *The Stained Glass of Gloucester Cathedral*, Frome (1985), p. 122.
[4] J. A. F. Thomson, *The Transformation of Medieval England*, Longman (1983), p. 348.

four and seven, and older pupils who had missed out. They also taught the Lord's Prayer, the Ten Commandments, the Creed and the basic principles of the Anglican catechism. Pupils generally stayed for no more than one or two years and attendance was often irregular, according to family means and the distance to be walked from home.[5]

The petty schools were open to girls as well as boys, but we have no idea of the numbers who benefited from them.[6] Young girls who did attend had little prospect of proceeding further. As females did not go to university or have a career at this time, there was no likelihood of a girl in medieval or Tudor Gloucester attending a more advanced school such as a grammar school. In some parts of the country a few schools did offer some education for girls in nunneries, but

Figure 44: Twentieth-century window in Gloucester Lady Chapel showing St Anne teaching the Virgin Mary.

there were none of these in the county of Gloucestershire.[7] Even girls from high-status families tended to get all the education they received inside their households. The main aim was to make a girl suitable for marriage.[8] She would have been taught reading, writing and enough arithmetic to help her keep household accounts, but the main thrust was on practical skills such as singing, music and the needlework required to make samplers and other pieces of embroidery.

It was in Elizabethan times that the number of petty schools across the

---

5   J. Lawson & H. Silver, *A Social History of Education in England*, Methuen (1973), p. 111.
6   H. M. Jewell, *Education in Early Modern England*, Macmillan (1998), p. 11.
7   N. Orme, *Medieval Schools from Roman Britain to Renaissance England*, Yale University Press (2006), p. 275.
8   T. Kelly, *Children in Tudor England*, Stanley Thornes (1987), p. 13.

country increased significantly. As well as catering for boys who were aiming for a grammar school and for some girls, also dipping in for a short time were some of the children of tradesmen and artisans who wished to acquire basic literacy before taking on apprenticeships.[9] The petty schools therefore contributed to a significant rise in the literacy rate in the years after the Reformation, especially in the early years of Elizabeth I's reign. Speaking of an 'English educational revolution' at this time, Lawrence Stone estimated that the average male literacy rate across the whole country rose to about 30 per cent and believed that half the male population of a town like Gloucester would have possessed basic reading skills.[10]

The petty school of St Owen

Set up by individuals, often women, in one room of their own homes, petty schools were private ventures. Although it has been estimated that by 1600 there were probably upwards of a dozen petty schools in Gloucester, few left any permanent records that historians can detect.[11] The beliefs of Puritanism with their emphasis on personal Bible reading, which took root in Gloucester in this period, are likely to have given literacy a particular boost in the city. The schools, however, were rarely in existence for long enough to become institutions in their own right; they catered for very small numbers, perhaps taking in no more than half a dozen or so pupils, and they sprang up here and there to meet local demand.[12]

We know of just one petty school that operated in Elizabethan Gloucester just outside the South Gate in the parish of the now lost Church of St Owen. John Taylor, who was to achieve national acclaim as England's 'water poet', was born in 1578 and attended this school before he was admitted to the Crypt. One of his earliest biographers, William Winstanley, explained that the School of St Owen was run by a Mr Green, who was treated as something of a joke by his pupils because of his short-sightedness and lack of business sense. 'Young Taylor', he wrote, 'had an odd

---

9   A. F. Leach, *Educational Charters and Documents*, Cambridge (1911), p. xlvi.
10 L. Stone, 'The Educational Revolution in England', *Past and Present* (1964), volume 28, p. 10.
11 P. Clark, 'The Ramoth-Gilead of the Good: Urban Change and Political Radicalism in Gloucester', J. Barry, *The Tudor and Stuart Town*, Longman (1990), p. 265.
12 C. Heighway, *Gloucester: A History and Guide*, Alan Sutton (1985), p. 113.

schoolmaster, upon whom some of his neighbours played a scurvy jest. The poor man was fond of new milk and went to market for the purpose of buying a milking cow, but being short-sighted and perhaps in other respects better qualified to deal with books than men, the seller, in sport it may be believed rather than roguery, sold him a bull, which poor Master Green drove contentedly home and did not discover the trick till he had called the maid to milk it'.[13]

The petty school curriculum

The petty schools were cheap and easy to set up. They required just one room in a cottage and little in the way of equipment beyond a few horn books. These horn books were sheets of paper containing the alphabet or Lord's Prayer mounted on a wooden tablet with a handle and covered with a thin layer of transparent horn for protection. Parchments displaying pictorial alphabets were also used to help boys and girls to learn to read.

The expansion of the printing press in Elizabethan times enabled those who made good progress with their reading to proceed onto a book known as a primer. There were numerous versions of these primers, but in 1545 Henry VIII tried to create one standardised text by issuing an authorised primer.[14] This was intended to give children the rudiments of the Christian religion and introduce them to the church services. It began with the alphabet and then moved on to the Ten Commandments, the Creed, the Lord's Prayer and the 'Hail Mary', using both Latin and English. It also contained various prayers and graces to be said at meals. In the preface the king expressed the expectation that 'every schoolmaster and bringer up of young beginners in learning, next after their ABC, now by use also set forth do teach this primer or book of ordinary prayers unto them in English'.[15]

Recognising the growing importance attached to the elementary stage of education and to help teachers at the petty schools, some experienced schoolmasters produced handbooks offering practical advice. One of them, *The English Schoolmaster: teaching all his scholars the order of distinct reading and true writing*, was the 1596 work of Edmund Coote, headmaster

---

13   W. Winstanley, *Lives of the Most Famous English Poets* (1687), p. 167.
14   D. W. Sylvester, *Educational Documents 800 – 1816*, Methuen (1970), p. 79.
15   H. G. Good, 'The First Illustrated School Books', *Journal of Educational Research*, volume 35 (1942), p. 339.

Figure 45: Woodcut of a Tudor schoolmaster using a horn book to teach the alphabet.

Figure 46: A 17th-century horn book.

of King Edward VI School in Bury St Edmunds.[16] It appeared in at least forty editions over the course of the next century, offering detailed guidance on alphabetic font styles and spelling. It aimed to move the pupil from single letters through rigorous tables of two-letter and three-letter combinations on to more complex prose and verse texts, ending with a catechism and a collection of prayers for daily use.[17] The *Ludus Literarius*, published by John Brinsley in 1612, described a method of teaching reading said to be so straightforward that it could be used by any would-be petty teacher and 'thus may any poor man or woman enter the little ones in a town together and make an honest living of it'.[18]

The most detailed description we have of an early petty school comes in a long book written in 1660 by Charles Hoole, a Yorkshire-born teacher and scholar, who eventually became Chaplain to the Bishop of Lincoln. Pupils generally started at the age of four or five. Their early lessons tended

---

[16] K. Charlton, *Education in Renaissance England*, Routledge & Kegan Paul (1965), p. 104.

[17] R. Shapiro, *Fixing Babel: An Historical Anthology of Applied English Lexicography*, Bucknell University Press (2017), p. 24.

[18] M. Hattaway, *A New Companion to English Renaissance Literature and Culture*, Wiley-Blackwell (2010), volume 1, p. 33.

to be designed with clear speaking and pronunciation in mind, after which familiarity with letters was the next step. 'The usual way to begin with a child, when he is first brought to school, is to teach him to know his letters in the horn-book, where he is to run over all the letters in the alphabet'.[19] To supplement this tradition, Hoole recommended games involving letters and letter sounds, including the use of flashcards with pictures and dice containing letters rather than numbers.

Fluent reading was the ultimate goal of a petty school. Hoole advocated beginning with the Lord's Prayer and the Ten Commandments, but within two years of starting at a good petty school he believed that a child should be capable of moving on to the Bible itself. 'When he can read any whit readily, let him begin the Bible and read over the book of Genesis by a chapter at a time. But acquaint him a little with the matter beforehand, for that will entice him to read it and make him more observant of what he reads'.[20] He also envisaged that they would read poetry in English, such as that written by George Herbert.

Hoole hoped to see an expansion of petty schools across the country and wanted them staffed by qualified teachers rather than women in reduced circumstances. 'The petty school is the place where indeed the first principle of all religion and learning ought to be taught and therefore deserveth that more encouragement should be given to teachers of it than that it should be left as a work for poor women or others whose necessities compel them to undertake it as a mere shelter from beggary'.[21] The qualifications he looked for in a good primary teacher were to have some knowledge of Latin, to write a fair hand and to possess good skill in arithmetic.

The petty schools continued to do important work as the first rung in Gloucester's educational ladder throughout the 17th and 18th centuries, though sadly we know very little about their location. It is recorded that John Collier kept a writing school in the city in the 1680s, having 'various writing tables and forms in his house and a small collection of teaching books'.[22]

---

19   T. Mark, *A New Discovery of the Old Art of Teaching School by Charles Hoole*, Manchester (1912), p. 33.
20   Ibid, p. 52.
21   Ibid, p. 59.
22   N. M. Herbert, *The Victoria History of the Counties of England: Gloucestershire*, volume 4, London (1988), p. 118.

These were also years in which the literacy rates continued to rise. By the early 17th century Gloucester had its own specialist bookseller, Toby Jordan, and several parishes operated small libraries, including one run from the Cathedral by the master of the College School, John Langley.[23] An analysis of the signatures recorded by those who appeared before the church courts at this time suggests that compared with other parts of the country Gloucester had a relatively high degree of adult male literacy. The literacy rate among those employed in the city in textiles during the 1630s has been estimated as 74 per cent. The corresponding figure for those working in food and drink was 70 per cent, for those in the clothing trade 64 per cent and for leather workers 62 per cent.[24] In the case of men appearing as witnesses in the church courts in the years between 1660 and 1685, no fewer than 88 per cent could sign their own names. Evidence from Gloucester wills shows a similar trend; 74 per cent of male testators and 49 per cent of female testators could sign their names in the years between 1660 and 1739.[25]

By 1818 there were said to be no fewer than fourteen petty schools offering their services in Gloucester and its surrounding hamlets.[26] As in earlier times, they were small schools meeting in private houses; they have left regrettably few records of their existence and sadly, despite the important work they did in preparing pupils for the grammar schools, they have passed into history largely undocumented.

[23] Ibid, p. 91.
[24] P. Clark, *The Ramoth-Gilead of the Good: Urban Change and Political Radicalism in Gloucester*, p. 265.
[25] N. M. Herbert, *The Victoria History of the Counties of England: Gloucestershire*, volume 4, p. 119.
[26] Ibid, p. 339.

CHAPTER NINE

The Early 17th Century:

Schools Dominated by Religious Controversy

When the 17th century dawned, Gloucester's educational provision based on the College School, the Cathedral Song School and the Crypt School seemed settled, each of these three institutions having its own clear function and niche in local society. The next forty years, however, saw the city's schools challenged by high-profile religious antagonisms. These involved the so-called High Church party, particularly strong within the Cathedral community, rallying to support the reforms of William Laud, who was Dean of Gloucester and eventually Archbishop of Canterbury. Pitted against the Laudians and in a majority on the City Council were those known as Puritans, who believed in simpler forms of worship based on a literal interpretation of the Bible. This conflict at a national level became one of the main causes of the English Civil War that began in 1642, but by then it had already been fought over inside the schools of Gloucester for several decades.

The College School in the early 17th century

Throughout the 17th century the College School, as set up by Henry VIII's statutes between 1541 and 1544, continued to meet in the room above the Cathedral cloisters that had previously served as the monastic library. This room received additional upgrades when it was refurbished in 1624 – 25 with 15s spent on repairing windows and 16s 6d on new classroom benches.[1]

The curriculum offered by the College School remained rooted in the mastery of Latin grammar, taught through the availability of influential

---

[1]   J. R. S. Whiting, *The King's School Gloucester*, Orchard & Ind (1990), p. 15.

teaching manuals such as the *Ludus Literarius*, which was written in 1612 by John Brinsley, the master of Ashby-de-la-Zouch grammar school, as a dialogue between two imaginary teachers. In his view the purpose of schools was 'to make scholars the most perfect grammarians, which all the learned do so highly commend'.[2] He continued to advocate the use of William Lily's grammar and summarised in great detail the most appropriate rules for use with syntax, parsing and translation in order to prepare the way for reading Virgil, Horace, Ovid and other writers.

Nonetheless, there were indications that changes were afoot and these would inevitably in due course bring tensions of their own to the school. The growth of Puritan religious feeling in Gloucester with its emphasis on personal Bible reading raised the importance of proficiency in the English language and increasingly there were calls for some of the work at the College School to be undertaken in English. Brinsley, himself of strong Puritan disposition, advocated that English should be taught side-by-side

Figure 47: No 4 Miller's Green, the house used by the College School headmaster and usher in the 17th century.

---

2   E. T. Campagnac, *Ludus Literarius or the Grammar School by John Brinsley*, London (1917), p. 88.

with Latin. His view was that a good grammar school should 'train up scholars so that they may be able to express their minds purely and readily in our own tongue and to increase in the practice of it as well as in Latin or Greek'.[3]

The College schoolmaster's house at this time was Number 4 Miller's Green. It was divided into two separate tenements for the master and the usher, and there was also space for them to take in boarders.[4] At the time of the bishop's visitation of 1613 it was reported to be 'very ruinate',[5] but a substantial refurbishment took place in 1637 – 38, when a sum of £14 was spent on 'ten bundles of lathes for the repair of his house, fourteen bushels of hair and two hundred tiles, and for workmen's wages'.[6]

Early 17th-century Headmasters and Ushers of the College School		
Masters	Ushers	
1605 – 1612: Thomas Potter	1605 – 1607: Thomas Wood	
	1607 – 1612: Thomas Lloyd	
1612 – 1616: John Clark	1612 – 1616: Christopher Pritchard	
1616 – 1618: John Hoare	1616 – 1618: John Langley	
1618 – 1635: John Langley	1618 – 1621: Daniel Williams	1628 – 1632: Giles Workman
	1621 – 1623: Thomas Daniel	1632 – 1634: Ezra Grayle
	1623 – 1628: John Angell	1634 – 1635: John Grayle

The longest serving headmaster of the early 17th century was John Langley (1618 – 35). He was born in Banbury and studied at Magdalen Hall, Oxford, achieving his B.A. in 1616. Langley began his association with the College School straight after his graduation and served as usher for two years under John Hoare, whom he succeeded as headmaster in 1618. Despite the puritanical outlook he developed, Langley was the only headmaster to be appointed by William Laud during the time he was Dean of Gloucester. Laud recorded the appointment in the Chapter Act Book, listing Langley as 'headmaster of the free school in the college or Cathedral

3   Ibid, pp. 21–2.
4   S. M. Eward, *No Fine But A Glass of Wine: Cathedral Life at Gloucester in Stuart Times*, Lymington (1985), p. 36.
5   J. R. S. Whiting, *The King's School Gloucester*, p. 13.
6   S. M. Eward, *No Fine But A Glass of Wine: Cathedral Life at Gloucester in Stuart Times*, p. 61.

church of Gloucester, the three articles required in that behalf being first signed by him and an oath being made by him to observe the statutes and ordinances of the said church and the oath of allegiance to King James'.[7]

Langley is considered by some to have been the first really highly regarded master to have been in charge of the College School since its foundation over seventy years earlier.[8] He was held in high esteem for his scholarship and teaching skills across a wide range of disciplines and was described as 'a general scholar and a great antiquary'.[9] A note in the Chapter Act Book for 1628 recorded that he had 'for diverse years before that enjoyed the good approbation of the Dean and Chapter'.[10] When Langley considered taking up a much better paid role at Dorchester School in 1628, the City Council stepped in and offered him an additional £10 a year to remain in post in 'regard of his good demeanour ... and his careful teaching and educating the youth of the city and the sons of diverse noblemen and gentlemen to the great grace and credit of this city'.[11] The Dean and Chapter raised his salary another 13s 4d as a mark of respect for him in 1635, his last year as headmaster.[12] The eulogy delivered at his funeral by Dr Edward Reynolds, Dean of Christ Church, Oxford, underlined Langley's reputation as 'learned in the whole body of learning, an excellent linguist and grammarian, historian, cosmographer, artist and a most judicious divine and a great antiquary'.[13]

Langley's approach to education was authoritarian, but complicated by his own individual character. It was said that he 'had a very awful presence and speech that struck a mighty respect and fear in his scholars which, however, wore off after they were a little used to him, and his management

---

[7]   W. Page, *The Victoria History of the Counties of England: Gloucestershire*, volume 2, London (1907), p. 324.

[8]   N. M. Herbert, *The Victoria History of the Counties of England: Gloucestershire*, volume 4, London (1988), p. 91.

[9]   J. Strype, *A Survey of the Cities of London and Westminster*, London (1720), volume i, p. 168.

[10] S. M. Eward, *Gloucester Cathedral Chapter Act Book 1616 – 1687*, The Bristol and Gloucestershire Archaeological Society Record Series, volume 21 (2007), p. 50.

[11] S. M. Eward, *No Fine But A Glass of Wine: Cathedral Life at Gloucester in Stuart Times*, p. 232.

[12] J. N. Langston, 'Headmasters and Ushers of the King's (College) School, Gloucester', *Records of Gloucester Cathedral*, volume III, H. Osborne Gloucester (1928), p. 177.

[13] E. Reynolds, *A Sermon Touching the Use of Humane Learning*, London (1658), p. 30.

of himself towards them was such that they both loved and feared him'.[14] The fact that no less than six ushers served under Langley may not be remarkable as the post was generally regarded as no more than a stepping stone to a higher appointment, but it could suggest that not everything was entirely well at the school and it may be that Langley was particularly difficult to get on with.[15]

Much of our knowledge about the lives of the masters and ushers of the school at this time is derived from the work of Anthony Wood, an antiquary who researched the ancestry and careers of those who graduated from Oxford University. He was the son of Thomas Wood, who was usher at the College School between 1605 and 1607.[16] His great work, which stretched to several volumes, was the *Athenae Oxonienses*, detailing the lives of all Oxford writers and churchmen in the 16th and 17th centuries.

This was a period of great religious controversy both nationally and at Gloucester. William Laud was Dean of Gloucester from 1616. On his appointment he said of the Cathedral that 'scarce ever was a church in England so ill governed and so much out of order'.[17] He immediately decreed that 'the communion table should be placed altar wise' at the east end of the

Figure 48: Boys at play in front of the College schoolroom on the north-east corner of the Cathedral (from an illustration by the 19th-century artist John Buckler).

---

[14]   S. Knight, *The Life of Dr John Colet*, Oxford (1823), p. 324.
[15]   D. Robertson, *The King's School Gloucester*, Phillimore (1974), p. 48.
[16]   A. Wood, *Athenae Oxonienses: the Fasti* (ed P. Bliss), London (1813), volume 1, p. 5.
[17]   W. Prynne, *Canterburies Doome*, London (1646), p. 77.

quire, where it should be railed off to create a powerful statement about holy space and the barriers needed to preserve it.[18] To take such action was regarded by many in the early 17th century as a deliberately provocative act. Altars had been moved from the east end of churches at the time of Edward VI and turned into communion tables, around which congregations could gather mindful of the fact that there were no longer any Catholic masses in the English Church. Laud's altar declared defiantly that he was not ashamed of the Catholic past. He also required all those taking part in a service from canons down to choristers to bow their heads as a mark of respect to the altar, 'making of their humble reverence to Almighty God, not only at their first entrance into the quire, but at their approach toward the holy table'.[19] For some, all this 'smacked of Popery'.[20] The offence caused to Puritan members of the Chapter was so strong that apparently the Bishop, Miles Smith, refused even to enter the Cathedral for several years.[21]

Two former headmasters of the College School who went on to become prebendaries in the Cathedral took opposing views of Laud's work. One of the keenest supporters of his High Church reforms was Elias Wrench (headmaster, 1588 – 98), who remained a force to be reckoned with in the Cathedral for more than thirty years until his death in 1633. He was opposed by William Loe (headmaster, 1598 – 1605), a Puritan sympathiser who may have been one of those responsible for a letter which 'appeared' in the pulpit of St Michael's Church, denouncing Laud's decision to move the Cathedral communion table from the middle of the quire to its east end as an act of Popery and criticising the canons for not having the spirit to prevent it.[22]

William Laud clearly took a great deal of interest in the running of the College School and was determined to make his mark on it. His influence has been seen behind the appointment of Daniel Williams and Thomas Daniel as ushers in 1618 and 1621 respectively; both of these young men

---

[18] C. Heighway, S. Hamilton et alii, *Gloucester Cathedral: Faith, Art and Architecture*, Scala (2011), p. 60.

[19] P. Heylyn, *Cyprianus Anglicus: History of the Life and Death of the Most Reverend and Renowned Prelate*, London (1668), p. 69.

[20] D. Welander, *The History, Art and Architecture of Gloucester Cathedral*, Alan Sutton (1991), p. 354.

[21] J. R. S. Whiting, *The King's School Gloucester*, p. 16.

[22] J. N. Langston, 'Headmasters and Ushers of the King's (College) School, Gloucester', p. 162.

matriculated from St John's College, Oxford, where Laud was president and would eventually be buried after his execution.[23] One of Laud's key reforms at Gloucester was the revival of early morning prayers at 6 a.m. in the Lady Chapel, which members of the school were expected to attend as part of the College or Cathedral Church.[24] The decision was recorded in Laud's Chapter Act Book with the words 'we, holding it unfit that so goodly and fair a building dedicated to the service of God should lose the use and end for which it was founded and consecrated, do order and decree that the said prayers at six of the clock shall be said and celebrated yearly in the said chapel from the Feast of the Annunciation of the Blessed Virgin St Mary unto the feast of St Michael the Archangel'.[25] This decision seems to have had the support of Headmaster John Langley and may be considered to be

the beginning of a formal act of worship or assembly involving the pupils of the King's School each morning in the Cathedral, a practice that continues in modern times.

It was also the custom in the Jacobean Church for Sunday services sung in the quire to be followed by a sermon preached in the nave.[26] The Chapter accounts make it clear that College School boys were expected to attend these services on special occasions. Pews were installed in the nave for the leading citizens and digni- taries of the city; and a charge

Figure 49: Portrait of William Laud by an unknown artist in the King's School Museum.

---

23 W. Page, *The Victoria History of the Counties of England: Gloucestershire*, volume 2, pp. 324–5.

24 E. Hayward, *Gloucester, Stroud and Berkeley*, Longman (1970), p. 102.

25 S. M. Eward, *Gloucester Cathedral Chapter Act Book 1616 – 1687*, p. 9.

26 S. J. A. Evans, 'Cathedral Life at Gloucester in the Early 17th Century', *Transactions of the Bristol and Gloucestershire Archaeological Society* (1961), volume 80, p. 9.

of £3 1s was recorded in 1628 for 'a gallery for the scholars to sit at sermons, of which Mr Langley paid twenty shillings'. In 1636 a locked door was added to the gallery, presumably to prevents boys trying to leave the sermon early.[27]

Langley worked as headmaster of the College School for seventeen years. His resignation in 1635 came about as a direct result of his religious convictions. William Laud was Archbishop of Canterbury by this point and the High Church reforms he promoted to 'beautify' the church were in full flow. Laud's Puritan critic, William Prynne, denounced the 'diverse crucifixes and images in the Cathedral at Gloucester ... and diverse altar cloths, pulpit cloths with other vestments, whereon crucifixes were embroidered to the great scandal of the people'.[28] Langley expressed agreement with him. Anthony Wood summarised his religious persuasion as follows: 'He was beloved of learned men, particularly Selden and those who adhered to the Long Parliament, but he had not much esteem for the orthodox clergy because he was a Puritan and afterwards a witness against Archbishop Laud'.[29] A later historian referred to Langley as 'an excellent theologist of the Puritan stamp'.[30]

In 1635, having long struggled with his convictions, Langley refused to take the oath of loyalty to the Church of England and its bishops, an oath which was binding on all schoolmasters. Consequently, Sir Nathaniel Brent, Vicar General of Canterbury, suspended him, commenting that he was 'a very good schoolmaster but thought to be puritanical'.[31] Langley did not wait for the reaction of the Dean and Chapter at Gloucester, but resigned with immediate effect. According to Dr Reynolds' funeral eulogy, this was caused by Langley 'fearing whether his conscience and his employment could consist together'.[32]

Despite his resignation, Langley's teaching skills remained in high regard in Gloucester. The Puritan-leaning City Council in 1640 praised him for having 'given good testimony in teaching and instructing many of the burgesses' sons of this city and others and enabling them for the

---

[27] S. M. Eward, *No Fine But A Glass of Wine: Cathedral Life at Gloucester in Stuart Times*, p. 48.
[28] W. Prynne, *Antipathy of the English Lordly Prelacy*, London (1641), p. 196.
[29] A. Wood, *Athenae Oxonienses: the Fasti* (ed P. Bliss), volume 3, p. 435.
[30] B. Brook, *The Lives of the Puritans*, (London) 1813, volume 3, p. 290.
[31] S. M. Eward, *Gloucester Cathedral Chapter Act Book 1616 – 1687*, p. 166.
[32] E. Reynolds, *A Sermon Touching the Use of Humane Learning*, London (1658), p. 30.

universities'.[33] He secured new employment as usher at the Crypt School and it seems that the Council's plan was eventually to offer him the headship there, but later in 1640 Langley left Gloucester and was appointed High Master of St Paul's School in London, where he was regarded as 'an able and religious schoolmaster'.[34] One of his pupils at St Paul's was the diarist Samuel Pepys. When Archbishop Laud was put on trial by the leaders of Parliament in 1643, Langley was one of those called to give evidence.[35] There he reported that, whilst Dean of Gloucester, Laud had moved the communion table to an altar position and insisted on 'due reverence' being paid by anyone entering the building. He also reported that Laud had John Workman, Puritan lecturer at St Nicholas' Church and brother of Giles Workman, the usher of the College School, barred from teaching after he had denounced the use of images in church and called for clergy to be elected by the people rather than appointed by bishops.[36]

The Cathedral Song School

The eight boy choristers provided for Gloucester Cathedral in Henry VIII's statutes continued throughout the 17th century to be educated in their own school separately from the boys of the College School. The Song School they attended was most likely part of the organist's house, which was situated at the east end of the old infirmary, then known by the intriguing name of Babylon.[37] This was a ramshackle two-storey half-timbered structure built around the Infirmary Arches that still remain in place today. At the time of the bishop's visitation of 1613, it was recorded that 'the number of our choristers is full and they have a master to teach them and order them, whom we cease not to put in mind of his duty'.[38] The quality of the education the choristers received in the Song School depended very much on the personality and aptitude of the individual appointed by the Dean and Chapter as the organist and master of the choristers, but on the whole in this era it appears not to have been of a very high standard.

33   R. Austin, *The Crypt School Gloucester*, John Bellows Gloucester (1939), p. 93.
34   T. Fuller, *The Church History of Britain*, London (1842), book 5, p. 168.
35   S. Eward, *Gloucester Cathedral Chapter Act Book 1616 – 1687*, p. xxviii.
36   C. Heighway, S. Hamilton et alii, *Gloucester Cathedral: Faith, Art and Architecture*, p. 62.
37   N. M. Herbert, *The Victoria History of the Counties of England: Gloucestershire*, volume 4, p. 286.
38   S. J. A. Evans, *Cathedral Life at Gloucester in the Early 17th Century*, p. 13.

Figure 50: The Infirmary Arches on the north side of the Cathedral, which mark the site of the 17th-century Song School.

We know the names of many of the boy choristers from the early Stuart period as their appointments were recorded in the Chapter Act Book begun by William Laud. The eight choristers in place when Laud arrived in Gloucester in 1616 were William Morgan, William Jennings, Thomas Brodgate, Thomas Goslin, Elias Smith, Thomas Smith, Abell Randall and Polidore Brodgate.[39] Unlike the pupils in the College School, these choristers were paid for their services to the Cathedral and the instruction it required. Their pay in the early 17th century was £3 6s 8d (as opposed to the £6 13s 4d earned by the adult lay clerks).[40] They also received an annual grant for material for their gowns, which they were required to renew each Christmas. The average length of a boy's service in the choir seems to have been between six and eight years, but there were exceptions. Richard Brodgate was a chorister for a full twelve years from 1618 to 1630; in addition to his pay he was also apprenticed to a barber-surgeon.[41]

---

[39]   S. M. Eward, *No Fine But A Glass of Wine: Cathedral Life at Gloucester in Stuart Times,* p. 18.

[40]   Ibid, p. 16.

[41]   S. M. Eward, *Gloucester Cathedral Chapter Act Book 1616 – 1687,* p. xiv.

Choristers in the 1620s	Year of Appointment
Constantine Smith, Richard Dobbs, Giles Dobbs & Mark Colman	1620
Berkeley Wrench	1621
Anthony Dobbs & Richard Price	1623
Thomas Lewes	1624
Anthony Smith	1625
Luke Turner	1626
William Hosier	1627
William Dobbs, Richard Longe & Richard White	1629

Although choristers were occasionally the sons of canons or organists, there was generally a great social gulf between them and the sons of the gentry in the College School. Most choristers combined their Cathedral duties with apprenticeships as glaziers, bell-ringers or barber-surgeons. Their working day consisted of singing and instrumental classes, periodic lessons on the catechism and the singing of offices, all of which had to be fitted around their trade apprenticeships.[42] Berkeley Wrench, who became a chorister in 1621, spent most of his adult life as sexton and later subsacrist in the Cathedral.[43] John Painter, a chorister in 1638, went on to become a Cathedral glazier.[44] A few bettered themselves markedly, one being Richard Longe, who was a chorister between 1629 and 1631. He went on to become a chorister at Magdalen College, Oxford, until 1637 and then returned to Gloucester Cathedral as a minor canon.[45]

Young choristers received their education from the Cathedral organist and master of the choristers. The two most long-serving individuals to fill this post in the first half of the 17th century were Elias Smith (1600 – 1620) and Philip Hosier (1620 – 38), neither of whom it seems carried out their role to the full satisfaction of the Dean and Chapter. Possibly the only organist in the Cathedral's history who was ordained, Hosier combined his role with being curate at St Mary de Crypt church and later also St John's, meaning that he may well have been simply too busy to spend sufficient

---

42 J. R. S. Whiting, *The King's School Gloucester*, p. 24.
43 S. M. Eward, *Gloucester Cathedral Chapter Act Book 1616 – 1687*, p. 22.
44 J. R. S. Whiting, *The King's School Gloucester*, p. 25.
45 S. M. Eward, *Gloucester Cathedral Chapter Act Book 1616 – 1687*, pp. 84 & 165.

time on the mundane task of providing the choristers with a well-rounded education. There were criticisms of the way Hosier organised the choir and Laud enacted that 'the master of the choristers shall appoint before the beginning of prayers one or more of the choristers to turn the books ready for such services as shall be appointed to be sung, and likewise for the anthem, and lay them ready upon the singing men's desks to avoid confusion and running to and fro in the time of divine service'.[46]

The religious instruction that the master of the choristers was meant to provide for the young as part of their education seems often to have been ignored. At the bishop's visitation of 1613 it was reported that 'the choristers are not well ordered and there is no one appointed to catechise them'. Their master, at the time Elias Smith, seems to have been failing in his duties and for many years it seems that the College School was asked to step in to fill this gap, causing considerable ill-feeling.[47] The Chapter Act Book for 1628 records that John Langley, the College School's headmaster, was pressing for the master of the choristers to be ordered to do his job of teaching 'the catechism and principles of the Christian religion' to the choristers. As a result of his action, the Dean and Chapter asked Philip Hosier specifically to find the time to take charge of a weekly class to ensure the catechism was taught.[48]

The Cathedral Chapter Act Book reveals that the management of the choir and the behaviour of the choristers were real causes for concern for William Laud and his immediate successors as Dean. The standards of musicianship among the lay clerks appear to have been low, which was a situation replicated in several other cathedrals at this time.[49] In 1620 it was recorded that 'Mr Dean this day in open chapter pronounced a solemn admonition against Christopher Hayes, a lay singing man, being the first warning given for his manifold negligence and especially for not applying himself to get more knowledge in singing'.[50] Neither did the day-to-day conduct of the adult lay clerks set a good example to the younger boys. Lay clerk Richard White was given a warning by Dean Laud in 1618 'for frequenting of alehouses and slothfulness in performing his service and

---

46   Ibid p. 19.
47   J. R. S. Whiting, *The King's School Gloucester*, Orchard & Ind (1990), p. 14.
48   W. Page, *The Victoria History of the Counties of England: Gloucestershire*, volume 2, p. 325.
49   A. Mould, *The English Chorister: A History*, London (2007), p. 99.
50   S. M. Eward, *Gloucester Cathedral Chapter Act Book 1616 – 1687*, p. 18.

other unseemly courses not befitting this church'.[51] Rowland Smith was accused of assaulting a tailor in the city in 1618 and two years later was expelled from the choir for being 'drunk in church in time of Divine prayers'.[52] In order to reduce the lay clerks' reputation for heavy drinking and rowdiness, in 1625 the Dean and Chapter introduced a night-time curfew, ordering that 'for the avoiding of night walking and scandal that may arise thereby, no member of the choir whose habitation is within the precincts of this church shall be abroad in the city or elsewhere after ten of the clock in the night'.[53]

This kind of unruly behaviour was sometimes mirrored by the boy choristers themselves. Archbishop Laud's visitation of the Cathedral in 1635 laid down the principle that 'those of the choristers and other ministers of your church who are disorderly, unruly or wilfully negligent in performance of their several duties, and do not after wholesome admonition or correction reform their lives and conform their manners, be expelled from their places'. It then went on to demand that 'Thomas Longe and Richard Longe, two of the choristers of this church, being presented for incorrigible boys, should forthwith be removed from their places'.[54] What they had done wrong is not known, but their dismissal seems to be indicative of some of the serious problems that were affecting the Gloucester Song School in the years approaching the Civil War.

The Crypt School in the early 17th century

At the Crypt School it seems that the early decades of the 17th century brought significant progress in the quality of education on offer to the boys, who continued to be drawn from local families of merchants, shopkeepers and artisans. The school was well-funded, the teaching of Latin appears to have been innovative and scholarly and for a short period Greek was added to the curriculum. At the same time, however, like the neighbouring College School, the Crypt was torn asunder by the bitter religious antagonisms that divided the city as Laudians and Puritans struggled for supremacy.

---

51   Ibid, p. 11.
52   B. Taylor, 'William Laud Dean of Gloucester' in *Transactions of the Bristol and Gloucestershire Archaeological Society* (1958), volume 77, p. 95.
53   S. J. A. Evans, *Cathedral Life at Gloucester in the Early 17th Century*, p. 12.
54   S. M. Eward, *No Fine But A Glass of Wine: Cathedral Life at Gloucester in Stuart Times*, p. 57.

We know very little about the first two 17th-century headmasters at the Crypt. The second was recorded as a Mr Floyde and it appears that he was dismissed from his post in 1611 following parental complaints. Although the nature of their concerns is not specified, the City Council Books claim that 'diverse and sundry persons of this city do much complain for that they have not a sufficient and diligent schoolmaster to teach scholars in the Christ School of this city and that for want thereof many are enforced to send their children abroad to be taught to their very great charge . . . and that this schoolmaster, Mr Floyde, is careless and negligent in performance of his duty towards his scholars'.[55] It is difficult to know how much credibility to attach to complaints of this kind made against Floyde and even more so against his controversial successor, John Bird, as they seem to have arisen more from conflicting religious allegiances than from deficiencies in the standard of instruction provided.

The early 17th century saw the government of Gloucester concentrated in the hands of fewer and fewer men, essentially the forty burgesses who made up the Common Council, and it was from their number that the positions of mayor, steward, sheriff and aldermen were filled.[56] This small ruling elite also became increasingly committed to radical forms of Puritanism and was responsible for the appointment of lecturers to preach Puritan sermons in the churches of the city centre.[57] By 1642, when the Civil War began, Gloucester was regarded as a Puritan stronghold and the Presbyterian leader Richard Baxter was able to praise its inhabitants as 'a civil, courteous and religious people'.[58] This outlook clouded the Council's judgement of the city's schools, which came to be regarded principally as building blocks for the creation of a new society referred to by Puritans as a godly commonwealth. The criticisms made of the Crypt School in this period therefore stemmed from the religious allegiance of its masters and do not necessarily prove underlying problems with the quality of the education offered to the boys.

That said, the Council does seem to have shown a genuine interest in the running of the school. In 1620 it voted to allocate more money to the

---

55   R. Austin, *The Crypt School Gloucester*, p. 91.
56   C. Heighway, *Gloucester: A History and Guide*, Alan Sutton (1985), p. 117.
57   P. Clark, *The Ramoth-Gilead of the Good: Urban Change and Political Radicalism in Gloucester*, p. 264.
58   N. M. Herbert, *The Victoria History of the Counties of England: Gloucestershire*, volume 4, p. 92.

school, increasing the master's salary to the sum of 40 marks (about £27), well ahead of the figure of £10 originally specified by Joan Cooke.[59] Also at this time financial provision was made for an usher. Whilst occasional temporary assistants had been appointed in Elizabethan times, steps were now taken to make the position of usher permanent. This decision was facilitated by a £100 bequest made to the Council in the will of Alderman Lawrence Wiltshire, who died in 1612 and, according to a brass plate once visible over his grave in the north transept of the Cathedral, was 'sometime mayor of this city, by his vocation a clothier, wherein he did much good to the poor'.[60] Edward Barwell was appointed as the first permanent usher in 1614, with an

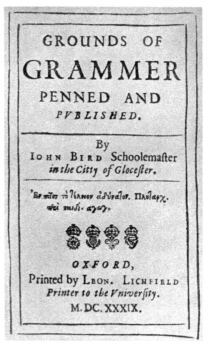

Figure 51: John Bird's text book in use at the Crypt in the 1630s.

annual salary of £8 and permission to live in one of the chambers above the schoolroom. Described on his appointment as 'a very able and sufficient man for his learning to teach school and to instruct scholars in the Latin tongue', Barwell stayed in post for fourteen years and may have combined his duties at the school with the post of Rector of St Mary de Crypt Church itself.[61]

These were positive steps and the next master, John Bird, seems to have been a promising choice. We do not know exactly when he became master; it may have been as early as 1611, although it is possible that there are gaps in the record. He was clearly an able academic who developed his own Latin grammar book out of lessons taught at the Crypt. This was eventually published in 1639 under the title *Grounds of Grammar Penned and*

---

59 C. Lepper, *The Crypt School Gloucester 1539 – 1989*, Alan Sutton (1989), p. 12.
60 S. Rudder, *A New History of Gloucestershire*, Cirencester (1779), republished by Alan Sutton in 2006, p. 176.
61 R. Austin, *The Crypt School Gloucester*, p. 121.

Published by John Bird Schoolmaster in the City of Gloucester.[62] It was based on a number of changes that Bird thought should be made to the standard textbook still in use at this time, that of William Lily, seeking to 'correct and amend some errors in the old grammar'. Bird thought it important to emphasise derivation and composition, criticising Lily for providing insufficient examples. He believed that the essentials of grammar needed more thorough reinforcement so that teachers did not 'have boys run before they can creep or go'. Bird also warned of the dangers of relying too much on attempting to translate English sentences into Latin; he wanted boys to understand Latin on its own merits and said that the two languages should 'not be mixed together nor one comprehended under another'.[63]

Early 17th-century Headmasters and Ushers at the Crypt School	
Masters	Ushers
1607 – ? : William Orton	1614 – 1628: Edward Barwell
? – 1611: Mr Floyde	1628 – 1633: Jonathan Bullock
1611? – 1641: John Bird	1633 – 1639: Robert Bird
	1639 – 1640: John Langley

Despite its promising start, Bird's period as master came to a very sad end when, like his predecessor, he too became engulfed in a long-running conflict with the City Council. In 1639 members of the Council dismissed John Bird's son, Robert, who had been usher at the Crypt since 1633. They also voted to halve the master's salary from 40 marks to a mere 20 marks and, if possible, to remove Bird from the headship subject to 'the placing of a more diligent man in that place'.[64] The Council Books of the same year record that 'whereas Crypt School, founded by the Lady Cooke with a schoolmaster to teach grammar, there is at this present and for diverse years last past hath been very negligently and carelessly supplied by Mr John Bird, schoolmaster, in so much that very few able scholars have been sent thence to the university in comparison of other free schools ... There is and hath been too much neglect by Mr Bird in teaching and instructing

---

62   Ibid, p. 103.
63   J. S. Pendergast, *Religion, Allegory and Literacy in Early Modern England*, Ashgate Illinois (2006), pp. 79–80.
64   C. Lepper, *The Crypt School Gloucester 1539 – 1989*, p. 13.

scholars in the school called Christ School within this city in so much that both aldermen and others shall be enforced to withdraw their sons from thence and to place them elsewhere, which will turn to their great charge and the disgrace of this city and contrary to the founder's intention'.[65]

The extent to which the Council's minutes present an accurate picture of the state of learning at the Crypt must remain a matter of conjecture. Personal animosities no doubt played a part. Some of the complaints arose from the fact that Bird had his wife and children living with him in the lodgings above the schoolroom contrary to the stipulations of the Tripartite Indenture of 1540. 'Mr John Bird', the Council recorded, 'hath had all the chambers but one and cocklofts over the said school and kept therein his wife, children and family contrary to the intention of the foundress'. Much more important though were deeply rooted religious disputes as Bird became caught up in the battle between the Puritans, who dominated the City Council, and High Church Laudians. Bird made his own religious allegiance clear when he published a second edition of his grammar book in 1641; he dedicated it to Laud, who he referred to as 'the Most Reverend Father in God William by Divine Providence Archbishop of Canterbury'.[66]

The intention of the City Council seems to have been to replace Bird with the strongly Puritan-minded John Langley, who had resigned as master of the College School in 1635. He was appointed at the Crypt initially as usher in 1639 'to teach Greek and other learning in the Crypt School and to have for his stipend forty marks yearly'. The inflated salary Langley was promised almost certainly meant that he had been marked out as a successor to Bird as headmaster.[67] The following year, however, in 1640 the Council received a letter from King Charles I expressly forbidding the change of staffing that had been envisaged. This letter, thought to have been influenced by Archbishop Laud, upheld Bird as 'a very sober man of conversation and learned in that way and hath deserved very well of you and that city in the instruction and education of the children'.[68] The king went on to command that 'you suffer the aforesaid John Bird to continue master in the school which he hath and fairly and peaceably to allow him all such fees and profits whatsoever belonging to his place as have heretofore been enjoyed by him without any

---

[65] R. Austin, *The Crypt School Gloucester*, pp. 93–95.
[66] Ibid, p. 105.
[67] C. Lepper, *The Crypt School Gloucester 1539 – 1989*, p. 13.
[68] W. Page, *The Victoria History of the Counties of England: Gloucestershire*, volume 2, pp. 326 & 348.

interruption or molestation'.[69] Langley on the other hand was denounced as 'a man factiously set against the government of the Church of England who … refused to conform himself to those things which were required of him according to law and forthwith deserted the school in Gloucester belonging to the Dean and Chapter'.[70]

Despite the king's personal intervention, the City Council refused to give way. Bird's salary was cut to just £9 per annum, the figure laid down for a lay teacher in Joan Cooke's original Tripartite Indenture a century earlier. They also secured nothing less than an Act of Parliament, which was passed in 1641 for the 'removing and putting out of Mr John Bird schoolmaster of Crypt School in the said city from being schoolmaster there'.[71] Bird was not, however, replaced by John Langley as originally envisaged. By the time the case was finally settled, Langley had already moved to St Paul's School in London.

Figure 52: The Crypt schoolroom in Southgate Street, which was presided over by John Bird for three decades of the early 17th century.

---

[69]   R. Austin, *The Crypt School Gloucester*, p. 97.

[70]   J. N. Langston, 'Headmasters and Ushers of the King's (College) School, Gloucester', pp. 178–9.

[71]   C. Lepper, *The Crypt School Gloucester 1539 – 1989*, p. 14.

Despite the high-profile disputes of this period, work continued at the Crypt to provide generations of boys with the grounding in Latin that remained so important to their prospects in later life. The absence of a Crypt School register before Victorian times makes it difficult to build up a picture of the pupils who attended in the 17th century or to discover how they perceived their school. One comment has been left for us by Richard Atkyns of Tuffley, who became a Royalist officer in the Civil War and a writer on matters relating to printing. He recalled how he was discouraged by John Bird's reaction to the discrepancy between the difficulty he found in reciting grammar and the apparent ease with which he was able to write in Latin. 'I was sent to a free school in Gloucester', he wrote, 'where I made exercises best of any in the seat, but repeated grammar rules and lessons worst ... so as my master suspected others to have made my exercises for me, which took me off from making them so well as I could'.[72] He also commented that he found his time at the Crypt in the 1620s to be a merciful release as his mother's uncle, who had previously been educating him at home, used to beat him for the slightest offence. Atkyns's final year at the Crypt was marred by serious illness. 'When I began to take some delight in learning', he said, 'I fell sick with the smallpox and was very near death and went to school no more'. He had, however, learnt enough to secure a place at Balliol College, Oxford, a fact which in itself does much to suggest a picture of sound learning being maintained at the Crypt, despite the many problems which the religious antagonisms of the age caused for the school.

---

[72]   R. Atkyns, *The Vindication*, London (1669), p. 3.

CHAPTER TEN

Civil War and Commonwealth:

The City's Schools under Siege

'It may be the case that historians of education have underestimated the amount of dislocation caused, at least in some parts of the country, by the Civil War' wrote Malcolm Seaborne in his study *The English School: Its Architecture and Organisation*.[1] Nowhere was the disruption likely to have been greater than in Gloucester, which was a city subjected to a five-week-long siege and a community torn apart by rival concepts of what constituted the true religion. The Cathedral's Song School closed for two decades. At the College School the pro-Royalist headmaster was forced to resign and the school was brought under radically new governance. The Crypt literally came under heavy artillery fire and was afflicted by controversies over its headmaster's religious beliefs, which were a step too far for Oliver Cromwell and the leaders of Parliament.

The Crypt School

The headmaster appointed to succeed John Bird at the Crypt in 1641 was John Biddle, a native of Wotton-under-Edge and a graduate of Magdalen Hall, Oxford. Whilst a boy at Katharine Lady Berkeley's School, Biddle was already credited with translating Virgil's *Eclogues* and the first two of Juvenal's *Satires* into English verse and composing an oration in Latin for the funeral of a schoolfellow.[2] Like his predecessor, Biddle was a

---

[1]   M. Seaborne, *The English School: Its Architecture and Organisation 1370 – 1870*, Routledge & Kegan Paul (1971), p. 63.

[2]   T. D. Fosbrooke, *An Original History of the City of Gloucester*, London (1819), reprinted by Alan Sutton (1986), p. 152.

distinguished academic; he was regarded as a brilliant scholar, who apparently could recite the whole New Testament by heart, in both English and Greek, apart from the last few chapters.[3] Many held high hopes that he would provide the inspired teaching necessary to maintain rising standards at the Crypt School.

The City Council Minute Book confirms that John Biddle was 'well commended to us and by us well approved for his piety, learning, integrity and discretion to be schoolmaster in the said school of Christ'.[4] It was reported that, on becoming master, Biddle 'was met with much joy and honour. Neither did he deceive their expectation; he discharged that employment with such skill and faithfulness that they thought themselves not a little happy in that behalf, who could commit their sons to his instruction'.[5] Presumably because of this, Biddle was granted a reasonably generous salary of £30 a year.[6] The Oxford antiquary Anthony Wood recorded that 'he became master of the Crypt School within the city of Gloucester, where for a time he was much esteemed for his diligence in his profession, severity of manners and sanctity of life'.[7] By all accounts, he was considered to be 'a learned and good man of a most amiable disposition'.[8]

Biddle's first usher, John Corbet, was another promising appointment. The son of a Gloucester shoemaker and in all likelihood a former pupil at the Crypt, he graduated from Magdalen Hall, Oxford, and acted as Rector of St Mary de Crypt Church as well as usher in the school.[9] He had distinct, though restrained, Puritan views and was said to be 'a man of great moderation, a lover of peace and of blameless conversation'.[10] He would go on to take a leading part in the Siege of Gloucester in 1643, acting as Chaplain to Lieutenant-Colonel Edward Massey, who directed Parliamentarian operations in the city. He also wrote a valuable account of the siege, 'A True and Impartial History of the Military Government of the

---

3   W. Hawkins, 'John Biddle, the father of English Unitarianism', *Glevensis,* volume 28 (1995), p. 32.
4   R. Austin, *The Crypt School Gloucester,* John Bellows Gloucester (1939), p. 106.
5   G. Smallfield, *The Monthly Repository of Theology and General Literature,* Hackney (1818), volume 13, p. 346.
6   C. Lepper, *The Crypt School Gloucester 1539 – 1989,* Alan Sutton (1989), p. 16.
7   A. Wood, *Athenae Oxonienses: the Fasti* (ed P. Bliss), London (1817), volume 3, p. 593.
8   W. P. W. Phillimore, *Gloucestershire Notes and Queries,* volume 6, London (1896), p. 80.
9   A. Grime, 'John Corbet 1619 – 80', unpublished PhD thesis, Edinburgh (1932), p. 4.
10   D. Neal, *History of the Puritans,* Harper New York (1855), volume 2, p. 296.

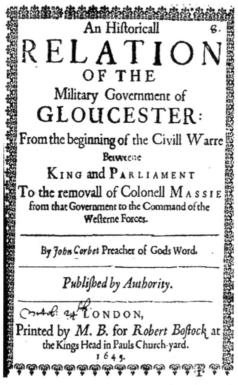

An Hiſtoricall 8.

RELATION
OF THE
Military Government of
GLOUCESTER:
From the beginning of the Civill Warre
Betweene
KING and PARLIAMENT
To the removall of Colonell MASSIE
from that Government to the Command of the
Weſterne Forces.

By *John Corbet* Preacher of Gods Word.

Publiſhed by Authority.

ᴸONDON,
Printed by *M. B.* for *Robert Boſtock* at
the Kings Head in Pauls Church-yard.
1645.

Figure 53: Title page of an account of the Siege of Gloucester compiled by the Crypt usher, John Corbet.

City of Gloucester'.[11] In this he argued that the main cause of the Civil War was that 'the ambition of the times hath endeavoured the undermining of true religion' and he attacked Laudianism as 'blind and irrational worship'.[12]

The school inevitably suffered disruption when Gloucester was besieged by Royalist forces, who based their heavy artillery scarcely a quarter of a mile away in Gaudy Green. One of the most talked about incidents in the five-week-long siege occurred close to the schoolroom, when an incendiary landed a few yards further along Southgate Street only to be extinguished by a quick-thinking woman who brought a pail of water from her house.[13] The Church of St Mary de Crypt itself was transformed into the main Parliamentarian gunpowder store in the city. 'A place was fitted up in the Crypt Church for ammunition', wrote the early 19th-century historian John Washbourn, 'probably in the vaults of the crypt itself, as a place of greater security they deposited the powder'. [14] A sundial on the south buttress of the chancel is said to mark the spot where a Royalist cannonball struck the church.[15] The nearby suburbs of the city were almost completely destroyed by the pounding of the

---

11   The full text of this account is to be found in T. D. Fosbrooke, *An Original History of the City of Gloucester*, pp. 223–34.
12   R. MacGillivray, *Restoration Historians and the English Civil War*, Springer Science and Business Media (2012), p. 18.
13   J. R. S. Whiting, *Gloucester Besieged*, Gloucester City Museum (1974), p. 12.
14   J. Washbourn, *Bibliotheca Gloucestrensis: A Collection of Scarce and Curious Tracts*, Gloucester (1825), p. 62.
15   M. Atkin and Wayne Loughlin, *Gloucester and the Civil War*, Alan Sutton (1992), p. 109.

artillery, including the Church of St Owen and eighty-eight houses.[16]

The Crypt School itself suffered a considerable amount of damage during the siege and it is clear that education would have been seriously disrupted. Immediately afterwards, the City Council accounts record substantial payments to 'repair Christ schoolhouse and the schoolmaster's rooms'.[17] A total of £5 14s 8d was spent, including new paving and seats for the schoolroom as well as making good the windows.[18] Many of the materials used in the repair were taken from St Owen's Church, which was never rebuilt.[19]

Figure 54: The Church of St Mary de Crypt, which acted as an ammunition store during the Siege of Gloucester and was struck by a Royalist cannonball.

The years of the Civil War also had the effect of ending episcopal authority in parts of the country, like Gloucester, that were controlled by Parliamentarians. The result was an intense debate of all kinds among radical groups ranging from the Levellers to the Fifth Monarchists. A whole range of differing religious groups began to campaign for support in Gloucester. It was in this setting that the Crypt School's usher, John Corbet, became a leading figure in a high-profile public theological debate that took place in the Cathedral quire in 1644. Pitted against Corbet was Robert Bacon, the leader of an Antinomian sect from Bristol, whose members believed that Christians should be exempt from moral law. The debate lasted for two whole days and ended with Bacon's expulsion from the city.[20]

---

16   Ibid p. 143.
17   C. Lepper, *The Crypt School Gloucester 1539 – 1989*, p. 16.
18   R. Austin, *The Crypt School Gloucester*, pp. 64–65.
19   N. M. Herbert, *The Victoria History of the Counties of England: Gloucestershire*, volume 4, London (1988), p. 311.
20   S. M. Eward, *No Fine But A Glass of Wine: Cathedral Life at Gloucester in Stuart Times*, Lymington (1985), p. 82.

John Biddle, the master of the Crypt, placed himself at the centre of an even more bitter controversy, one which was ultimately to cost him his job. As the Civil War continued, he emerged as a leading Unitarian; his writings attracted great attention and led to serious charges of heresy against him. His pamphlet entitled *Twelve Arguments against the Doctrine of The Trinity*, drafted in 1644, put forward an emphatic argument that neither Christ nor the Holy Spirit, however important they were, could be ranked as equal to God. Biddle's writings circulated privately among his friends at first, but his views were quite quickly reported to the city magistrates as heretical, some say by his former usher, John Corbet.[21] One of the most vociferous of Biddle's opponents was none other than the headmaster of the College School, William Russell, who wrote a counter work entitled *Blasphemoklonian: the Holy Ghost Vindicated*.[22]

By the end of the Civil War the leaders of Parliament were mainly Presbyterians, who believed in an orderly church with elected leaders and set up committees to eject church ministers and schoolmasters they deemed unsuitable.[23] Biddle was removed from his position as headmaster at the Crypt in 1645 and imprisoned in Gloucester by commissioners working for Parliament. Throughout the remainder of his life, he was constantly at the centre of controversy, building up a body of followers in London, for which he has been styled the 'Father of English Unitarianism'.[24] The tract he published in 1654, *A Twofold Catechism*, was burnt on the orders of Oliver Cromwell, resulting in Biddle himself being exiled to the Isles of Scilly. He died in Newgate debtors' prison in 1662 and has been castigated by historians of Gloucester ever since.[25] Thomas Rudge referred to him as 'an infamous character, the author of several blasphemous books, for which he was punished during all the changes of government in the rebellious times'.[26] Thomas Fosbrooke added that 'in denying the divinity of the Holy Spirit, the rest of his days were passed in misery and imprisonment'.[27]

---

[21] W. Hawkins, *John Biddle, the father of English Unitarianism*, pp. 31–32.
[22] J. Stratford, *Good and Great Men of Gloucestershire: A Series of Biographical Sketches*, Cirencester (1867), pp. 124–25.
[23] H. M. Jewell, *Education in Early Modern England*, Macmillan (1998), p. 35.
[24] W. Turner, *Lives of Eminent Unitarians*, London (1840), p. 23.
[25] P. Lim, *The Crisis of the Trinity in Early Modern England*, Oxford (2012), p. 183.
[26] T. Rudge, *The History and Antiquities of Gloucester*, J. Wood Gloucester (1811), p. 129.
[27] T. D. Fosbrooke, *An Original History of the City of Gloucester*, p. 152.

The departure of John Biddle from the headship of the Crypt left the school deeply unsettled. James Allen, who had succeeded Corbet as usher, was elected master in Biddle's place. He stayed for just two years (1645 – 47) and it seems that there was no new usher appointed to assist him. Five short-lived headmasters then followed in less than a decade between 1647 and 1656. One of these, John Cooper, is thought to have shared Biddle's controversial Unitarian beliefs.[28] With its masters embroiled in the most bitter controversies of the day, the Crypt really struggled throughout this period, its reputation and ability to provide a sound education inevitably declining.[29]

Mid-17th-century Headmasters and Ushers at the Crypt School	
Masters	Ushers
1641 – 1645: John Biddle	1641 – 1643: John Corbet
1645 – 1647: James Allen	1643 – 1645: James Allen
1647 – 1651: John Cooper	
1651: Thomas Bevan	1648 – 1653: Thomas Smith
1651 – 1652: Nicholas Taylor	1653 – 1656: Abraham Heague
1653 – 1654: William Rawlins	1656 – 1658: Isaac Heague
1654 – 1656: Francis Stedman	

The College School during the Civil War and Commonwealth

In the Cathedral and the College School, unlike most of Gloucester city, Royalist sympathies remained strong throughout the Civil War. Thomas Widdowes (1635 – 46) was headmaster at the College School during most of this turbulent period. Appointed in 1635, he had matriculated from Gloucester Hall and Magdalen College in Oxford. He quickly established a good reputation for himself as an able teacher and strong academic, publishing a book entitled *Certain Matters Pertaining to the*

---

28 N. M. Herbert, *The Victoria History of the Counties of England: Gloucestershire*, volume 4, p. 101.

29 C. Lepper, *The Crypt School Gloucester 1539 – 1989*, p. 17.

Faculty of Grammar for the use of Scholars.[30] Within a year it was reported that he was 'very diligent in his instruction to the youths under his charge, as well as in their manners as learning, to the great good liking of us the Dean and Chapter and to the credit of the said school' and his salary was raised by an extra £2 13s 4d as mark of respect. [31] Widdowes's loyalty to the Crown and the Established Church was not in question, but somehow he managed to survive in a city of Parliamentarians and rose to meet the great challenges posed by the Civil War, remaining in post until its very end.

Widdowes had a succession of young ushers at the College School, but it may be that he had to cope alone for his last few years as it is not clear at what point his final usher, William Eldridge, left the school. These were uncertain times. The Dean and Chapter fled from Gloucester in 1643, many taking refuge in the Royalist capital at Oxford. What remained of the Cathedral community was in consternation and Widdowes deserves great credit for providing the school with the continuity and stable leadership it required to survive.

The events of the Civil War were almost as disruptive to education in the College School as they were at the Crypt. Although there is no evidence of the boys taking part, they would have witnessed the women and children being sent to cut turf from the nearby Paddock in order to strengthen the defensive ramparts of the city.[32] With victory accomplished following the Battle of Naseby, Parliament confiscated the estates of the Cathedral in November 1645. Increasingly the Cathedral itself was used for non-religious purposes; assizes and quarter sessions were held in the nave and the cloisters acted as stables for a Scottish cavalry unit based in Gloucester. The lay cemetery became a mustering ground for Parliamentarian troops and marks left by musket balls on the south side of the Cathedral testify to the building being used for target practice.[33]

In these circumstances Thomas Widdowes, who had always been pro-Royalist, resigned as headmaster in 1646, moving to take charge of the

---

[30]   J. R. S. Whiting, *The King's School Gloucester*, Orchard & Ind (1990), p. 19.
[31]   W. Page, *The Victoria History of the Counties of England: Gloucestershire*, volume 2, p. 326.
[32]   M. Atkin and Wayne Loughlin, *Gloucester and the Civil War*, p. 72.
[33]   C. Heighway, S. Hamilton et alii, *Gloucester Cathedral: Faith, Art and Architecture*, Scala (2011), p. 63.

Figure 55: Bishop Edward Fowler, who was a pupil at the College School in the 1640s.

Figure 56: Artist's reconstruction showing turf being cut from the Paddock during the Siege of Gloucester.

school at Woodstock and later at Northleach.[34] Some say that he was ejected under pressure from the City Council, although that is not clear.[35] To keep the school afloat whilst other parts of the Cathedral's work crumbled, Giles Workman, who had been usher fifteen years earlier, stepped in as temporary headmaster, since his religious views were more acceptable to the Presbyterian majority on the Council. Described as 'a quiet and peaceable Puritan', he combined his responsibility for the school with the position of lecturer to preach the word of God at St Nicholas' Church.[36]

The survival of the school in these turbulent times was greatly assisted the following year, in 1646, when William Russell became headmaster. A former pupil of Katharine Lady Berkeley's School at Wotton-under-Edge and an Oxford graduate, he brought considerable experience to his new

---

[34] J. N. Langston, 'Headmasters and Ushers of the King's (College) School, Gloucester', *Records of Gloucester Cathedral*, volume III, H. Osborne Gloucester (1928), p. 188.

[35] S. M. Eward, *Gloucester Cathedral Chapter Act Book 1616 – 1687*, The Bristol and Gloucestershire Archaeological Society Record Series, volume 21 (2007), p. 170.

[36] A. Wood, *Athenae Oxonienses: the Fasti* (ed P. Bliss), p. 255.

role, having previously been headmaster at Chipping Sodbury. His appointment was another inspirational one that helped the school to manage the difficult period of Oliver Cromwell's Commonwealth. Russell seems to have been a committed Presbyterian with religious views aligned with the majority of those in Parliament and in Gloucester City Council at this point.[37] His salary was paid for by Parliament out of the lands and revenues of the Dean and Chapter and in some years it was raised very considerably to a sum of £30.[38]

Anthony Wood praised William Russell's many skills, commenting that 'by his singular, happy ways of teaching, and by his great skill in tongues and in holy scripture, many learned youths were sent thence to the universities'.[39] The monument to his memory erected in St Michael's Church, which was demolished in the mid-20th century, spoke of his erudition, piety and singular aptitude in instructing boys.[40] One of the pupils under his care in the late 1640s was Edward Fowler, who would go on many years later to become Bishop of Gloucester (between 1691 and 1714); Russell was married to Fowler's elder sister.[41]

Mid-17th-century Headmasters and Ushers of the College School	
Masters	Ushers
1635 – 1646: Thomas Widdowes	1635 – 1636: Christopher Prior
	1636 – 1637: William Collins
	1637 – 1639: Richard Lovell
	1639 – ??: William Eldridge
1646: Giles Workman	
1646 – 1659: William Russell	1655 – 1657: William Bennett
	1657 – 1659: Edward Batten
1659 – 1660: Benjamin Master	1659 – 1660: Samuel Bayes

---

[37] W. Page, *The Victoria History of the Counties of England: Gloucestershire*, volume 2, p. 327.

[38] W. A. L. Vincent, *The Grammar Schools: Their Continuing Tradition*, John Murray (1969), p. 13.

[39] A. Wood, *Athenae Oxonienses: the Fasti* (ed P. Bliss), p. 474.

[40] S. Rudder, *A New History of Gloucestershire*, Cirencester (1779), republished by Alan Sutton in 2006, p. 170.

[41] L. Stephen, *Dictionary of National Biography*, Macmillan 1889, volume 20, p. 84.

The College School continued to occupy the room above the Cathedral cloisters which it had used since Henry VIII's day, as is underlined by graffiti bearing the date '1645' on one of the staircases leading up to it.[42] The use of this room was, however, threatened throughout the years of the Commonwealth by uncertainties over the future of the rest of the Cathedral. Deprived of proper management, the Cathedral fell into poor repair and some members of the City Council considered pulling it down. Work to dismantle it began in the Lady Chapel and in Little Cloister. The rest of the building, including the schoolroom, was saved only by a last-minute reprieve that followed an appeal by John Dorney, the town clerk, 'to hold up the stately fabric of the College Church, the great ornament of this City, which some do say is now in danger of falling'.[43] One of his reasons for wishing to save the Cathedral is said to have been that he thought the College School was too important an institution to lose.

The survival of the school was also jeopardised by severe financial difficulties at this time. An Act of Parliament in 1649 abolished the national church and all cathedral establishments, but allowed their schools and charities to continue, paid for out of revenues from their estates.[44] In Gloucester the intention was that revenues from the former Cathedral manor at Tuffley should fund the salary and house repairs of the headmaster, while his usher was to be supported from profits derived from the manor at Rudford. The management of these funds was beset with troubles and it is far from clear that they were ever adequate. The City Council had to intervene in 1650 and on other occasions, petitioning Parliament for a grant for the 'constant reparation of the goodly fabric of the College and for the maintenance of a schoolmaster and usher in the College School'.[45] Another petition of 1656 drew attention to the salary arrangements in the original statutes of Henry VIII's reign. At the time of his death in 1659 it seems that Russell's salary was in significant arrears as the Council took pity on his widow and paid her a maintenance annuity.[46]

---

[42]   S. M. Eward, *No Fine But A Glass of Wine: Cathedral Life at Gloucester in Stuart Times*, p. 105.

[43]   C. Heighway, S. Hamilton et alii, *Gloucester Cathedral: Faith, Art and Architecture*, p. 65.

[44]   S. M. Eward, *No Fine But A Glass of Wine: Cathedral Life at Gloucester in Stuart Times*, p. 89.

[45]   J. N. Langston, 'Headmasters and Ushers of the King's (College) School, Gloucester', p. 194.

[46]   J. R. S. Whiting, *The King's School Gloucester*, p. 21.

The governance of the school was almost as pressing a problem as concerns about fabric and finances. In 1657 another Act of Parliament handed over the Cathedral library, cloisters and school to the mayor, burgesses and City Council 'for the public worship of God, the education of children in learning and for other public, religious and charitable uses'.[47] The mayor of Gloucester, six burgesses, the town clerk and four others were named as the 'governors of the said free grammar or College School for the time being'.[48] They immediately ratified William Russell's position as headmaster 'so long as he shall well behave and demean himself in the said place' and confirmed the appointment of William Bennett as his usher. It is possible, however, that the long-term plan was to combine the College School and the Crypt School into a single institution under a common management. The two schools were treated as a single unit in 1657 when they were refurbished with seats removed from St Michael's Church, 'placing them fit for the scholars of the two schools in this city'.[49]

The leaders of the Commonwealth period generally seem to have been well-disposed towards education. A number of visionaries, such as James Harrington, Gerrard Winstanley and John Milton, advocated a compulsory universal state educational system.[50] One modern historian has praised the grants schools received from the confiscated lands of Deans and Chapters as 'a brave and forward-looking brief experiment, which suffered suffocation after 1660 for over a century and a half'.[51] We can but surmise how the College School may have fared under its new management, but it does seem that the City Council shared the outlook of its times and took its responsibilities very seriously. As well as refurbishing the seating, a genuine attempt was made to improve the financial position of the school by funding the salary of its headmaster at a higher level. Benjamin Master, who was appointed in 1659 – 60 received an extra £10 in addition to the sum he was paid from the profits of the Tuffley manor.[52] Following his premature death, the Council went to great lengths to 'headhunt' John Gregory as the next headmaster early in 1660. A special delegation was sent

[47]   D. Welander, *The History, Art and Architecture of Gloucester Cathedral*, Alan Sutton (1991), p. 364.
[48]   W. Page, *The Victoria History of the Counties of England: Gloucestershire*, volume 2, p. 329.
[49]   R. Austin, *The Crypt School Gloucester*, p. 65.
[50]   J. Lawson & H. Silver, *A Social History of Education in England*, Methuen (1973), p. 154.
[51]   H. M. Jewell, *Education in Early Modern England*, Macmillan (1998), p. 5.
[52]   W. Page, *The Victoria History of the Counties of England: Gloucestershire*, volume 2, p. 330.

to interview him at Woodstock, he was allowed £10 removal expenses and the pay he received was raised to £20 13s 4d, in addition to the £19 6s 8d he could take from the Cathedral estates.[53] This package was three times that received by his Tudor predecessors and represented a significant move to improve salaries; if it had become a permanent settlement, it would undoubtedly have strengthened the school's position and the quality of education it could provide in the centuries yet to come.

The Song School

The Song School that educated the boy choristers of Gloucester in the Cathedral organist's living quarters in the old infirmary was not so fortunate in the way it was able to respond to the threats posed by the Civil War.

John Okeover, who had previously been organist at Wells, became Cathedral organist and took over the Song School in Gloucester in 1640. His time in charge was, however, short-lived. Interesting graffiti survives inside the back cover of a bass book written in 1641 and still preserved in the Cathedral Library. It lists the names of some of the choristers in office at this point: 'Thomas Barber, Richard Elliotts, John Tyler and John Painter; these be the choristers of decani side, 1641'.[54] It was almost as if they felt a cloud of impending doom about to engulf them. The following year, with the beginning of the Civil War, Parliament passed an order that 'such part of the common prayer and service as is performed by singing men, choristers and organs in the Cathedral Church be wholly forborne and omitted, and the same be done in a reverent, humble and decent manner without singing or using the organs'.[55] In 1643 the Bishop, Godfrey Goodman, was forced to flee from Gloucester after a mob attacked his palace; it was at this point that the operation of the Cathedral choir and Song School was suspended.[56]

Throughout the Civil War and the period of Oliver Cromwell's Commonwealth that followed there was no choral music to speak of in the Cathedral. There were no choristers and no organist. Laudian altars, altar

---

[53]   J. R. S. Whiting, *The King's School Gloucester*, p. 22.
[54]   S. M. Eward, *No Fine But A Glass of Wine: Cathedral Life at Gloucester in Stuart Times*, p. 63.
[55]   D. Welander, *The History, Art and Architecture of Gloucester Cathedral*, p. 362.
[56]   C. Heighway, S. Hamilton et alii, *Gloucester Cathedral: Faith, Art and Architecture*, p. 63.

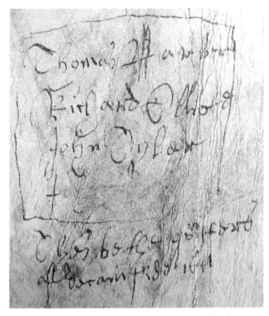

Figure 57: The names of the choristers in the Song School, as recorded in a document of 1641.

rails, candlesticks, crucifixes and all holy pictures were removed from churches across the entire country in 1644. In their place came a much simpler form of worship based on preaching the word of God in spoken form, extempore prayer and singing of metrical psalms. Against this backdrop, Gloucester's small Song School ceased to exist.

CHAPTER ELEVEN

The Late 17th Century:

Normality Restored

The Restoration of the monarchy under King Charles II in 1660 brought the return of the Dean and Chapter to Gloucester and the revival of Laudian forms of worship enforced by the 1662 Prayer Book. As far as education was concerned, the overwhelming desire was to return to the normality of the past and banish the memory of the upheavals of the Civil War and Commonwealth period.

Even as the Restoration was taking place, the educational writer Charles Hoole was working on a new illustrated translation of the *Orbis Sensualium Pictus* by the Czech philosopher John Amos Comenius. Beneath the picture of a schoolroom, he provided in English and Latin a caption that could easily have been written 200 years previously. 'A school is a shop', he wrote, 'in which young wits are fashioned to virtue and it is distinguished into forms. The master sitteth in a chair, the scholars in forms. He teacheth; they learn. Some things are writ down with chalk on a table. Some sit at a table and write. The master mendeth their faults. The boys stand and rehearse things committed to memory. Some talk together and behave themselves wantonly and carelessly; these are chastened with a ferula and a rod'.[1]

The return of the Song School

Within Gloucester Cathedral the return to past norms involved the revival of the choral tradition and the re-establishment of the Song School, which had closed in 1643. There had been little music in the Cathedral throughout the time of Cromwell's rule. The reintroduction of anthems was

---

[1]   C. Hoole, *John Amos Comenii Orbis Sensualium Pictus*, 12th edition, New York (1810), p. 138.

an ambitious task, so it was fortunate that several of the pre-Civil War choristers were still alive. Among them was Richard Brodgate, who had first become a chorister in 1618 and his contemporary William Jennings. They were joined by John Tyler, a chorister in the 1630s, and John Painter, who had joined the choir in 1638 and worked as one of the Cathedral glaziers. It was around lay clerks like this, who had been boys before the outbreak of the Civil War, that the Cathedral choir was recreated, most of its newer members having no previous experience. Amateurish they may have appeared, but they did their best at what was a daunting task, even if they did not always live up to expectations and occasionally had to be reprimanded. Brodgate and Painter, for example, received a warning in 1665 'to depart this church for their often absence and contempt of the Dean and Chapter's authority in not asking their leave, when many times commanded the contrary by the said Dean, and particularly for neglecting the morning prayer on Sundays at seven of the clock'.[2]

By 1663, when Bishop William Nicholson held a visitation of the Cathedral, there were seven lay clerks and eight choristers in place. The first group of boy choristers after the Restoration were: John Browne, Richard Elliotts, Godfrey Faunes, William Howell, John Lugg, Charles Thomas, Edward Thomas and John Wells.[3] The revival of musical life was only just beginning and at this early stage there was no permanent organist or master of the choristers. Robert Webb was appointed as organist and chorister master in 1662 and was followed by Thomas Lowe, who moved from Salisbury but may have fallen victim to an outbreak of bubonic plague that occurred in Gloucester in 1665.[4]

Gradually, a much more professional choir began to emerge. An impressive new organ was built at Gloucester in 1665 – 66, displaying on its case the coats of arms of both Charles II and his brother, James II.[5] Daniel Henstridge was appointed as master of the choristers and held the post from 1666 to 1674. Standards began to rise as he adopted new anthems

---

[2] S. M. Eward, *Gloucester Cathedral Chapter Act Book 1616 – 1687*, The Bristol and Gloucestershire Archaeological Society Record Series, volume 21 (2007), p. 96.
[3] S. M. Eward, *No Fine But A Glass of Wine: Cathedral Life at Gloucester in Stuart Times*, Lymington (1985), p. 128.
[4] W. Bazeley, 'The Organ of Gloucester Cathedral', in *Records of Gloucester Cathedral 1885 – 97*, volume III, p. 89.
[5] D. Welander, *The History, Art and Architecture of Gloucester Cathedral*, Alan Sutton (1991), p. 37.

written for the Chapel Royal, providing Gloucester's Song School with a much more stable foundation on which to grow.[6] The Chapter Act Book records, albeit in piecemeal fashion, the names of a succession of new choristers recruited in this period. They included Edward Tyler, Thomas Wilcox and John and Jesse Painter, the sons of former chorister John Painter, all appointed in 1666 – 67.[7] Jesse Painter was listed 'in place of John Lug, who has left, his voice for a long time not in tune'; he remained a chorister until 1679 and may have been one of those, not unknown in the 17th century, whose treble voices held until they were eighteen or nineteen.[8] His brother, John, continued living in Babylon and died in 1696; he is buried in the south transept of the Cathedral, where there is a ledger stone in his memory.

Figure 58: Gloucester Cathedral's organ dates from 1665 – 66 and helped to foster the revival of the Song School under Daniel Henstridge.

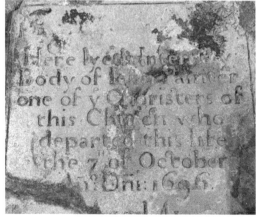

Figure 59: Gravestone of John Painter, appointed a chorister in 1666.

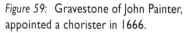

---

6   J. R. S. Whiting, *The King's School Gloucester*, Orchard & Ind (1990), p. 24.
7   S. M. Eward, *Gloucester Cathedral Chapter Act Book 1616 – 1687*, pp. 106 & 124.
8   A. Mould, *The English Chorister: A History*, London (2007), p. 128.

Choristers in the 1670s	
Charles Twinning (1670-73)	William Beard (1674-78)
Joseph Browne (1671-76)	John Swain (1675-79)
Ben Crooker (1672)	William Harrison (1676-1680)
John Pree (1672-79)	William Brown (1677-79)
John Soudely (1673-74)	Abraham Wood (1677-79)
William George (1673-78)	

Daniel Henstridge proved a much more competent teacher for the choristers than many of his predecessors, meaning that the education they received improved considerably. He is regarded as 'one of the first really responsible organists at Gloucester Cathedral'. A composer in his own right, he had a small organ installed in the Song School itself 'for instructing the singing boys'. He took on the responsibility of teaching catechism to the boys himself and prepared them for confirmation, working under clear guidelines from the Dean and Chapter. Bishop Nicholson's 1668 visitation underlined the good work achieved by Henstridge. It confirmed the expectation that 'the master of the choristers be very diligent in teaching the choristers to sing, and given his approbation of the voice and aptness of the boy who is to be chosen chorister, and one day in every week catechise the choristers in the principles of Christian religion as is set down in the Church Catechism the better to prepare them for Confirmation'. The Bishop also found that for the first time a period of probation had been introduced in order to improve the recruitment of choristers. He noted that 'for the first year choristers be admitted as probationers only, that so, if they fit not themselves to do the choir service by the end of the year, they may be removed; yet be it provided that they receive the usual stipend for that year of probation quarterly, as if they were actually admitted'.[9]

---

[9] S. M. Eward, *No Fine But A Glass of Wine: Cathedral Life at Gloucester in Stuart Times*, p. 134.

The College School after the Restoration

The Restoration of 1660 brought the College School's short-lived period of management by the City Council to an abrupt end.[10] The Cathedral estates returned to the Dean and Chapter, who were quick to reassert their control over the school once more. In 1661 the Dean, William Brough, imposed restraints on the school's finances, resolving that 'the pay of the schoolmaster of the College School and of the usher . . . shall be according to the allowance in the time of Mr Langley, if they shall be pleased to accept thereof'.[11]

The intention was to return to the quieter days that had existed before the outbreak of the Civil War. Education reflecting mainstream Anglican values was encouraged throughout the country in a move to curtail the religious antagonisms of the chaotic middle years of the century. The 1662 Act of Uniformity required 'every schoolmaster keeping a public or private school and every person instructing or teaching youth in any house or private family as a tutor' to swear the illegality of taking up arms against the king and to declare their conformity to the liturgy of the Church of England as by law established.[12] Three years later Gilbert Sheldon, the Archbishop of Canterbury, issued a letter calling on all bishops to find out if teachers were well-affected to the doctrine and discipline of the Established Church and whether they encouraged their pupils to attend its services.[13]

The College School was absolutely dominated by the Gregory family during the years of the Restoration. The headmaster, John Gregory (1660 – 73), was described by Anthony Wood as having 'a great deal of ancient learning, especially as to criticism and the languages'.[14] A number of aspects of his career were somewhat unusual. He was one of the few masters not to have graduated from Oxford, but was an alumnus of Trinity College, Cambridge.[15] He was a High Church Laudian who combined his post at the school with a range of offices in the diocese, as Rector of St Mary

---

10 See Chapter Ten.
11 J. N. Langston, 'Headmasters and Ushers of the King's (College) School, Gloucester', *Records of Gloucester Cathedral,* volume III, H. Osborne Gloucester (1928), p. 207.
12 H. M. Jewell, *Education in Early Modern England*, Macmillan (1998), p. 37.
13 W. A. L. Vincent, *The Grammar Schools: Their Continuing Tradition*, John Murray (1969), p. 110.
14 A. Wood, *Athenae Oxonienses: the Fasti* (ed P. Bliss), London (1817), volume 3, p. 259.
15 J. Venn & J. A. Venn, *Alumni Cantabrigienses*, Cambridge (1922), p. 263.

Figure 60: Abraham Gregory, usher at the College School (1660 – 71).

de Crypt, Rector of Hempsted and Archdeacon of Gloucester. He can have had little time for the school and it is difficult to see this as a very good period for the development of its educational prowess.

Also unusual was the fact that John Gregory's usher for most of his headship was his younger brother, Abraham, appointed at the young age of seventeen before he had taken his degree.[16] The comments attributed to him in the Chapter record books have left the impression that he was 'a precise, rather aggressive man with a keen legalistic mind …, a stickler for constitutional procedure, pernickety and contentious over what he thought were his rights'.[17] This in turn has given rise to the view that the boys of the College School probably had a hard time working under him.[18]

Late 17th-century Headmasters and Ushers of the College School	
Masters	Ushers
1660 – 1673: John Gregory	1660 – 1671: Abraham Gregory
1673 – 1684: Oliver Gregory	1671 – 1674: Nathaniel Lye
1684 – 1712: Maurice Wheeler	1674 – 1687: Thomas Trippett
	1687 – 1709: John Hilton

When John Gregory resigned in 1673, the headship went to his nephew, Oliver Gregory (1673 – 84), who had previously been usher at the Crypt

---

[16] S. J. A. Evans & S. M. Eward, 'Dr Abraham Gregory: Prebendary of Gloucester Cathedral', *Transactions of the Bristol and Gloucestershire Archaeological Society* (1977), volume 95, p. 59.

[17] S. M. Eward, *No Fine But A Glass of Wine: Cathedral Life at Gloucester in Stuart Times*, p. 158.

[18] J. R. S. Whiting, *The King's School Gloucester*, p. 23.

School.[19] Despite the strong suggestion of nepotism, this proved to be a reasonably wise move. The testimonial letter written by Bishop Robert Frampton to support Oliver Gregory's appointment described how 'he had cultivated pious and sober morals, performed his work with painstaking devotion and always demonstrated the utmost loyalty to His Majesty the King'.[20] It does indeed seem that Gregory went on to gain a reputation for being a rigorous teacher and was regarded as particularly skilful where the teaching of Greek was concerned.

The school over which the Gregory family presided was described as 'a long, spacious, lightsome school'; its library was considered extensive with a number of historical, geographical and mathematical works.[21] We know a good deal about how a school such as the College School would have operated from Charles Hoole's writings.[22] The overall aim remained to speak and read Latin and acquire a familiarity with Classical authors. In the first three forms in Lower School boys worked on the declensions of verbs, tenses and the genders of nouns. They built up their vocabulary and became familiar with Latin phrases by using colloquies, which were books written in the form of dialogues dealing with everyday life. They also practised the 'making of Latins', usually by writing letters in Latin. In Upper School the older boys embarked on more challenging 'theme-writing', which required them to create their own extended compositions in the style of various Classical authors such as Ovid, Terence, Virgil, Sallust, Livy or Tacitus. Much of their time was spent on private study, though boys of any age could be called up by either the usher or the master to repeat parts of their work and be examined on their understanding of it. Occasionally the master might give a lecture to the whole school, with the boys then being expected to reproduce what had been said from notes.

The Restoration was a period of consolidation and stable routines. These could in turn be seen as preparing the way for the much more exciting educational developments that were about to occur at the College School on the appointment of Maurice Wheeler as headmaster in 1684.[23]

---

19   W. Page, *The Victoria History of the Counties of England: Gloucestershire*, volume 2, London (1907), p. 331.

20   Gloucestershire Record Office D9125/2/7120.

21   N. M. Herbert, *The Victoria History of the Counties of England: Gloucestershire*, volume 4, London (1988), pp. 118–19.

22   W. A. L. Vincent, *The Grammar Schools: Their Continuing Tradition*, pp. 75–77.

23   See Chapter Thirteen.

The Crypt School

The Crypt School also benefited from a period of stability at the end of the 17th century. Abraham Heague was the master from 1656 until 1696, an unusual unbroken stint of forty years, and one of his ushers, Thomas Merrett, held office from 1675 to 1709, the longest term served by any of the Crypt School ushers.

Heague was a distinctly colourful character who indulged in a boisterous social life with his friend the Revd Richard Littleton, Rector of St Mary de Crypt. Heavy drinking left them open to charges of immorality and other unseemly conduct, their behaviour eventually being the subject of a legal case heard in 1694 by the Consistory Court in the Cathedral.[24] Here it was alleged that Heague and Littleton had 'misbehaved' with the daughters of a local tavern keeper following a visit to Barton Fair and had become so drunk that they had to be carried home by a group of maid servants.

Despite his risqué personal life, however, Heague seems to have paid careful attention to his school and to have shown the professionalism that enabled it to recover a sense of purpose after the bitter religious controversies that had surrounded his predecessor, John Biddle. The City Council noted the rising reputation of the school by recording in its minutes of 1675 that Heague 'bred several scholars, some whereof are now eminent men in the university'.[25] He also maintained close links with the College School throughout his time in office. Two of the ushers who worked with him were Oliver Gregory (1670 – 73), who later became master at the College School, and Thomas Trippett (1673 – 75), who moved to become usher there. According to a statement made by Trippett, 'Abraham Heague did keep his school at Crypt very carefully and diligently'.[26]

---

24 C. Lepper, *The Crypt School Gloucester 1539 – 1989*, Alan Sutton (1989), p. 19.
25 N. M. Herbert, *The Victoria History of the Counties of England: Gloucestershire*, volume 4, p. 118.
26 C. Lepper, *The Crypt School Gloucester 1539 – 1989*, p. 19.

Late 17th-century Masters at the Crypt	
1656 – 1696:	Abraham Heague
1696 – 1697:	John Grubb
1697 – 1701:	William King
Late 17th-century Ushers	
1656 – 1658:	Isaac Heague
1658 – 1670:	William Wood
1670 – 1673:	Oliver Gregory
1673 – 1675:	Thomas Trippett
1675 – 1709:	Thomas Merrett

Figure 61: George Townsend, who endowed scholarships to support boys from the Crypt at Pembroke College, Oxford.

It was also during Abraham Heague's time that the school received one of the most important boosts in its history. This came through the inauguration of Townsend Scholarships, which allowed a succession of Crypt boys to proceed to complete their education at Oxford. The funds were left in the will of George Townsend of Roel, a prosperous Lincoln's Inn lawyer who died in 1682; he left various properties to the master and fellows of Pembroke College, Oxford, the profits from which he specified should be used to support scholars from the free grammar schools of Gloucester, Cheltenham, Northleach and Chipping Campden.[27] The result was that a series of Townsend Scholars from the Crypt began to attend Oxford, a system that continued right up to the 1980s. The first to take a place at Pembroke, perhaps rather predictably in 1684, was the headmaster's own son, Henry Heague, but others who followed him were William Eaton (1696), John White (1700) and John Gregory (1704).

To have a scholarship of this kind was one of the most valued possessions a school could actually gain.[28] Within Gloucester it was a unique distinction, something which enhanced the profile of the Crypt School beyond measure and was used to its advantage throughout the next century in enticing ambitious pupils away from potential competitors.

---

[27] W. Page, *The Victoria History of the Counties of England: Gloucestershire*, volume 2, p. 354.
[28] J. Lawson & H. Silver, *A Social History of Education in England*, Methuen (1973), p. 197.

CHAPTER TWELVE

Sir Thomas Rich's Hospital:

The Arrival of the Bluecoat Boys

As well as making the headlines for its Civil War and regicide, the 17th century also witnessed a quiet proliferation of philanthropy. In Gloucester a growing number of the city's leading citizens left funds to endow apprenticeship charities to benefit young boys from poor and modest backgrounds. One was William Halliday, an alderman living in London, who left £500 in his will of 1623, a sum sufficient to support six Gloucester apprenticeships each year.[1] Abraham Blackleech, who died in 1639, left £50 for apprenticeships. Jasper Clutterbuck, by a will dated 1658, left funds for apprenticing two boys annually. Alderman John Punter also used his will in 1666 to fund two or more boys.

It was against this background that a completely new kind of school emerged in Gloucester, a school with a model radically different from that of the established grammar schools with their central focus on the rigours of Latin. This new school was Sir Thomas Rich's Blue Coat Hospital for poor boys; it was established in 1668 to increase the number of boys with the right kind of education to take advantage of the apprenticeships that were being created. The school aimed to take in twenty boys and to offer them elementary and practical schooling within a new boarding setting. It was based on the model of Christ's Hospital in London, which had been founded in 1552 for 'fatherless children and other poor men's children'.[2]

Thomas Rich, the founder of this new school, was born in Gloucester in 1601, the son of a wealthy textile merchant who had been mayor of the city. He was baptised in St John's Northgate Church, but he was sent to London for his education, eventually graduating from Wadham College, Oxford, at

---

[1]   N. M. Herbert, *The Victoria History of the Counties of England: Gloucestershire*, volume 4, London (1988), pp. 356–57.

[2]   H. M. Jewell, *Education in Early Modern England*, Macmillan (1998), p. 95.

the age of seventeen. He entered the world of commerce and became a liveryman of the Vintner's Company and an alderman of the City of London. The trade he conducted in importing malmsey wine from Turkey and the investments he made with the East India Company were especially profitable.[3] Thomas's political sympathies lay with the Royalists during the Civil War and he ran a safe house to harbour persecuted Anglican clergy, including the Bishop of Exeter, who had been ejected from their livings. At the same time he acted skilfully and intelligently to ensure that his livelihood did not suffer whatever the political climate.[4] He acquired the manor of Holme Park in Sonning in 1654 and was appointed Sheriff of Berkshire whilst Cromwell was in power; after the Restoration he was created a baronet by Charles II and became MP for Reading.[5] Today an ornate marble table monument in the space under the tower of St Andrew's Church at Sonning commemorates the life of Sir Thomas Rich, who died in 1667.

Figure 62: Sir Thomas Rich (born in Gloucester in 1601), portrait by an unidentified artist.

---

3   N. M. Herbert, *The Victoria History of the Counties of England: Gloucestershire*, volume 4, p. 336.

4   D. J. Watkins, *The History of Sir Thomas Rich's School*, Gloucester (1966), p. 7.

5   L. L. Peck, *Women of Fortune: Money, Marriage and Murder in Early Modern England*, Cambridge (2018), p. 64.

Figure 63: The Classical façade of the Bluecoat School in Eastgate Street from an artwork of 1880.

A substantial sum of money was bequeathed for a variety of religious and social causes in Sir Thomas Rich's will, dated 1666. In particular, he left 'to the mayor and burgesses of the county of the city of Gloucester where I was born ... and unto their successors for ever all my capital messuage or tenement with the appurtenance in the Eastgate Street near the Barley Market in the said city of Gloucester to be an hospital and to be only employed by them as an hospital for ever for the entertainment and harbouring of so many Blue-coat poor boys therein as hereafter in and by this my will are expressed'.[6] In addition to his house in Eastgate Street, the will proceeded to grant to the mayor and burgesses another £6,000 for the purchase of land, the profits from which were to go towards 'the yearly maintenance for ever of twenty boys with diet, lodging, washing, clothing or other necessities in blue coats and caps according to the laudable usage of Christ Church Hospital in London'.

---

[6] Gloucestershire Record Office, D9125/2/7575.

The endowment was received by the mayor and burgesses in 1668 and invested in several farms in Awre and Lydney, the rents from which were intended to provide the new school with a steady income of £160 a year. The Bluecoat School, attended by twenty boys, was set up in the same year in the house that had belonged to Sir Thomas Rich in Eastgate Street, which was on the site now occupied by the Guildhall.[7] It was administered until 1836 by the mayor and councillors of Gloucester, who took all important decisions on the appointment of staff and the admission of boys.

Among the first intake of pupils was John Lugg, the son of the porter at the Tolsey, the building at the Cross where Council meetings took place. Another early pupil was Amity Clutterbuck, who was at the school in the 1670s and in adult life went on to become one of the school's principal benefactors following a career in the navy.[8] The school was described as a 'hospital', which meant that it was both a teaching establishment and a home that provided boys 'with diet, lodging, washing, clothing and other necessaries'.[9] The boys taken in were between the ages of ten and sixteen, the original expectation probably being that they would stay for up to six years. They were required to wear the uniform which Sir Thomas Rich had seen at Christ's Hospital. This comprised a navy-blue coarse drugget coat, cap, yellow stockings, a leather belt, white collar and tabs. In addition, each boy was given a numbered silver medallion, which he had to wear. This uniform, with minor modifications, remained in use until 1882, when modern equivalents – eventually today's distinctive blue blazer – were introduced.

As the school was a boarding institution, the Bluecoat Boys were under the supervision seven days a week of a live-in master, who was provided with his own accommodation and paid a salary of £20 a year.[10] If the master was ever out of the building during the daytime, the schoolroom was supervised by the oldest boy, who was known as the 'observator', a title still applied to the senior prefects in the modern-day Sir Thomas Rich's School. A matron, sometimes referred to as the 'mother woman', was also employed. She was given a modest budget to prepare food for the boys,

---

[7]   A. Platts and G. H. Hainton, *Education in Gloucestershire: A Short History*, Gloucestershire County Council (1954), p. 42.

[8]   T. Rudge, *The History and Antiquities of Gloucester*, J. Wood Gloucester (1811), p. 132.

[9]   S. Rudder, *A New History of Gloucestershire*, Cirencester (1779), republished by Alan Sutton in 2006, p. 198.

[10]   Ibid, p. 198.

which had to be basic and cost effective. Bread and cheese were all that was on offer for both breakfast and supper each day. Soup and limited amounts of boiled meat and vegetables were provided for dinner most days, but on two days per week simply bread and cheese. It was not until 1818 that a parliamentary report recommended substituting some of the bread for milk.[11] Parents had no say in the way the charity was run and were allowed to see their sons only during designated holiday times. Each Sunday the boys were required to form part of the mayor's solemn procession to the Cathedral, where they sat on their own special benches on the left-hand side of the north door of the quire.[12]

The Bluecoat School was completely different from the city's two grammar schools, the College School at the Cathedral and the Crypt School. It was a boarding institution or hospital that offered elementary and practical teaching designed to meet the needs of families with a background in trade. Its main aim was to prepare boys for apprenticeships in Gloucester, but also in London, Worcester, Bristol and elsewhere. Sir Thomas Rich's will specifically stated that six boys were to be apprenticed each year and that 'three or four of them should be apprenticed in London to some honest handicraft trades there and with honest masters, not adhering in their opinions to the novelties of the times'.[13] A special ceremony took place each year on St Thomas's Day, 21st December, to acknowledge the boys who were about to leave the school to begin their apprenticeships.[14] Until the end of the 19th century, therefore, the curriculum was an elementary one designed to prepare its boys for their immediate future. It covered reading, writing, arithmetic, religion and some practical subjects. The school also ring-fenced funds designed to clothe and support boys once their apprenticeships had begun.

Sir Thomas Rich's will envisaged that the master selected to lead his Bluecoat School would be 'an honest, able schoolmaster'.[15] The first master appointed was the Revd John Beard, who ran the school with his matron, Mrs Anne Smallman. The setting up of the school presented them with a

---

[11] D. J. Watkins, *The History of Sir Thomas Rich's School*, pp. 38–39.
[12] Ibid, p. 13.
[13] W. Page, *The Victoria History of the Counties of England: Gloucestershire*, volume 2, London (1907), p. 352.
[14] J. Barlow, *A Calendar of the Registers of Apprentices of the City of Gloucester*, The Bristol and Gloucestershire Archaeological Society (2011), p. xxiii.
[15] Gloucestershire Record Office, D9125/2/7575.

number of teething problems to work through. On several occasions Mrs Smallman had to ask the Council for extra money to provide basic food because 'the price of bread and cheese and meat is increasing double'.[16] A pressing concern for Beard as master was that the first intake of boys was found to contain three who were under the minimum age of ten, which led to two of them being expelled. Another problem was the level of contact that should be permitted between the boys boarding in a school in their own city and their relatives living nearby. The resolution to this came in the Council's minutes of 1670, which stated that 'if any parent of either of the said boys do hereafter taunt, reproach or vex the schoolmaster or mother woman there, then upon complaint the said Bluecoat boy shall be removed from there'. The question of whether boys could be apprenticed in businesses run by their own parents also caused controversy. Responding to a request from the mother of Anthony George that her son should be apprenticed with her, the Councillors took the view that generally parents in this situation were more interested in the money they could gain than in teaching their children the skills of their trades and laid down the rule that, in the future, apprentice payments would be paid only when the boys were bound to people other than their parents.[17]

Some of the Masters of Sir Thomas Rich's School	
1668 – 1677: John Beard	1741 – 1788: Luke Hook
1677 – 1687: Thomas Merrett	1788 – 1789: Thomas Mutlow
1687 – 1688: Richard Reeve	1789 – 1796: Henry Lye
1689 – 1733: John Abbott	1796: Charles King
1733 – 1736: Edward Estcourt	1796: William Luke
1736 – 1741: Revd Elliott	1796 – 1810: Thomas Villiers
1741: John Price	

---

[16]   D. J. Watkins, *The History of Sir Thomas Rich's School*, Gloucester (1966), p. 15.
[17]   Ibid, pp. 12–14.

The appointment of suitable masters proved problematic for the school on some occasions. John Price, for example, remained in post for barely a month in 1741, when the Council minutes recorded that he was accused of 'several immoralities and scandalous misbehaviours to which being required he has not given any satisfactory answer'.[18] Again, in 1796, the school had two masters, Charles King and William Luke, who lasted only a few months between them. Occasional outbreaks of serious indiscipline were also reported. Some of these involved the boys finding a way over the wall that separated the school from the Saracen's Head Inn, which was next door to the school in Eastgate Street, an issue not solved until 1792 when the Council had the height of the wall raised.[19]

Richard Reeve, who briefly held the position of master in 1687 and 1688, was a figure of national importance. Born in Gloucester in 1642, he suffered from a lifelong disability from a childhood stroke and attended both the Crypt (1650 – 54) and the College School (1655 – 58) as a pupil.[20] After taking his degree at Oxford, where he was known for his skills in poetry, rhetoric and Greek, he became master at Magdalen College School, where his religious views began to bring him great notoriety. He converted to Roman Catholicism in 1667 and spent the next eight years at the French Catholic seminary in Douai, emerging as a Benedictine monk. The English Catholic king, James II, called on him to return to Oxford, but instead he chose to come back to his native city of Gloucester, where he was appointed to the mastership of the Bluecoat School with a salary augmented by royal grant.[21] We can but wonder what such an eminent scholar made of the apprentice boys that were his responsibility and the requirement to prepare them for apprenticeships in trade. Whatever his feelings, however, his time at the school was relatively short-lived due to the so-called Glorious Revolution that brought William and Mary of Orange to the throne. He was charged with being a Jesuit, arrested at a Catholic refuge in Bourton-on-the-Water and imprisoned for eight months in Gloucester Castle. Anthony Wood, who compiled biographies of hundreds of Oxford-educated men, wrote that Richard Reeve 'was accounted a perfect philologist, admirably well-versed in all Classical learning, a good Grecian,

18   Ibid, p. 19.
19   Ibid, p. 21.
20   R. Austin, *The Crypt School Gloucester*, John Bellows Gloucester (1939), p. 81.
21   A. Wood, *Athenae Oxonienses: the Fasti* (ed P. Bliss), London (1813), volume IV, p. 386.

and has been so sedulous in his profession of pedagogy that he has educated sixty ministers of the Church of England and about forty Roman priests. Having been lame from the beginning, so consequently taken off from the rambles of the world, he spent his time altogether in studies and devotion'.[22]

Apart from this unusual complication with national political events, for the most part the Bluecoat School benefited from several long and remarkable periods of stability. One of these was under John Abbott, master in the first third of the 18th century. Another long-serving master was Luke Hook, a scrivener who had attended the school as a boy in the 1720s and continued to operate his own business alongside running the school from 1741 until 1788.[23]

Figure 64: A 19th-century impression of life inside the Bluecoat School by local artist John Kemp; he depicts the boys at work wearing their distinctive drugget coats, tabs and yellow stockings.

---

[22] Ibid, p. 387.
[23] D. J. Watkins, *The History of Sir Thomas Rich's School*, Gloucester (1966), p. 18.

Assisted by these well-established masters, the City Councillors on the whole seem to have provided the school with effective support. It was inspected each month by four representatives of the Council and each quarter by the governors of St Bartholomew's Hospital 'to head and examine all complaints, disorders and abuses there'.[24] A full cohort of twenty boys was maintained and the school functioned reasonably efficiently in the second half of the 17th century and throughout the 18th century. When Bishop Benson made his visitation in the 1740s, he found there were eighteen boys at the school and, as envisaged in Sir Thomas Rich's will, six left each year to take up apprenticeships.[25] Unlike the Crypt, the Bluecoat School was not starved of the financial resources it needed to flourish in the 18th century. Rents from the estates it owned brought in a total income of £320 a year in 1731, a sum sufficient to cover the expenses of running the school and the cost of supporting new apprentices, taking rising salaries and other inflationary pressures into account.[26] The charity also benefited from a number of important additional endowments in these years. Lady Napier contributed a gift of £50 in 1715; Amity Clutterbuck left it £1,000 in stock in his will of 1722; and Alderman Thomas Browne made a donation of £400 in 1731.[27] Two additional farms were bought for the school in Awre in 1749 and 1766.[28] Richard Elly, who died in 1755, left £500 to be used 'in such a beneficial manner as Luke Hook, the present master, shall from his experience think expedient'.[29] He decided that the interest on the first £170 of this donation should be allocated to buy new shoes and stockings for the boys each Easter and the interest on the remainder used for periodic repairs to the school building. Thomas Gunter of Massachusetts, a native of Gloucester, left £1,000 in his will in 1760, much of which was used to buy additional land to increase the endowment.[30] By 1800 the annual

---

24 Ibid, pp. 13–14.
25 J. Fendley, *Bishop Benson's Survey of the Diocese of Gloucester*, The Bristol and Gloucestershire Archaeological Society (2000), p. 83.
26 N. M. Herbert, *The Victoria History of the Counties of England: Gloucestershire*, volume 4, p. 336.
27 S. Rudder, *A New History of Gloucestershire*, p. 199.
28 'Report from Commissioners in England and Wales', House of Commons (1926), volume XII, p. 26.
29 J. Fendley, *Bishop Benson's Survey of the Diocese of Gloucester*, p. 83.
30 N. M. Herbert, *The Victoria History of the Counties of England: Gloucestershire*, volume 4, p. 357.

income of the school from its lands had been raised to £452 a year, making its finances healthy and in surplus.[31]

As a sign of their care for the school, the councillors and others associated with the school's management paid 5s each for an annual dinner called the Audit Feast, to which the master and the twenty boys were all invited. The proceedings began with an inspection of written work produced in the school.[32] As the 18th century progressed, this occasion was held as part of the St Thomas's Day celebrations each December and became an increasingly lavish affair. Right up until 1792, a doe hunted in the Forest of Dean was the centrepiece of the meal, often supported by a couple of turkeys, a salmon and oysters. The celebration was opened with a peal of bells from nearby St Michael's Church and, it is said, the event invariably passed off with great jollity. Another feature of the event was the singing of a hymn in praise of charity, which made particular reference to the school's founder; and out of this it is thought that the song now known as the 'Tommy Psalm' originated. Although the oldest copy to exist on paper dates from 1811, it has all the marks of a composition from the 18th century.[33]

Writing his Gloucester history in 1829, George Counsel reflected on the high regard in which the Bluecoat School was held. 'Some of the most respectable persons in this city and neighbourhood', he wrote, 'have received their education at this most admirable establishment'.[34] A few years later still, the school was described as 'a large salubrious establishment, with a good schoolroom and a large playground behind. There are twenty boys educated and maintained'.[35]

Only in one important respect was the will of Sir Thomas Rich frustrated. He had originally intended that the school would be for the exclusive benefit of the children of the poor and that they would attend for up to six years between the ages of ten and sixteen. These provisions were ignored by the City Council, partly because of the intense competition for places and partly in order to maintain the privileges of the ruling elite.

---

31 Ibid, p. 336.
32 T. Rudge, *The History and Antiquities of Gloucester*, p. 132.
33 D. J. Watkins, *The History of Sir Thomas Rich's School*, p. 26.
34 G. W. Counsel, *The History and Description of the City of Gloucester*, Gloucester (1829), p. 180.
35 *Parliamentary Gazetteer of England and Wales*, London (1847), p. 163.

From the outset the decision was taken to limit the length of schooling to just three years and to admit only the sons of Gloucester freemen.[36] This was a status either inherited, purchased or conferred on someone who had completed an apprenticeship under an existing freeman of the city. The decision in effect meant that, rather than catering for the children of the poor, the school fulfilled the practical purpose of assisting the sons of middle-ranking tradesmen to secure apprenticeships and to carry on businesses similar to those of their fathers. For them the grammar schools were either too expensive or inappropriate with their focus entirely on the Classics.

Providing an ongoing and suitable education for the boys of the Gloucester trading community was certainly a worthwhile task and one that differed greatly from the older grammar schools already established in the city. It was not, however, quite what the founder, Sir Thomas Rich, had intended. As was so often the case, those who were genuinely poor in late 17th- and 18th-century Gloucester remained excluded and deprived.

---

[36] N. M. Herbert, *The Victoria History of the Counties of England: Gloucestershire*, volume 4, p. 336.

CHAPTER THIRTEEN

Maurice Wheeler:

Gloucester's Most Celebrated Schoolmaster

Of all those associated with education in Gloucester in the 17th and 18th centuries, one individual stands out. This man was Maurice Wheeler, who held the position of headmaster of the College School with great distinction for twenty-eight years from 1684 until 1712 and gained a national reputation as a far-sighted educationalist.

As well as introducing important curriculum reforms and showing unprecedented pastoral care towards his pupils, Wheeler was the first master to begin using the phrase 'the King's School' to refer to his establishment. Although 'College School' remained the more common term until the mid-19th century, it was now used alongside the terms 'King's School' and 'Cathedral School'. The three were interchangeable, but for the sake of consistency it is the now more familiar King's School that will be used in this book. Wheeler also prepared the ground for a permanent merger with the Song School, encouraging choristers to join his school. For these reasons the years of Wheeler's headship were pivotal to the development of the King's School known by later generations.

Wheeler's background

Maurice Wheeler was a self-made Oxford man. He was born in 1648, probably at Wimborne St Giles in Dorset.[1] It is not known where he went to school, but he rose from an undistinguished background by becoming a

---

[1] S. M. Eward, *No Fine But A Glass of Wine: Cathedral Life at Gloucester in Stuart Times*, Lymington (1985), p. 278.

'batteler' at New Inn Hall at Oxford at the age of sixteen. A batteler was a member of the college who lacked the financial resources to pay for full board and would have taken on some domestic duties to support his upkeep. Through this route, Wheeler graduated from New Inn with a B.A. in 1667 and remained at Oxford as a minor canon of Christ Church, where he took his M.A. degree in 1670.[2]

In the decade before his arrival in Gloucester, Wheeler had already become a well-known academic figure. He served for ten years as Rector of St Ebbe's in Oxford, where he married his wife, Anna, and quickly gained recognition through his studies.[3] In 1673 he published a compendium of knowledge known as an almanac, a lengthy work containing diverse facts on topics such as the calendar and the weather. Almanacs of this type were often best-sellers in the 17th century, second only to the Bible, and Wheeler's was no exception. It contained particularly useful information on the history of Oxford and the counties of England, but it was unusual for deliberately omitting astrology, which Wheeler regarded as unscientific.[4] Thirty-thousand copies are said to have been printed with a beautiful cover adorned with hieroglyphic figures under the title of *The Oxford Almanac for the Year of Our Lord 1673*. As a member of the Oxford

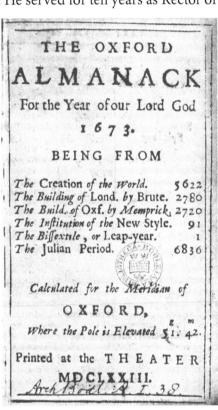

Figure 65: Front page of Wheeler's best-selling Almanac compiled in Oxford in the 1670s.

---

2   *Dictionary of National Biography*, London (1899), volume 60, p. 441.
3   J. N. Langston, 'Headmasters and Ushers of the King's (College) School, Gloucester', *Records of Gloucester Cathedral,* volume III, H. Osborne Gloucester (1928), p. 213.
4   J. Skelton, *Antiqua Restaurata: One Hundred and Ninety Engravings of Buildings in Oxford*, London (1843), p. iii.

Philosophical Society, Wheeler also demonstrated a strong aptitude for architecture and engineering at this time. He was part of a team that designed an inclined plane clock and a hygroscope, inventions for which he took the credit. He also worked with Henry Aldrich on structural improvements to the University Church and created an engraving of the timberwork in the new Sheldonian Theatre.[5] It was during this period, too, that Wheeler's interest in teaching grew as he became private tutor to a number of individuals, including William Wake, who later became Archbishop of Canterbury.[6]

The year 1680, however, brought unfortunate tragedy. A monument in St Ebbe's Church records the death of Wheeler's twin sons, Maurice and William, in that year. Probably prompted by this loss, the Wheelers decided to leave Oxford and spent the next four years at the Rectory at Sibbertoft in Northamptonshire. Along with their surviving children, they arrived in Gloucester in September 1684, taking up residence in the Schoolmaster's House, now known as 4 Miller's Green.[7] It seems that about this time, too, the neighbouring house, previously reserved for the usher, was vacated in order to provide extra space for Wheeler to expand the number of boarders that could be taken into the school.[8]

The development of the King's School under Wheeler

In the King's School of today Maurice Wheeler is remembered in the name of one of the school houses. Several of the procedures he adopted, especially the publication of the annual School List and the use of the 'Combat of the Pen' to reward good work, have continued until very recent times.

Wheeler arrived in Gloucester with a reforming educational outlook influenced by that of the educational writer Charles Hoole.[9] Although recognising the continued primacy of Latin, Hoole advocated a broadening

5   J. R. S. Whiting, *King's School Gloucester*, Orchard & Ind Gloucester (1990), p. 26.
6   N. Sykes, *William Wake, Archbishop of Canterbury*, Cambridge University Press (1957), vol 1, p. 96.
7   D. Welander, *The History, Art and Architecture of Gloucester Cathedral*, Alan Sutton (1991), p. 384.
8   S. M. Eward, *No Fine But A Glass of Wine: Cathedral Life at Gloucester in Stuart Times*, p. 178.
9   See Chapter Eleven.

of the curriculum to include English poetry and rhetoric, he was fond of Aesop's Fables, he supported the use of frequent encouragement rather than excessive punishment and he recommended that schools develop their own library and use their outdoor spaces to create recreational gardens.[10] These were all aspects of school life in which Wheeler was set to engage with gusto.

One of the first steps Wheeler took on his appointment to the headship was the decision to create a School List, a comprehensive admission register. He called his book the 'Scholae Regiae Glocestriensis Liber Censualis'. It is a major source of information about the boys who attended the school not simply in Wheeler's day but for many generations later. The title page, designed by Wheeler himself, was striking in two key respects. First, it represented the beginning of a volume maintained continuously in handwritten form by successive headmasters from 1685 right up to 1923. Second, the reference to 'Scholae Regiae Glocestriensis' represents the first use of the phrase 'King's School Gloucester'. Although the king referred to is its founder, Henry VIII it is thought that the political circumstances of the time may have influenced Wheeler's use of the term. The year 1685 marked the accession of James II, a king anxious to emphasise the principle of hereditary monarchy in the lead-up to what became known as the Glorious Revolution.[11] The Cathedral and the school associated with it at this time very much prided themselves on their royal con-nections, whereas many others in

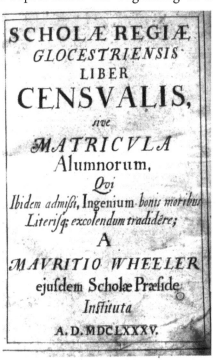

Figure 66: Title page of the King's School List begun by Wheeler in 1685.

---

10 T. Mark, *A New Discovery of the Old Art of Teaching School by Charles Hoole*, Manchester (1912), p. 240.
11 J. R. S. Whiting, *King's School Gloucester*, p. 28.

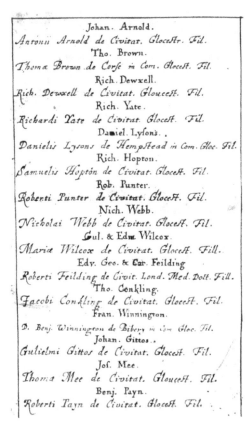

Johan. Arnold.

Antonii Arnold de Civitat. Gloucstr. Fil.

Tho. Brown.

Thomæ Brown de Corse in Com. Glocest. Fil.

Rich. Dewxell.

Rich. Dewxell de Civitat. Gloucest. Fil.

Rich. Yate.

Richardi Yate de Civitat. Glocest. Fil.

Daniel. Lysons.

Danielis Lysons de Hempstead in Com. Gloc. Fil.

Rich. Hopton.

Samuelis Hopton de Civitat. Glocest. Fil.

Rob. Punter.

Roberti Punter de Civitat. Glocest. Fil.

Nich. Webb.

Nicholai Webb de Civitat. Glocest. Fil.

Gul. & Edw. Wilcox.

Mariæ Wilcox de Civitat. Glocest. Fill.

Edv. Geo. & Car. Feilding

Roberti Feilding de Civit. Lond. Med. Dott. Fill.

Tho. Conkling.

Jacobi Conkling de Civitat. Glocest. Fil.

Fran. Winnington.

D. Benj. Winnington de Bibery in Com. Gloc. Fil.

Johan. Gittos.

Gulielmi Gittos de Civitat. Glocest. Fil.

Jof. Mee.

Thomæ Mee de Civitat. Gloucest. Fil.

Benj. Payn.

Roberti Tayn de Civitat. Glocest. Fil.

Figure 67: **Page in Wheeler's own immaculate writing; it lists some of the boys he found in the school on his arrival.**

Gloucester regretted the loss of the prestige the city had enjoyed in the Commonwealth period. Charles II had deprived Gloucester of its charter, levelled its walls and given its gates to the City of Worcester as a punishment for the stance it had taken during the Siege of Gloucester.[12]

During Wheeler's time there seems to have been on average between 80 and 100 boys in the school.[13] He initially divided them into two groups. The 'Scholares Aborigines' were the ones already in the school when he arrived. The first to be recorded was Samuel Mee, but in total there were fifty-seven of them, thirty-one from the City of Gloucester itself, twenty-one from villages mainly in the west of the county, three from London and one each from Worcester and Bristol. The second group were the 'Scholares Ascripti'. They were boys admitted by Wheeler himself. There were twenty-five in the year 1685 – 86 and thirty-four the following year. Included among them were two of Wheeler's own sons, Charles and George, who entered the school in 1688 and 1692 respectively. A total of 647 boys were educated at the school during the twenty-eight years of Wheeler's headship. The register records their names, their age, details of their father and their actual entry date into the school. It is clear that boys joined on whatever date suited, so there could not have been any rigidly defined terms around which teaching was organised. Nor was there any set

---

12   C. Heighway, *Gloucester: A History and Guide*, Alan Sutton (1985), p. 127.
13   F. Hannam-Clark, *Memories of the College School*, Packer Gloucester (1890), p. 8.

age for boys to join. The most common age was eight, but almost as many arrived at the ages of seven, nine, ten and eleven. Older boys were taken in up to sixteen, but there were occasional exceptions. Charles Snell came to the school at the age of five in 1692 and three years later Richard Bassett also joined aged five; fortunately, both seem to have had older brothers in the school. George Taylor of Hartpury on the other hand was admitted at the grand old age of twenty-four! We do not know why.

School fees in Wheeler's day stood at £2 4s a year, plus an entrance fee of 5s 6d, meaning that the school's clientele was drawn from the sons of local gentry, clergy and professional people.[14] Among the pupils were the three sons of Robert Fielding, a London doctor, who had once been Cathedral librarian at Gloucester and clearly had sufficiently fond memories to want his boys to be brought up there.[15] Others included the son of the Dean, Knightly Chetwood, the two sons of Canon Abraham Gregory, the two sons of former headmaster Oliver Gregory and the five sons of the local bell-founder Abraham Rudhall. The list of those Wheeler admitted shows the school drawing on some of the most well-to-do families of Gloucestershire. The Selwyns of Matson, the Lysons of Hempsted, the Guises of Rendcomb, the Bretts of Cowley, the Hyetts of Painswick and Over, the Pauncefoots of Newent, and the Bathursts of Lechlade all sent their sons to King's at this time and ensured that its reputation grew in Wheeler's hands.

Our main source about the school in Wheeler's time and his unique approach to education is a book published nearly a century later. It was rather obscurely entitled *Illustration of the Engraved Subjects which compose the First Number of the Copper-Plate Perspective Itinerary*. Its author, Thomas Bonnor, was one of the most prolific topographical artists of his day, and he was a frequent visitor to Gloucester. An acquaintance of Robert Raikes, he married Mary Fley, daughter of one of the vergers at Gloucester Cathedral, where most of his children were baptised.[16] One of the engravings he published was of the schoolroom, which he showed as two distinct units, Upper and Lower School, separated by a wooden

---

[14]   J. R. S. Whiting, *King's School Gloucester*, p. 31.
[15]   S. M. Eward, *No Fine But A Glass of Wine: Cathedral Life at Gloucester in Stuart Times*, p. 285.
[16]   H. Jones, 'A Bibliographical Note on Thomas Bonnor', *Transactions of the Bristol and Gloucestershire Archaeological Society*, volume 130 (2012), pp. 296–97.

screen; beneath his engraving he wrote a detailed description of what could be remembered of the school under Wheeler.

Wheeler worked alongside three ushers during the twenty-eight years of his headship.[17] The first (1684 – 87) was Thomas Trippett, who had previously been usher at the Crypt. There then followed a long period from 1687 until 1708 when the usher was John Hilton, a graduate of Queen's College, Oxford. He combined his role in the school with the post of Vicar of St Nicholas' Church in Westgate Street. Wheeler's final usher was Henry Abbot, who had been taught by Wheeler as a pupil. After graduating from Trinity College, Oxford, and Caius College, Cambridge, he became usher in 1709, a position he held with that of Vicar of Longney and Barnwood.

The admission of choristers to the King's School

One of the things that struck Wheeler as something to require his attention immediately on his arrival in Gloucester was that none of the Cathedral choristers attended the King's School. The statutes of Henry VIII had provided for the eight choristers to be educated in their own separate Song School with their own master, and this remained the case with varying degrees of success throughout the 17th century. It was a state of affairs that Wheeler began the process of changing.

Wheeler's ambition was to create one single school of choristers and other pupils, so he began to integrate as many of the choristers as he could into the main body of the King's School. He began with the organist's son, William Jefferies, who became a chorister at the same time as he entered King's in 1687. His younger brother joined the choir at the age of eight in 1689 and then entered the school two years later. Another boy, John Tyler, became a chorister in 1695 and a full member of King's in 1698. The task of fully integrating the two establishments would not come to complete fruition until Victorian times; Wheeler found the process difficult, but an important change had begun. Out of the fifty-three choristers in the choir during his time as headmaster, at least fifteen were admitted as full members of King's.[18] The barriers that prevented greater success lay in harsh financial reality. There was a huge social gulf separating most of the

---

[17]   J. N. Langston, 'Headmasters and Ushers of the King's (College) School, Gloucester', p. 216.
[18]   J. R. S. Whiting, *King's School Gloucester*, Orchard & Ind Gloucester (1990), p. 30.

boys in the King's School from the choristers, who were drawn mainly from the artisan class. This meant that not only were they unlikely to be able to afford the King's School fees, but many of them actually combined their choir roles with an apprenticeship.[19]

The progress Wheeler made in integrating choristers into the King's School was eased by the character of the two men who served as organists and masters of the choristers at this time. Stephen Jefferies, who held the role for twenty-five years after his appointment in 1682, seems to have had little inclination for supervising the day-to-day education of his boys. He was a prolific composer best known for the anthem he wrote in commemoration of the coronation of Queen Anne in 1702. He was also regarded by others in the Cathedral community as an awkward eccentric who stayed out drinking in local taverns until the late hours of the night. In 1699 the Dean and Chapter complained of 'his frequent absences, especially on Sunday mornings, but more particularly for his not educating the choristers in the grounds of music, which may prove very prejudicial for the future'.[20]

The second master of the choristers with whom Wheeler dealt was also predisposed towards having the general education of the choristers taken care of by the King's School, but for entirely different reasons. William Hine, who was married to Alicia Rudhall, daughter of the city's bell-founder, became organist about 1707. It quickly became apparent that he was intent on bringing 'a new professionalism to the musical life and choral tradition of the Cathedral and he established new standards of excellence'.[21] Under his leadership the Cathedral organ was moved from its original location beneath the south crossing arch to its current central position over the west entrance to the quire. About the same time Hine began to host music meetings involving the choirs from Worcester and Hereford Cathedrals as well as Gloucester, beginning what we now know as the Three Choirs Festival. The increasing ambition and complexity of the music being performed meant that the organist and master of the choristers was only too content to focus more or less exclusively on the musical education of the boys under his care, leaving other aspects of their general education to others and, for those who could afford the fees, to the King's School.

---

[19] D. Welander, *The History, Art and Architecture of Gloucester Cathedral*, p. 575.
[20] Ibid, p. 398.
[21] A. Boden & P. Hedley, *The Three Choirs Festival: A History*, Boydell Press (2017), p. 11.

Discipline and religion

Maurice Wheeler's personal views lay at the Puritan end of the religious spectrum. He believed that people were responsible for acquiring their own salvation rather than needing to rely on a priest to act as go-between with God.[22] Before Wheeler's time the schoolroom had contained a large cross called a tripos, beneath which the master used to bow before taking his seat each morning. Wheeler had the cross removed and abandoned the ceremony 'on account of it savouring somewhat of the religious ceremonies of the Roman church'.[23] Nor was the Cathedral itself used for school 'assemblies' in Wheeler's day. The practice recommended by the High Churchman William Laud that the school attend early morning prayers in the Lady Chapel seems to have been discontinued. Instead, Bishop Thomas Ken's morning and evening hymns were said at the beginning and end of each day in the actual schoolroom. The marginal comments, which Wheeler wrote in some of the books presented to the school library, also confirm his essentially puritanical outlook. Some of these warned boys against the evils of idleness and time-wasting and, in the Puritan tradition, extolled the virtues of hard work. One particular comment, which Wheeler wrote in 1691, demonstrates his strong anti-Catholic feelings: 'Whoever shall read this will understand no Popish kings are fit to rule this land'.

That said, the moderation of Wheeler's religious position also comes across in the way he viewed the execution of Charles I with revulsion, seeing to it that each anniversary of the king's death was commemorated sympathetically in the schoolroom with passages read aloud from Richard Perrinchief's *Life and Death of King Charles the First*. Wheeler also had no reservations about participating fully in the rituals and musical life of the Cathedral. He collaborated with Stephen Jefferies, the organist, in writing words for a three-part choral arrangement entitled 'A Meditation upon Death'.[24] These words conjure up the melancholy of human lives being like clock weights, running down to their inevitable end until they reach the point when they will never again be wound up. Wheeler and Jefferies set

---

[22] S. M. Eward, *No Fine But A Glass of Wine: Cathedral Life at Gloucester in Stuart Times*, pp. 290–92.
[23] T. Bonnor, *Illustration of the Engraved Subjects which compose the First Number of the Copper-Plate Perspective Itinerary*, London (1796), p. 18.
[24] J. Mackechnie-Jarvis, 'The Life and Times of Gloucester's Chimes', *Transactions of the Bristol and Gloucestershire Archaeological Society* (2017), volume 135, p. 255.

Figure 68: 'A Meditation on Death', a three-part choral arrangement written by Wheeler and set to the Cathedral chimes in collaboration with the organist, Stephen Jefferies.

the Cathedral chimes to play their piece with the result that it echoed over Gloucester three times each Tuesday for the next 200 years.[25]

As far as the discipline and treatment of his pupils was concerned, Wheeler accepted many of the conventions of his day. He was a strict disciplinarian who expected boys to maintain the standards he demanded. We do not know what offences they had committed, but Wheeler expelled three boys during his time as headmaster and had their names deleted from the admission register. In the case of one of the older boys he expelled, John Atkins, the name is still just legible in the register and alongside it Wheeler had written in Latin: 'The memory of the just will be eternal, but the name of the wicked will rot'. One theory is that Atkins may have repeatedly

---

[25]   D. Welander, *The History, Art and Architecture of Gloucester Cathedral,* p. 562.

refused to attend Sunday worship, as this tended to be the most common reason behind an expulsion in this period.[26] In a practice that seems particularly gruesome to the modern mind, Wheeler also attempted to create a sense of fear in the minds of his charges by displaying two skulls in the schoolroom. One of these, the skull of a young man hanged for stealing books, he intended as a warning against breaking rules; the other, the skull of a person who lived to a great age, he used to encourage the boys to live moderate and upright lives.[27] Wheeler had no qualms about using harsh corporal punishment on boys who were tempted to break his rules. He had his own version of the birch known as the 'manubrium', which was described by Bonnor as 'an instrument of punishment used rather to terrify'. Wheeler also thought nothing of sentencing young boys to periods of solitary confinement in a small room with strong bars on its door; he rather gruesomely named this room the 'tullianum', the name of one of the dungeons of ancient Rome.

Figure 69: **Page in the School List, on which Wheeler deleted the name of John Atkins, whom he expelled from the school.**

Harsh though some of it was, Wheeler's approach towards instilling good behaviour, as with many other aspects of his educational thinking, did contain his own unique twist. Especially important was his desire to encourage his boys to take on responsibilities in the running of the school. A good example of this can be found in the admissions register, where he recorded the appointment of Richard Gregory and John Foyle as school secretaries in 1698. Wheeler was also keen to see that the boys themselves were consulted on the enforcement of school rules. He wanted them not just to receive punishment but to be actively involved in the

---

26   W. A. L. Vincent, *The Grammar Schools: Their Continuing Tradition*, John Murray (1969), p. 90.
27   T. Bonnor, *Illustration of the Engraved Subjects which compose the First Number of the Copper-Plate Perspective Itinerary*, p. 18.

decision-making process, so that they could be given an insight into the workings of the legal system. This led Wheeler into some policies that even today seem remarkably progressive. Bonnor explained an interesting procedure he adopted to use a pupils' court to establish the guilt of any boy accused of wrong doing. 'An 'urna delatoria' was provided, into which was dropped the name of any boy accused of breaking the rules, along with the names of his accusers and any witnesses. Wheeler then organised a formal court hearing; the offender was placed at the bar; the censors performed the functions of public accusers; the class of orators supplied the counsel on both sides; and the event was determined by the verdict of a jury composed of nine boys. Unless two-thirds at least of the jury united in pronouncing him guilty of his charge, the party accused was acquitted'.[28] Through devices like this, Wheeler emerges in many respects as a pioneering, enlightened educationalist well ahead of his generation in terms of the innovations he introduced.

We get another intriguing glimpse into the pastoral care Wheeler extended to his pupils in an often-overlooked monument to Thomas Ware, which is situated in the Cathedral's north tribune gallery. Thomas was a young boarder from Latton, near Cricklade, who fell ill and died in 1698 at the age of seventeen. The inscription on the monument states that he grew up to become 'a conscientious and intelligent young man, who was trained to nurture his mind with good literature and sound morals at the famous school adjacent to the wall of this majestic Cathedral'. It goes on to say that Thomas was 'greatly mourned by his kinsfolk and schoolfellows and in truth he is lamented by everyone, with no one more sad than his teacher, Master Maurice Wheeler, under whose tutelage

Figure 70: Memorial to Thomas Ware, which expresses Wheeler's great sadness at the death of one of his most conscientious and intelligent pupils.

---

28   Ibid, p. 19.

he had never cried'. It is rare for a church monument specifically to mention a teacher. The fact that Wheeler is named reflects the esteem in which he would have been held by the boy's family; the reference to the fact that Thomas had never shown sadness, despite his illness, is a detail that seems to confirm Wheeler's genuine sense of loss and sorrow.

Curriculum changes

Maurice Wheeler showed a similar innovative approach towards the curriculum and the methods of teaching he adopted. He was a strong supporter of combining rigorous intellectual pursuits with outdoor and physical activities.

At a time when opportunities for sport were severely limited in schools, Wheeler had both a vaulting bar and a target post for darts erected in the school grounds.[29] These were the physical education lessons of his day, a novel aspect of the curriculum 200 years before the Victorians began to emphasise the importance of sport with the phrase 'a healthy mind in a healthy body'. Another area in which Wheeler showed his imagination was in the introduction of gardening as a school activity. He saw gardening as a way of combining the benefits of physical exercise with projects that would have a lasting effect. To this end, he organised some of his boys into a workforce, which he led himself, to transform an area of neglected land known as 'the Grove' at the north-east end of the Cathedral. This space had in earlier times been part of the monks' orchard and cemetery.[30] Wheeler found it overrun with rubbish, weeds and timber from a nearby sawpit and in its place he created a new formal garden. 'He thus promoted his own health', wrote Bonnor, 'called forth the laborious exertion of the inactive, contributed very essentially to the occasional improvement of the Grove and to the keeping of it at all times in good order at very little expense; and in addition to these salutary purposes, he at the same time conferred the highest distinction on those who, being made the companions of his work, were for the time placed upon a level with himself'.[31]

---

[29] Ibid, p. 19
[30] R. Auckland, 'Common Ground and Sacred Space: A Study in Gloucester Cathedral's Precincts' (2018), p. 62.
[31] T. Bonnor, *Illustration of the Engraved Subjects which compose the First Number of the Copper-Plate Perspective Itinerary*, p. 17.

Wheeler went to great lengths not simply to promote physical activities such as gardening but to combine them with new ways of approaching academic disciplines. He used the garden he created in the Grove as a space for encouraging philosophical, ethical and moral education, which ranked high among his priorities. At the centre of the garden he created a large mound of earth, on which he planted a striking tree which he referred to as the 'arbor vitae', a representation of happiness and immortality. He had two cypress trees planted at the bottom of the mound as emblems of death, a reminder to his boys that one day they would all have to pass through death on their road to immortality. Conjuring up a picture of the Garden of Eden, he planted a birch tree with a vine twining up it as a representation of good and evil. The various walks around the garden he named the Orators' Walk, the Poets' Walk and the Historians' Walk and he encouraged the boys in Upper School to walk through them when memorising their key texts. Wheeler's far-reaching educational aims are clear to see in the way he promoted his garden as a philosophical experience. Bonnor's comment was that 'his object was not merely to convert a neglected and offensive place into a playground; his views were much more extensive. They were not less

Figure 71: Nineteenth-century illustration by the artist William Bartlett, showing the landscaped garden or Grove created by Wheeler and his boys at the east end of the Cathedral.

directed to encourage habits of industry, to promote activity and to excite in young minds a taste for practical gardening, and for the cultivation of a nursery, than they were to the inculcating of elevated and classical ideas'.[32]

Another innovation actively promoted by Wheeler to enrich the curriculum was a significant expansion of the school library at King's. In doing this, as in many of his other reforms, Wheeler was echoing the advice of the educational writer Charles Hoole, who stated 'it were to be wished that in every school of note there might be a library, where in all the best grammars that can be gotten might be kept and lent to those boys who are more industriously addicted to grammar and who intend to be scholars'.[33] Another voice recommending libraries was that of Christopher Wase, the printer at Oxford University, who undertook a survey of grammar schools across the country in the 1670s. 'The greatest benefit to learners', he wrote, 'after the master is a good library'.[34]

The way Wheeler's library was begun demonstrates many of his personal attributes: his charisma, business acumen and willingness to involve his pupils in all aspects of the running of the school. Wheeler inherited a custom which required each boy in the school to contribute 6d to a special fund during the six weeks of Lent. The fund was used partly for the headmaster's own discretionary purposes and partly to buy cakes as treats for the boys. In 1686 Wheeler took a risk when he proposed to go without his own share of the fund in order to begin purchasing books for a new school library, but only on the condition that the boys also agreed to give up their cakes.[35] It was a calculated risk that paid off, presumably because of the respect in which Wheeler was held. The boys agreed and the new library began to take shape. Wheeler also took the opportunity to ensure that the boys were fully involved in the cataloguing of the books and the general running of the library as pupil-librarians. Bonnor states that 'two of the scholars best skilled in figures were appointed treasurers, to keep an account of this fund and its appropriation; and there were likewise two censors, two procensors and two secretaries chosen by ballot from among the best penmen; and a keeper of the diary roll'.[36]

32   Ibid, p. 18.
33   T. Mark, *A New Discovery of the Old Art of Teaching School by Charles Hoole*, p. 173.
34   C. Wase, *Considerations Concerning Free Schools*, Oxford (1678), p. 97.
35   S. M. Eward, *A Catalogue of Gloucester Cathedral Library*, Gloucester (1972), p. x.
36   T. Bonnor, *Illustration of the Engraved Subjects which compose the First Number of the Copper-Plate Perspective Itinerary*, p. 19.

Wheeler also understood the educational value to be derived from instilling a competitive spirit among his boys, encouraging them to strive for the highest academic standards they could manage. A key part of this strategy involved identifying and rewarding those boys who achieved the very best pieces of work in the school each month through a competition, which he named the Combat of the Pen. A version of this is still used at the King's School today to reward academic achievement. The procedure Wheeler set up is described clearly by Bonnor: 'To excite emulation in penmanship, the scholars once a month had a Combat of the Pen. From the several specimens exhibited, the master chose the twelve best; and from these the scholars, by ballot, selected six which were honoured with a premium. By this arrangement, encouragement was extended to double the number of those who were adjudged the premiums; for to be one of the twelve distinguished by the master's preference was to establish a credit but little capable of diminution by the decision of those inferior judgements which ultimately awarded the prizes'.[37]

We gain a good insight into the type of academic work the boys undertook at the end of the 17th century from some of the books that survive in the Cathedral Library. Wheeler set aside part of each Thursday for the reading of tales from these books, dwelling on those that stimulated the imagination or helped in building up character.[38] One of the books, a 1692 translation of Aesop's Fables by Sir Roger L'Estrange, contains a number of stories written by the boys themselves under the heading 'Fables Collected by the Industry of Ingenious Scholars'.[39] It seems that the boys would have read the tales in L'Estrange's book as a stimulus to creating their own fables. Possibly as part of the Combat of the Pen, Wheeler then invited the authors of the most successful pieces to copy their short stories into the back of the printed book, where they remain to this day. One of the best was that written by fourteen-year-old Thomas Andrews, the son of a Cardiff doctor. His subject was the greed of an innkeeper who presented his guests with exorbitant bills. When the innkeeper found his premises infested with rats, Thomas showed his wit by putting the following words into the mouth of one of the guests in

---

[37]   Ibid, p. 18.
[38]   S. M. Eward, *No Fine But A Glass of Wine: Cathedral Life at Gloucester in Stuart Times*, p. 290.
[39]   Gloucester Cathedral Library, Wheeler 155.

his fable: 'I know a ready way to clear the house of your sort of vermin. I will present you with a gallon of the best wine', said the innkeeper, 'if you please to impart the secret.' 'Well! Go then', said the gentleman, 'to where the rats haunt most; there lay some of the strongest cheese, finest manchet, fattest bacon, etc. When you have thus entertained them, do but bring them such a reckoning as you have brought me and I'll engage that they will never trouble your house more.'[40]

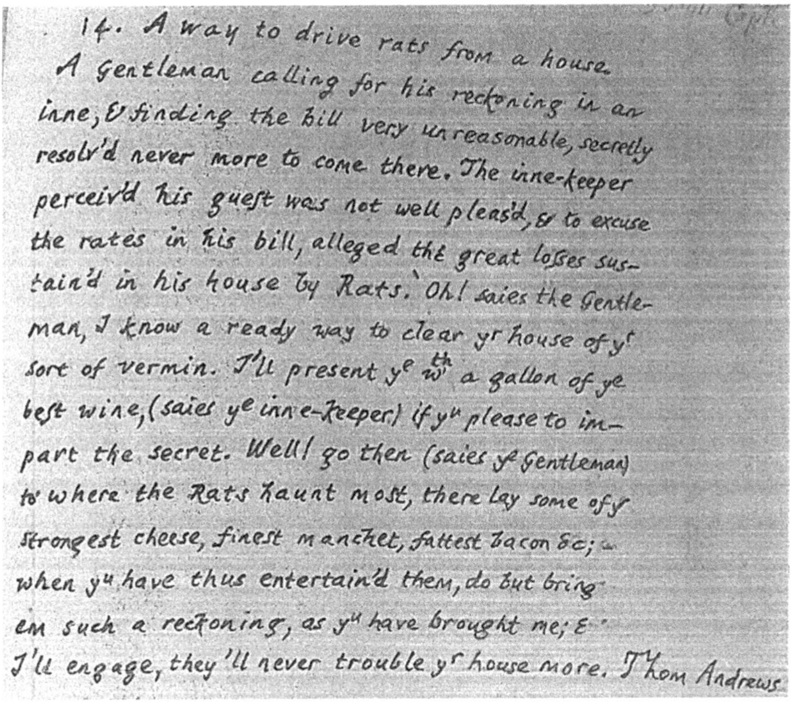
14. A way to drive rats from a house
A Gentleman calling for his reckoning in an
inne, & finding the bill very unreasonable, secretly
resolv'd never more to come there. The inne-keeper
perceiv'd his guest was not well pleas'd, & to excuse
the rates in his bill, alleged the great losses sus-
tain'd in his house by Rats. Oh! saies the Gentleman, I know a ready way to clear yr house of yr
sort of vermin. I'll present ye wth a gallon of ye
best wine, (saies ye inne-keeper) if yu please to impart the secret. Well! go then (saies ye Gentleman)
to where the Rats haunt most, there lay some of ye
strongest cheese, finest manchet, fattest bacon &c;
when yu have thus entertain'd them, do but bring
em such a reckoning, as yu have brought me; &
I'll engage, they'll never trouble yr house more. Thom Andrews

Figure 72: Witty fable in the style of Aesop written by fourteen-year-old schoolboy Thomas Andrews.

The stories preserved in this book represent the oldest surviving examples of written work by pupils in any school in Gloucester. Another account of interest it contains, but written a little later – in 1702 – by sixteen-year-old George Gwinnett, was a description of the festivities in Gloucester that marked the coronation of Queen Anne. It was an occasion that saw 'a banquet of wine and sweet meats and the heartiest acclamations of prosperity to the

40 A. Nandhla, E. Chan & R. Cooke, 'The Scholars Tales' Transcript, King's School (2018), p. 5.

three united nations, under the glorious reign of our most gracious and beloved Queen, as the bells all the while ringing, bonfires blazing and illuminations glittering closed up the celebrations of the day'.[41]

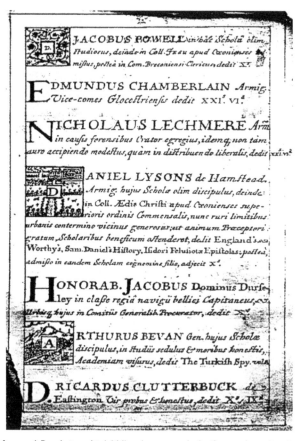

Figure 73: Benefactors' Book, in which Wheeler recorded gifts to the school and details of the donors.

Improvements to fabric and facilities

Alongside his keen interest in education, Wheeler also set about improving the furnishings and equipment to be found in the schoolroom. He completely grasped that schools in this period required generous benefactions in order to flourish; the key resources needed could not come

---

41   Ibid, p. 7.

simply from the limited capital generated by fees. Wheeler seems to have possessed a particular gift for persuading benefactors to make contributions and he used his beautiful handwriting proudly to record their gifts in a Benefactors' Book, which is still preserved in the Cathedral Library. In each record he described the nature of the gift and in many cases included comments about the biography and characters of the 200 donors.[42] Among the first to contribute was Robert Frampton, the Bishop of Gloucester, who donated new desks 'of improved design'. The Dean, William Jane, paid £3 for 'a new seat for the schoolmaster' and in the following year made additional payments for new wood panelling in the schoolroom.[43] Examples of other donations included: 10 shillings from 'James Rowell, one time a pupil in the school and sent on to Jesus College Oxford, afterwards a clerk in Holy Orders in the county of Brecon'; 21s 6d from 'Edmund Chamberlain Esquire, Sheriff of Gloucester'; 21s 6d from 'Nicholas Lechmere Esquire, distinguished diplomat in foreign affairs, a man not so much known for his moderation in receiving gold as for his generosity in distributing it'; and 10s from Thomas Rich, 'a former pupil of this school and son of the founder of the charity hospital of the Bluecoat boys in the city of Gloucester'.[44]

The new library was built up by encouraging donations from local dignitaries and former pupils. A Latin inscription in Wheeler's own hand was inserted into each book provided, recording the date of the book's acquisition, the name of the donor and his thanks for the gift. Daniel Lysons of Hempsted, a former pupil and later fellow of Christ Church, Oxford, gave copies of *The History of the Worthies of England*, Samuel Daniel's *History* and *The Letters of Isadorus Pelusiota*. John Churchill, a London bookseller, donated a copy of Chillingworth's *Works*; John Bennett, a pupil at the school, donated a copy of the *Historia Anglicana*; and Henry, Duke of Beaufort gave a copy of Dr Scott's *Christian Life*.[45] There are a total of 161 books recorded by Wheeler in the Benefactors' Book. Today fifty-six of these still survive as the 'Wheeler Library', a part of the main Cathedral Library.[46] Wheeler created a catalogue for these books

---

42 S. M. Eward, *No Fine But A Glass of Wine: Cathedral Life at Gloucester in Stuart Times*, p. 286.
43 J. R. S. Whiting, *King's School Gloucester*, p. 28.
44 Gloucester Cathedral Archives (Benefactors' Book), Kirby 206, p. 31.
45 Ibid, p. 36.
46 D. Welander, *The History, Art and Architecture of Gloucester Cathedral*, p. 586.

in his own writing, putting his own inscriptions and annotations in many of the volumes that were donated.[47] Several of his comments were written in verse and reflected both his wide knowledge of literature and his interest in how books could be used in an educational setting.[48] On the basis of his work in building up these resources Wheeler was appointed Cathedral librarian in 1709, a post he combined with his headship for his last three years in Gloucester.[49]

One of the most interesting gifts to the school was a new school clock, which Wheeler designed himself. Financed by Gloucester's MP John Hanbury, a former pupil of the school, it was a very elaborate clock indeed.[50] The hours were marked by twelve capital letters, the first letter of the words in this inscription: 'Most Loving King John Hanbury's Gift; For Every Day Celestial Bless the Author'. The four corners were each ornamented with one of the four cardinal virtues explained by a Latin motto.[51]

Wheeler's retirement and reputation

Maurice Wheeler's wife, Anna, died in 1711 and was buried in the Cathedral. This, and the fact that his own health had begun to cause him problems, probably led to Wheeler's decision to resign as headmaster in 1712. A translation of his final Latin entry in the Benefactors' Book records his feelings at that point: 'With eyes tired out by long hours of reading and writing and of late almost failing with partial blindness, here I lay down my pen, now inert and feeble, into the hand of some scholar more skilful, my far happier successor, praying that all good things may attend him as I take my leave and say to all in city and countryside my last short farewell'.[52] He was sixty-four years of age.

Wheeler left Gloucester in 1712, but he continued to serve the church in retirement, first as Rector of Wappenham and then of Thorpe Mandeville, two villages about ten miles apart in Northamptonshire. He died in 1727 and was buried in Wappenham churchyard.

---

47 S. M. Eward, *A Catalogue of Gloucester Cathedral Library*, p. x.
48 J. R. S. Whiting, *King's School Gloucester*, p. 37.
49 D. Welander, *The History, Art and Architecture of Gloucester Cathedral*, p. 386.
50 S. M. Eward, *No Fine But A Glass of Wine: Cathedral Life at Gloucester in Stuart Times*, p. 287.
51 T. Bonnor, *Illustration of the Engraved Subjects which compose the First Number of the Copper-Plate Perspective Itinerary*, p. 18.
52 Gloucester Cathedral Archives (Benefactors' Book), Kirby 206, p. 41.

Figure 74: Wheeler's final resting place at Wappenham, Northamptonshire.

There survives in Gloucester Cathedral one interesting and unique memorial to Wheeler. On the wall of the famous Whispering Gallery above the Great East Window his contemporaries immortalised some of his words in a short poem inscribed on a memorial stone:[53]

> Doubt not but God who sits on High
> Thy secret prayers can hear,
> When a dead wall thus cunningly
> Conveys soft whispers to the ear.

An inscription nearby confirms that these words are those of Wheeler, although they were re-chiselled in 1946 as the original had become decayed.

Among the headmasters of the King's School, Maurice Wheeler is

---

[53] S. M. Eward, *No Fine But A Glass of Wine: Cathedral Life at Gloucester in Stuart Times*, p. 278.

remembered as the most prestigious. He is credited with raising the fortunes of the school to such an extent that for a time it became one of the leading schools in the country, attracting boys from all over Gloucestershire, Bristol and the south of England. An early indication of this praise can be found in the *Athenae Oxonienses* written in 1692 by Anthony Wood, whose life work was to research the lives of eminent men listed in the Oxford University registers. Wood wrote of Wheeler that 'he is now master of the College School in Gloucester and is in a capacity of doing greater matters'.[54] Another near contemporary tribute is that provided by Bonnor in his *Itinerary* of 1796. It stated that the school had been 'a first-rate seminary of learning for centuries, and its character was greatly raised by the judicious arrangements and rules laid down by the celebrated Mr Wheeler ... His learning, ingenuity, ability and strict attention were happily applied to the improvement of the school in various ways. He new modelled it in every respect, both within doors and without'.[55]

---

[54] A. Wood, *Athenae Oxonienses: the Fasti* (ed P. Bliss), London (1813), volume 2, p. 297.
[55] T. Bonnor, *Illustration of the Engraved Subjects which compose the First Number of the Copper-Plate Perspective Itinerary*, p. 17.

CHAPTER FOURTEEN

Private Schools and Academies:

The Proliferation of New Types of School

New private schools

As England settled into a period of political stability in the 18th century and memories of the Civil War upheavals faded, a wave of new schools came into existence and a higher proportion of Gloucester's population than ever before began to receive an education of some kind. Literacy rates rose, the city's first newspaper was established in 1722 and several booksellers launched themselves in business.[1]

Underpinning these developments was the creation of a number of small private schools. Some of these, as in previous centuries, were elementary schools that taught basic literacy and acted as the first stage in the educational process. Sadly, we continue to hear regrettably little about their activities, but documentary references have survived of several more advanced privately run schools that made their appearance in the years after 1700. These tended to be small enterprises, taking in just a few children mainly from families in the middle of the social spectrum. They were free to depart from traditional grammar school subjects and positioned themselves to provide a curriculum more suitable for those destined for careers in business or commerce.[2] They generally offered a more specialised curriculum than elementary schools, including English grammar, geography and business-related skills; they took in pupils up to the age of ten or even twelve.

As these schools were relatively informal and usually met in a room that was part of a private dwelling, they are difficult to trace in historical records. One of them was a school kept from 1748 by Thomas Rudge, a young clergyman who several decades later became master of the Crypt

---

1   N. M. Herbert, *The Victoria History of the Counties of England: Gloucestershire*, volume 4, London (1988), p. 119.

2   L. W. Cowie, *Hanoverian England*, Bell & Hyman (1967), p. 33.

School and eventually Archdeacon of Gloucester. At this point in his life, he styled himself as a writing master and accountant, and the curriculum he provided included bookkeeping and accountancy.[3] His school originally met in St Mary's Square near the Church of St Mary de Lode, but in 1769 it was recorded as having moved to Miller's Green.[4] Another small private school was the business and writing school known as Lewis's Day School. It met in Westgate Street in the 1780s and had a programme of study described as including 'English grammar, writing and accounts, both vulgar and decimal, mensuration of superficies and solids, both plane and spherical, extraction of the square and cube roots, merchant accounts, the Italian method of bookkeeping, gauging in all its extensive variety, both in the theory and the practice'.[5]

The Gloucester Priory School was one of the more ambitious private schools of the late 18th century. It met in Priory House, which was a ramshackle residence created when most of the remains of the medieval St Oswald's Priory were demolished in 1655. An advertisement of 1791 described it as 'a spacious dwelling house called St Oswald's Priory with a garden, stable and convenient offices'.[6] Benoni Peach was in charge of this school in 1793 and offered a practical curriculum with instruction in 'reading, grammar, writing, arithmetic, history, geography, astronomy, the use of the globes, algebra, geometry, trigonometry, navigation and mathematics in general'. In providing details of the school, he stressed the supportive boarding community he had established as its unique feature, which provided an environment centred entirely around learning. 'The scholars will be compelled', wrote Mr Peach, 'to enter upon business early every morning. As particular attention will be given to the explaining of their lessons before they are imposed, their labour must become pleasant and happy progress ensue. It is very general among youth to find upon examination that they have utterly lost the preceding day's acquisition; but to obviate this, the pupils for their evening's amusement will be frequently taken through their former exercises, the repetition of which will stamp a

---

3   N. M. Herbert, *The Victoria History of the Counties of England: Gloucestershire*, volume 4, p. 350.
4   S. M. Eward, *No Fine But A Glass of Wine: Cathedral Life at Gloucester in Stuart Times*, Lymington (1985), p. 324.
5   *Gloucester Journal*, 2nd May 1785.
6   Ibid, 11th July 1791.

Figure 75: Priory House, where Benoni Peach and John Hart ran a school (from a 19th-century watercolour by John Buckler).

lasting impression on their tender minds. The young gentlemen will at all times be encouraged in freedom and ease in conversation and company, which will induce them to be inquisitive for knowledge without reserve and consequently increase the happiness of this little society'[7].

Like many other schools from which little documentary evidence survives, it is impossible to make any judgement about the success or otherwise of the Priory School. Fees were set at sixteen guineas per annum, which included board, washing and tuition, plus an initial entrance fee of one guinea.[8] By 1797 it was reported that the school was being run by John Hart and had been broadened to take in 'young gentlemen and ladies'.[9]

We hear in passing of three other small private schools in Gloucester at the end of the 18th century from a court case brought by William Cole against the Berkeley Estate in 1811.[10] In proceedings heard in court, three brothers – Theodore, Charles and John Gwinnett – described memories of their childhood; they walked most days from their home in Barnwood to

---

[7] Ibid, 30th December 1793.
[8] Ibid, 19th September 1796.
[9] Ibid, 16th January 1797.
[10] *The Glocester Herald*, issue 521, 21st September 1811.

collect their friend, William Cole, continuing with him into the city, where they attended a school run by John Cooke in the Oxbode. Referring to the years between 1779 and 1782, their witness statements also mentioned other schools, including one run by a Mr Mutlow 'down behind the College wall' and a girls' school kept by Mrs Middleton in Lower Northgate.[11]

Schools for girls

It is from the early 18th century that we begin to hear of the first private schools, other than elementary ones, that set out specifically to cater for middle-class girls. They tended to be fairly small establishments set up by individual ladies; most were relatively short-lived and have left no detailed impression on the historical records. One of the earliest of the girls' schools was established in 1723 by Mrs Shelton 'in a house near the Cathedral'; the advertisement she placed in the *Gloucester Journal* that year stated that 'young ladies may be boarded at reasonable rates and taught several sorts of work'.[12] The school continued for several decades and was run by Mrs Fitzwilliams in the 1740s, when it offered tuition in 'all sorts of needlework after the best manner' and optional lessons in writing, dancing, music and French.[13]

The creation of girls' schools did not in any sense indicate a progressive change in attitudes to female rights at this time. The sentiment attributed to Dr Johnson that 'a man in general is better pleased when he has a good dinner upon his table than when his wife speaks Greek' would have struck a familiar note in 18th-century Gloucester.[14] Prospects for girls remained as limited as ever. The curriculum in the new schools was designed to provide girls with the skills to manage a household and to educate their own children in the future. Whilst some literature and arithmetic may have been included, the main emphasis was on teaching 'ornamental accomplishments' thought likely to secure a girl an eligible husband, putting the focus on music, dancing, painting, needlework and deportment rather than academic subjects.[15]

---

11   *A Narrative of the Minutes of Evidence Respecting the Claim to the Berkeley Peerage*, London (1811), p. 108.

12   *Gloucester Journal*, 11th February 1723.

13   Ibid, 23rd December 1740.

14   L. W. Cowie, *Hanoverian England*, Bell & Hyman (1967), p. 35.

15   H. M. Jewell, *Education in Early Modern England*, Macmillan (1998), p. 12.

Figure 76: College Green landscaped with its tree-lined walks, location of Ann Counsell's
18th-century school for young ladies.

From 1743 Ann Counsell is recorded as keeping a private school for girls
in a house in College Green, where she taught music, dancing and
needlework 'after the newest manner'[16] and employed Mr Sexton Allen as
visiting dancing master.[17] The Green was landscaped about this time to
create a genteel shaded walkway, where the girls would have joined the
ladies of the Cathedral community for their afternoon turns. Ann
Counsell's daughter, Elizabeth Counsell, took on the running of the school
in 1756 and sought to strengthen its curriculum by adding English
grammar.[18]

The number of girls' schools increased as the 18th century progressed
and by 1791 there were no less than four small privately run boarding

---

[16] *Gloucester Journal,* 1st March 1743.
[17] Ibid, 9th April 1751.
[18] Ibid, 31st August 1756.

schools of this kind for young ladies operating in the city.[19] One of these, run by Mrs Pierrepont, was based at Number 7 Westgate Street.[20]

The Barton Street Dissenting Academy

Across the country as a whole one of the most significant developments of the 18th century was the setting up of dissenting academies. These were schools which over time developed a strong reputation for the grammar and university-style curriculum they offered and several of them produced students of great distinction.[21] Although Gloucester had only a single short-lived academy of this type in the early 18th century, it was one of the first to exist anywhere in England.

The original purpose of a dissenting academy was to teach boys brought up in Protestant families that did not accept the Church of England and to provide academic training for the ministers of the churches they attended. The Dissenters were mainly Quakers and Congregationalists who advocated elected leaders for the church rather than bishops appointed by the Crown. They included some 1,760 clergy across the country ejected from the Church of England under Charles II's Act of Uniformity of 1662.[22] The 1689 Toleration Act granted most of them the right of freedom of worship as a reward for their loyalty to William and Mary during the Glorious Revolution, but other barriers continued, including a ban on Dissenters attending university. It was also the case that Dissenters were prevented from teaching in schools, although this law began to fall into disuse as the 18th century progressed and was repealed in 1719.[23]

As the universities were closed to Dissenters, there was little point in them attending the grammar schools that prepared young men for university admission. This led to a range of new fee-paying schools known as academies that catered for the sons of middle-class Dissenting families. With university excluded, these boys aspired to mercantile or professional careers. The academies they attended began to develop a new curriculum

---

[19] N. M. Herbert, *The Victoria History of the Counties of England: Gloucestershire*, volume 4, p. 350.

[20] *Gloucester Journal*, 16th January 1797.

[21] N. Hands, *New Trends in Education in the 18th Century*, Routledge & Kegan Paul (1951), p. 15.

[22] J. Lawson & H. Silver, *A Social History of Education in England*, Methuen (1973), p. 164.

[23] L. W. Cowie, *Hanoverian England*, Bell & Hyman (1967), p. 33.

of their own, one which included many aspects of subjects taught at university level as well as in the grammar schools. Instead of focusing exclusively on the Classics, the new dissenting academies placed equal emphasis on French, Italian, history, geography, English literature, mathematics, science, political theory and logic.[24] This type of curriculum won many accolades for its breadth and its dynamic forward-looking nature. 'The traditional education of a gentleman at a grammar school and at Oxford and Cambridge', one historian has written, 'might fit him to ruminate on the past and observe the present, but the Dissenting Academies equipped a man to build the future'.[25]

The academies tended to be small, domestic establishments, typically with between twelve and twenty boys and young men living there as boarders. The Gloucester academy had a strong theological focus and functioned from 1696 until 1712.[26] It was set up by the Scottish minister James Forbes, who ran a small brick-built meeting house for Dissenters in Barton Street near the old East Gate. He had a long association with Gloucester, initially having been appointed as a Presbyterian lecturer based in the Cathedral during the time of the Commonwealth. He remained in Gloucester after the Restoration, despite a period of imprisonment in the dungeons of Chepstow Castle for his preaching against the Anglican Prayer Book.[27]

One of the teachers employed by Forbes was Samuel Jones, a scholar of great repute educated at Leiden University in the Netherlands. Between 1708 and 1712 Jones took over the running of the Gloucester academy, which he moved into a house in the Barton Street area owned by Henry Wintle. He took in a considerable number of students and developed what for a time was the largest dissenting academy in the south of England.[28] The education he offered covered a range of subjects centring around the theology of the Reformed Church, mathematics and logic, but it also included Latin, Greek and a number of other ancient languages. Such were the number of lectures and the required sessions of private reading that the

---

[24] H. M. Jewell, *Education in Early Modern England*, p. 41.
[25] D. Jarrett, *Britain 1688 to 1815*, Longman (1965), p. 72.
[26] B. S. Smith & E. Ralph, *A History of Bristol and Gloucestershire*, Phillimore (1972), p. 59.
[27] G. W. Counsel, *The History and Description of the City of Gloucester*, Gloucester (1829), p. 162.
[28] N. M. Herbert, *The Victoria History of the Counties of England: Gloucestershire*, volume 4, p. 119.

Figure 77: Engraving of James Forbes, Presbyterian minister who founded the Barton Street Dissenting Academy in 1696.

Figure 78: Archbishop Thomas Secker, who was educated at the Barton Street Academy (as shown in a portrait in the style of Sir Joshua Reynolds).

daily timetable there apparently began at 5 a.m.[29] Under Jones's leadership, the Gloucester academy gained a reputation as 'a most flourishing academy famed for as much learning as any one seminary among the Non-Conformists. The languages and mathematics were very much studied here'.[30]

So successful were some of the dissenting academies, like the Barton Street one, that many progressive Anglican families preferred them to traditional schools and used them as a stepping stone towards Scottish or Dutch universities.[31] Over its brief existence the Barton Street Academy educated up to a hundred students and drew young men from across the entire country, both Dissenters and others from a professional or commercial background who were attracted by the high-quality

---

[29] A. Platts and G. H. Hainton, *Education in Gloucestershire: A Short History* (1954), p. 14.
[30] I. Parker, *Dissenting Academies in England: Their Rise and Progress*, Cambridge (1914), p. 97.
[31] J. Lawson & H. Silver, *A Social History of Education in England*, p. 166.

curriculum. Jones's pupils included some who would become the religious leaders of the future, including Joseph Butler, Bishop of Durham between 1750 and 1752, and Samuel Chandler, an influential Nonconformist preacher and pamphleteer. The most famous of his pupils, however, was Thomas Secker. He came from London to the academy in 1710 at the age of fifteen, following encouragement by the great hymn-writer Isaac Watts. Secker studied for four years under Jones's guidance, learning elements of the Hebrew, Chaldee and Syriac languages as well as reviving his interest in Latin and Greek. In adult life Secker chose to join the Church of England and rose up through its ranks, becoming Bishop of Oxford in 1737 and Archbishop of Canterbury between 1758 and 1768.

In a letter written to Isaac Watts in 1711, Thomas Secker painted a glowing picture of the abilities of Samuel Jones as a teacher at this point in his career. 'Mr Jones', he wrote, 'I take to be a man of real piety, great learning and an agreeable temper, one who is very diligent in instructing all under his care, very well qualified to give instructions, and whose well-managed familiarity will always make him respected. He is very strict in keeping good order and will effectually preserve his pupils from negligence and immorality. And accordingly, I believe there are not many academies freer in general from those vices than we are'.[32]

In the same letter Secker provided a careful description of the pattern of study in the Barton Street Dissenting Academy, which at that time contained sixteen students. 'I began to learn Hebrew', he continued, 'as soon as I came hither and find myself able now to construe and give some grammatical account of about twenty verses in the easier parts of the Bible after less than an hour's preparation. We read every day two verses a-piece in the Hebrew Bible, which we turn into Greek. And this with Logic is our morning's work. Mr Jones also began about three months ago some critical lectures about the antiquity of the Hebrew language. This is what we first set about in the afternoon, which being finished we read a chapter in the Greek Testament, and after that Mathematics. We have gone through all that is commonly taught of algebra and proportion, with the six first books of Euclid. This is our daily employment, which in the morning takes up about two hours and something more in the afternoon. We are obliged to rise at five of the clock every morning and to speak Latin always, except

---

[32]   T. Gibbons, *Memoirs of the Rev Isaac Watts*, London (1780), p. 347.

when below stairs amongst the family. The people where we live are very civil and the greatest inconvenience we suffer is that we fill the house rather too much, being sixteen in number'.[33]

Whilst maintaining his academy with such apparent success, Samuel Jones was also subject to prejudice and a certain amount of persecution. The requirement for educational establishments to be licensed, as they had been since the Middle Ages, by the local bishop remained in force. In 1712 Jones found himself charged with instilling into his students 'seditious and anti-monarchical principles very prejudicial to the present Establishment in Church and State'.[34]

Jones transferred his academy to the High Street in Tewkesbury later that year. The move came about partly because of his desire to secure larger premises, but other factors played their part, such as the sudden death of James Forbes and the prejudice he faced in Gloucester. However, the success he had achieved with the Gloucester academy was not replicated at Tewkesbury. His new premises were attacked by High Church rioters celebrating the coronation of George I in 1714.[35] Shortly after this, there is a suggestion that the quality of Jones's teaching went into sharp decline as he became a heavy drinker in his later years. According to Secker's memoirs, Jones began 'to relax of his industry, to drink too much ale and small beer and to lose his temper'.[36] He died in 1719 and what was left of his academy was moved by his nephew, Jeremiah Jones, to fresh premises in Nailsworth.

The model of small dissenting academies taking in twenty or so pupils was recommended on a national scale in 1720 by John Clarke, the master of a school in Hull, in his 'Essay on the Education of Youth in Grammar Schools'.[37] He considered most grammar schools up and down the country to be little more than houses of correction for unruly boys and recommended that they be replaced with private academies to safeguard the children's morals and religious upbringing and to introduce more non-Classical subjects.

---

[33] Ibid, pp. 349–351.
[34] R. G. Ingram, *Religion, Reform and Modernity in the 18th Century*, Boydell Press (2007), p. 30.
[35] A. Randall, *Riotous Assemblies: Popular Protest in Hanoverian England*, Oxford (2006), p. 46.
[36] H. McLachlan, *English Education under the Test Acts*, Manchester (1931), p. 130.
[37] M. Seaborne, *The English School: its Architecture and Organisation 1370 – 1870*, Routledge & Kegan Paul (1971), p. 94.

Following the academy's move to Tewkesbury in 1712, however, Gloucester itself appears to have had no formal educational provision for Dissenters of any kind for most of the remaining years of the 18th century. With the grammar schools still barred against them, the sons of Nonconformist families were confined to being taught by itinerant preachers, tutors and their own parents, whereas in other comparable cities a number of Friends' Schools sprang up.[38]

It was not until comparatively late in the century that the Dissenting community in Gloucester attempted to revive the academy they once had. A project led by the Revd J. Tremlett in 1787 opened a school for young gentlemen 'in a commodious house in a very healthy and pleasant situation near the City'.[39] It offered places for twelve boarders, all of whom were 'furnished with single beds', and an additional number of day pupils keen to be instructed in the English, Latin and Greek languages, geography, writing and arithmetic. Fees were £25 per year.

---

[38] R. Lacock, 'Quakers in Gloucester; the First Fifty Years', *Transactions of the Bristol and Gloucestershire Archaeological Society* (2007), volume 125, p. 289.
[39] *Gloucester Journal*, 19th November 1787.

CHAPTER FIFTEEN

The Crypt in the 18th Century:

A School Confronting its Financial Constraints

Challenging problems

After the long period of stability the school had enjoyed under the colourful character of Abraham Heague at the end of the 17th century,[1] the fortunes of the Crypt began to suffer from a range of challenging issues. The following century saw a school in good heart continuing to provide great service to the people of Gloucester, despite the problems it faced.

One of these problems was a national decline in the attractiveness of grammar schools, which began to face difficulties virtually everywhere in the country at this time.[2] The education they provided based on Latin grammar appeared increasingly old-fashioned and anachronistic, especially in the way it neglected mathematics, which some were beginning to regard as the fundamental tool for technical progress in an age of commercial and industrial expansion.[3] One modern survey of schooling over the centuries has consequently spoken of an 'educational recession in the 18th century'.[4]

The other key challenge that faced the Crypt School in particular was a funding shortage as the school was starved of the finances it required by the City Council.[5] This was in part a reflection of changes that occurred

---

[1] See Chapter Eleven.
[2] A. C. Percival, 'Gloucestershire Grammar Schools from the 16th to the 19th Centuries', *Transactions of the Bristol and Gloucestershire Archaeological Society* (1970), volume 89, p. 114.
[3] L. W. Cowie, *Hanoverian England*, Bell & Hyman (1967), p. 31.
[4] J. Lawson & H. Silver, *A Social History of Education in England*, Methuen (1973), p. 177.
[5] N. M. Herbert, *The Victoria History of the Counties of England: Gloucestershire*, volume 4, London (1988), p. 146.

within the small elite that made up Gloucester's ruling class. As the 18th century progressed, the city merchants and traders, who in the previous century had sent their sons to the Crypt, gradually slipped out of prominence. More and more of the leading office holders instead were drawn from the ranks of the gentry who lived in the surrounding countryside and the lawyers, surgeons and other professionals of the city, all of whom tended to patronise the rival King's School.[6] Amid an atmosphere that criticised any degree of extravagance in public expenditure, the result was that insufficient funds were made available to maintain the Crypt in a flourishing state or even to pay its master an adequate salary.

The first headmaster of the 18th century, Philip Collier, seems particularly to have suffered from the tight financial constraints imposed by the Council. His annual salary was squeezed to a mere £10, which was a full £20 below the level enjoyed by his predecessor. The figure of £10 had been laid down by the foundress of the school, Joan Cooke, nearly 200 years previously. As he was not a priest, Collier was even threatened on occasions with a pay cut as Joan Cooke had originally envisaged that only £9 would be offered if a lay man took charge of the school.[7] Such a salary was woefully inadequate. More than fifty years previously one well-respected national writer on educational matters had recommended the payment of £100 a year to masters in charge of the country's best schools.[8] Although salaries rarely reached such a level, there were several schools in the country who paid their teachers between £50 and £80 in the early 18th century.[9] Under such circumstances, it comes as no surprise to find that the Crypt began to face difficulties and that complaints were raised about the quality of the education it could provide.

By 1719 the City Council was already reporting that 'the school is at present reduced to such a condition that it is of little benefit to this city and, though admonition had been freely given, no amendment has been made or is likely to be made. Parents, though burgesses, are obliged to send their

---

6   C. Heighway, *Gloucester: A History and Guide*, Alan Sutton (1985), p. 134.
7   R. Austin, *The Crypt School Gloucester*, John Bellows Gloucester (1939), p. 112.
8   T. Mark, *A New Discovery of the Old Art of Teaching School by Charles Hoole*, Manchester (1912), p. 244.
9   W. A. L. Vincent, *The Grammar Schools: Their Continuing Tradition*, John Murray (1969), p. 161.

children to other schools for education at great charges'.[10] Against the background of such complaints, Philip Collier was deprived of the headship that year.

18th-century Headmasters, Ushers and Pupils of the Crypt School	
Masters	Ushers
1701 – 1719: Philip Collier	1675 – 1709: Thomas Merrett
1719 – 1724: Richard Furney	1709 – 1724: Daniel Bond
1724 – 1750: Daniel Bond	1724 – 1727: Joseph Gegg
	1727 – 1732: Henry Church
	1732 – 1737: James Commeline
	1737 – 1750: Thomas Garner
1750 – 1788: Thomas Garner	1750 – 1753: Charles Bishop
	1753 – 1756: William Boyce
1788 – 1803: Thomas Rudge	
Well-known pupils of the 18th century: Daniel Bond; John Lightfoot; Daniel Lysons; John Moore; George Whitefield	

Under circumstances of financial constraint, the fortunes of the school were not good and it became increasingly inward-looking. Two of Collier's 18th-century successors had already served in the school as usher before their appointment as headmaster, suggesting that the Council found it difficult to attract a pool of strong candidates.[11] Daniel Bond, a graduate of Magdalen Hall, Oxford, was promoted from usher to master in 1724, holding his new post for a further twenty-six years. His successor, Thomas Garner, a Balliol graduate, had previously been Bond's usher, giving him a total length of service to the school of fifty-one years.

Although there were about fifty boys on the roll, in 1765 the condition of the Crypt was rather alarmingly described as 'fatal'.[12] It was in this year that

---

[10]   W. Page, *The Victoria History of the Counties of England: Gloucestershire*, volume 2, London (1907), p. 349.
[11]   R. Austin, *The Crypt School Gloucester*, John Bellows Gloucester (1939), p. 115.
[12]   N. M. Herbert, *The Victoria History of the Counties of England: Gloucestershire*, volume 4, p. 146.

Figure 79: The 18th-century stone-clad façade of the Crypt School (from an illustration made by John Buckler in 1827).

a meeting of the leading men of Gloucester was called at the Booth Hall to investigate the future of the school. The local press commented that 'the present fatal state of the school will induce many, 'tis presumed, to favour the steward with their company, in order to consider proper measures to revive its interest and to raise it to its late flourishing condition'.[13] The underlying problem continued to be the low level of funding and the constraints on the salary that could be offered to the master. When Bishop Benson made his visitation in the 1730s, he reported that Daniel Bond was paid a salary of £30 a year, whilst the usher, James Commeline, received £16.[14] In 1779, when Samuel Rudder wrote his *New History of Gloucestershire*, he reported that the master was still paid £30 a year, a salary well below the average for similar institutions at that time.[15]

The financial problems facing the school were tackled partly by making

[13] *Gloucester Journal*, 13th May 1765.
[14] J. Fendley, *Bishop Benson's Survey of the Diocese of Gloucester*, The Bristol and Gloucestershire Archaeological Society (2000), p. 87.
[15] S. Rudder, *A New History of Gloucestershire*, Cirencester (1779), republished by Alan Sutton in 2006, p. 128.

economies. The average amount spent by the Council in the 18th century on maintenance and the provision of books and stationery was reduced to a little over £2 a year.[16] Even greater savings came with the abolition of the post of usher after 1756. William Boyce was dismissed by the Council in September of that year, 'the deputy town clerk to give him proper notice of such discharge'.[17] It does not appear that anyone else was formally appointed to the role for the remainder of the century. 'Only one schoolmaster is now appointed' was the comment made by Thomas Rudge, headmaster from 1788, in the *History and Antiquities of Gloucester*, which he wrote in 1811.[18]

Another solution adopted by Rudge, and one common to many other late 18th-century grammar schools, was to take in extra pupils who boarded with local families and to charge them tuition fees, which meant that for the first time in its history the Crypt was no longer a 'free school' in any real sense.[19] The advertisement he placed in the local press in 1788 gave an indication of Rudge's new terms and conditions. His initial plans were for basic tuition fees of two guineas and full boarding fees of fifteen guineas. The advert ended optimistically by emphasising that 'Mr Rudge flatters himself that, by a strict attention to the moral and Classical improvement of his pupils, he shall ensure the approbation of those who may be pleased to honour him with their confidence'.[20] Within a year there had been an increase for the most senior pupils, who now faced fees of sixteen guineas for both boarding and tuition in the Classics, although younger boys aged seven and requiring teaching only in reading and English grammar continued be admitted at lower rates.[21] An advertisement of 1794 makes clear the position as the 18th century came to an end: 'Young gentlemen prepared either for the university or trade, the best assistance being procured in the writing and arithmetic branches; boarders are instructed in the Classics and treated on the most liberal principles, at sixteen guineas per annum'.[22] Nicholas Carlisle, the Somerset Secretary of

---

16 R. Austin, *The Crypt School Gloucester*, John Bellows Gloucester (1939), p. 66.
17 Ibid, p. 132.
18 T. Rudge, *The History and Antiquities* of Gloucester, J. Wood Gloucester (1811), p. 128.
19 M. Seaborne, *The English School: its Architecture and Organisation 1370 – 1870*, Routledge & Kegan Paul (1971), p. 79.
20 *Gloucester Journal*, 17th March 1788.
21 Ibid, 12th January 1789.
22 Ibid, 9th June 1794.

Antiquities who completed a survey of 475 schools across the land, said of the Crypt in 1818, 'as to the school itself, it is now in every sense a private school – the exertions of the instructor being rewarded by payments from the friends of the pupils'.[23] Some historians have expressed the view that across the country schools like the Crypt 'tended to become sinecures for their masters, who corruptly charged fees for the few pupils who came to them'.[24] In 1827 it was reported of the Crypt that there were only twelve boys at the school, each paying tuition fees of eight guineas a year.[25]

Another aspect of the poor management and governance from which the school suffered can be seen in the way in which the annual visitations made by the mayor and aldermen of Worcester degenerated into nothing more than lavish social occasions. Their visits were required by the tripartite indenture made by Joan Cooke in 1540 and were meant to support the councillors of Gloucester and make sure that they were providing adequately for the school's needs.[26] In the early 18th century these visitations seem to have achieved very little of any benefit. An account of the 1700 visitation, for example, shows that £3 1s 5d was spent on hiring a barge to transport the delegation from Upton-on-Severn, providing a 'rib of ox beef roasted for the occasion, bread, cucumber, ale, wine, candles, tobacco and pipes'. The banquet that followed the visitation was that year held at the New Bear Inn in Westgate Street, where the total bill came to a mouth-watering £55 10s 4d. In 1708 the celebration was held at the Bell Inn in Southgate Street, where the father of the future evangelist George Whitefield was landlord; the bill came to £57 2s.[27] Possibly as a result of protests from the ratepayers, the Worcester visitation came to an end in 1728, leaving no constraints on the way the school could be treated by the City Council. The situation would not improve until the 19th century, which brought a wholescale reform of urban administration in the Municipal Corporations Act of 1835.

---

23 N. Carlisle, *Concise Description of the Endowed Grammar Schools in England and Wales*, London (1818), volume I, p. 453.
24 A. Platts and G. H. Hainton, *Education in Gloucestershire: A Short History* (1954), p. 10.
25 W. Page, *The Victoria History of the Counties of England: Gloucestershire*, volume 2, p. 350.
26 See Chapter Six.
27 R. Austin, *The Crypt School Gloucester*, John Bellows Gloucester (1939), pp. 58–59.

The continuing tradition of sound instruction

Despite the very real difficulties that existed, it would be wrong to paint the 18th century as an entirely dismal period for the Crypt School. Like many other institutions in this period, the abilities and efforts of individual headmasters made all the difference to a school's fortunes and it is clear that many former pupils looked back with gratitude on the education they received at the Crypt.[28]

Two headmasters of the Crypt served the city with great distinction as record-keepers and historians of considerable note. Richard Furney, a graduate of Oriel College, Oxford, was master of the Crypt for a short period between 1719 and 1724. He has been described as 'a man of outstanding ability and learning' and was one of the first Gloucester men to take a serious interest in the city's past.[29] He catalogued the Llanthony Priory registers and reorganised the city archives.[30] Amongst other things, he wrote one of the first histories of Gloucester, which was used as a valuable source by several later writers, although he did not produce a published version himself.[31] Similarly, the final headmaster of the 18th century, Thomas Rudge, a Gloucester boy and graduate of Merton College, Oxford, published another history of the city and went on to a career of distinction as Archdeacon of Gloucester. The Crypt was fortunate to have these able men at its helm and in some decades was able to offer much coveted instruction in Greek as well as Latin.

Nor did the provision of the basic Classical education provided by the Crypt appear to suffer as a result of the school's financial difficulties, especially in the case of boys who were keen to work hard on their lessons. Academic lessons no doubt remained something of an endurance test as they required the memorisation of endless grammatical rules and procedures, but the lure of university or the ability to access a professional career helped most boys to maintain their motivation. The school benefited from the existence of the prestigious Oxford Townsend

---

28 W. A. L. Vincent, *The Grammar Schools: Their Continuing Tradition*, John Murray (1969), p. 17.

29 C. Lepper, *The Crypt School Gloucester 1539 – 1989*, Alan Sutton (1989), p. 20.

30 J. Rhodes (ed), *A Calendar of the Registers of the Priory of Llanthony by Gloucester*, Bristol and Gloucestershire Archaeological Society Record Series (2002), volume 15, p. 50.

31 Archdeacon Furney's Unpublished History of Gloucester, c. 1750, Gloucestershire Record Office D327/1.

Scholarships, which had been set up in the 1680s and enabled the Crypt to attract a number of very promising scholars throughout the 18th century.[32]

Great camaraderie clearly existed amongst those who were members of the school at this time. The one large schoolroom continued to be used for teaching much as it had been 200 years previously. A few of the boys left traces of the time they spent there in the form of carvings still visible in the wooden panelling of the schoolroom today.[33] They still sat on benches, which they referred to as forms, with the master's desk strategically placed in front of them. Writing in 1819, the Gloucestershire antiquarian Thomas Fosbrooke preserved a story about how boys and masters in schools such as the Crypt bonded over the smoking of their pipes in this period. 'After tobacco came into use', he wrote, 'the children carried pipes in their satchels with their books, which their mothers took care to fill, that it might serve instead of breakfast. At the accustomed hour everyone laid aside his book and lit his pipe, the master smoking with them and teaching them how to hold their pipes and draw in the tobacco'.[34]

Several 18th-century Crypt boys went on to win great distinction in adult life. Daniel Lysons graduated from Magdalen College, Oxford, in 1745 and after a few years practising medicine in Gloucester became physician at the General Infirmary in Bath.[35] John Lightfoot of Newent gained one of the Townsend Scholarships to attend Pembroke College, Oxford, and was elected as a Fellow of the Royal Society in 1785; a keen botanist, he became curator of the private natural history collection of Margaret Bentinck, the Dowager Duchess of Portland, and wrote a pioneering study of plants and fungi, the *Flora Scotica*, which was based on his travels around Scotland. Another Crypt pupil was Daniel Bond, nephew of the headmaster of the same name; he enjoyed a long career in the 1770s and 1780s as a Birmingham landscape artist.

It was common in the 18th century, as now, for pupils to move from one school to another. Within Gloucester boys regularly seem to have passed from the Crypt to King's and vice versa for a variety of reasons. One of those who did so was John Moore, a talented boy who lived in a butcher's

---

32   See Chapter Eleven.

33   H. W. Allen, *The Crypt School: 475 Years*, Bristol (2014), p. 10.

34   T. D. Fosbrooke, *An Original History of the City of Gloucester*, London (1819), republished by Alan Sutton in 1986, p. 151.

35   *The Gentleman's Magazine*, London (1800), volume 70, p. 392.

Figure 80: Dr Daniel Lysons, a Crypt pupil in the 1730s.

Figure 81: Archbishop John Moore, a Crypt pupil in the 1740s.

shop and house next to the Fleece Inn. He enrolled at King's at the age of seven in 1737, but moved to the Crypt in 1739 probably to take advantage of one of the Townsend Scholarships, which he secured in 1744.[36] An outline of his biography states that: 'born in 1730, John Moore in course of time became a scholar at the Crypt Grammar School, then under the mastership of the Rev Daniel Bond. His progress was good and his general conduct satisfactory. While diligently gaining acquaintance with Latin nouns and Greek verbs, he was helpful to his father in business. His persevering ability rendered him successful at school.'[37] In later life Moore rose up through the ranks of the church eventually to become Archbishop of Canterbury in 1783, in which capacity he presided over the marriage of the Prince Regent and Caroline of Brunswick.

Another boy with a similar story was the future evangelist George Whitefield, who was born in the Bell Inn in Southgate Street in 1714. He also moved to the Crypt after a short spell at King's, where he was enrolled in January 1726.[38] Whitefield's father had died when he was two, leaving his wife, Elizabeth, to run the inn and look after seven children, of whom George was the youngest.[39] It is likely under such circumstances that raising the fees for King's was a struggle for the family, whereas the cost of attending the Crypt would have been significantly lower. In the memoirs he published in adult life, Whitefield wrote: 'when I was about twelve, I was placed at a school called St Mary de Crypt in Gloucester, the last grammar school I ever went to.'[40]

At the Crypt Whitefield was given a number of opportunities for public speaking, especially on important occasions which were the equivalent of a modern speech day.[41] 'Having a good elocution and memory', he wrote, 'I was remarked for making speeches before the corporation at their annual visitation.'[42] He also showed a keen interest in drama, preferring it to the study of the Classics, and he took part in a number of school plays. These plays, usually tragedies or comedies adapted from those written by

---

36 J. R. S. Whiting, *King's School Gloucester*, Orchard & Ind Gloucester (1990), p. 44.
37 J. Stratford, *Gloucestershire Biographical Notes*, Gloucester (1887), p. 145–46.
38 D. Robertson, *The King's School Gloucester*, Phillimore (1974), p. 85.
39 J. Gillies, *Memoirs of the Life of the Revered George Whitefield*, London (1772), p. 2.
40 'Memoirs of George Whitefield' printed in *The Scots Magazine*, Edinburgh (1770), volume 32, p. 591.
41 A. D. Belden, *George Whitefield*, London (1961), p. 7.
42 'Memoirs of George Whitefield' printed in *The Scots Magazine*, volume 32, p. 591.

Classical authors, were put on at various points in the school year, particularly Christmas, and were seen as a good way to encourage boys to speak Latin. So keen was Whitefield to take part that it is said that on occasions he played truant from normal lessons in order to master his parts fully.[43] Whitefield's own account was as follows: 'During the time of my being at school I was very fond of reading plays together to prepare myself for acting them. My master, seeing how mine and my schoolfellows' vein run, composed something of this kind for us himself and caused me to dress myself in girl's clothes (which I had often done) to act a part before the corporation. The remembrance of this has often covered me with confusion of face and I hope will do so even to the end of my life'.[44] Despite the embarrassment he felt in taking on female roles, it was to his participation in the plays written by his teacher, Daniel Bond, that Whitefield attributed the powerful and exceptionally clear voice he developed as a preacher. He went on to acknowledge 'my particular thanks

Figure 82: Evangelist George Whitefield, a Crypt pupil in the 1720s.

---

43   F. A. Hyett, *Gloucester in National History*, John Bellows Gloucester (1906), p. 133.
44   'Memoirs of George Whitefield' printed in *The Scots Magazine*, volume 32, p. 592.

Figure 83: Eighteenth-century carving still visible in the old Crypt schoolroom today.

due to my master for the great pains he took with me and his other scholars in teaching us to speak and write correctly'.[45]

The decision to leave the Crypt in 1729 was apparently Whitefield's own and was made against the wishes of his mother. 'Before I was fifteen', he wrote, 'having – as I thought – made a sufficient progress in the Classics and at the bottom longing to be set at liberty from the confinement of a school, I one day told my mother, since her circumstances would not permit her to give me a university education, more learning I thought would spoil me for a tradesman and therefore I judged it best not to learn Latin any longer. She at first refused to consent, but my corruptions soon got the better of her good nature'.[46] For about a year, 'wearing my blue apron', he worked in the family inn, serving ale and cleaning, but eventually with the help of extra tuition from Daniel Bond, he secured a place as a servitor at Pembroke College, the Oxford college with which the Crypt was associated. This enabled him to study for a degree whilst carrying out domestic duties in lieu of paying student fees. He preached his first sermon in 1736 with great impact from the pulpit that still stands in St Mary de Crypt Church today. Remembering it many years later, he recalled: 'Some few mocked, but most for the present seemed struck and I have since heard that a complaint had been made to the bishop that I drove fifteen mad. The worthy prelate, I am informed, wished that the madness might not be

---

45   C. Lepper, *The Crypt School Gloucester 1539 – 1989*, p. 22.
46   'Memoirs of George Whitefield' printed in *The Scots Magazine*, volume 32, p. 592.

forgotten before next Sunday'.[47] Thereafter Whitefield spent much of his life energetically preaching at open air meetings throughout Britain and the American colonies. His loud voice and the oratorical skills he had developed at the Crypt stood him in good stead; Benjamin Franklin calculated that he could be heard by 30,000 people at any one time.[48]

Whitefield, like many of his contemporaries, remained indebted throughout his life to the education he had received, albeit with some reluctance, at the Crypt, a school still in good heart, despite the financial difficulties the 18th century imposed on it.

---

[47] S. Drew, *Sermons on Important Subjects by the Rev George Whitefield*, London (1832), p. v.
[48] B. M. Miller, *Benjamin Franklin: American Genius*, Chicago (2010), p. 39.

CHAPTER SIXTEEN

The 18th Century at King's:

A School of Fluctuating Fortunes

A difficult first half century

Gloucester's other 18th-century grammar school, King's, differed from the Crypt in a number of striking ways. Still generally known as the College School, it had a more exclusive feel to it. Whereas the Crypt was situated on the busy thoroughfare of Southgate Street, the schoolroom at King's could only be accessed by using one of the narrow spiral staircases inside the Cathedral. Whereas the City Council formed the dominant influence on the fortunes of the Crypt, the governing body of King's was formed entirely by the Dean and members of the Cathedral Chapter. The Crypt catered essentially for the sons of Gloucester traders and businessmen, but the clientele at King's drew on the whole of Gloucestershire and a sizeable proportion of its pupils were boarders. There were also curriculum differences. Although both schools successfully provided their pupils with a strong grounding in Latin grammar, the programme at King's was broader, including 'modern' subjects such as French and dancing, and crucially the opportunity for advanced study in Greek, which was regarded as the high point of an 18th-century education and was not always available at the Crypt.

The qualities looked for in an 18th-century King's School headmaster were outlined when an advertisement was placed in the *Gloucester Journal* in 1787. 'We, the Dean and Chapter of Gloucester, do hereby invite such gentlemen as may think themselves qualified to undertake that office to apply to us as candidates for the same, at the same time requesting that none may take the trouble to apply who is not in priest's orders, completely skilled in the Greek and Latin languages, a graduate of one of the two universities and furnished with unexceptionable testimonies of his sound faith, piety and good morals'.[1]

---

[1]   *Gloucester Journal*, 19th November 1787.

Early and Mid-18th-century Headmasters and Ushers at King's	
Masters	Ushers
1712 – 1718: Benjamin Newton	1709 – 1718: Henry Abbot
1718 – 1742: William Alexander	1718 – 1727: Jeremiah Butt
	1727 – 1739: Joseph Gegg
	1739 – 1742: Edward Sparkes
1742 – 1777: Edward Sparkes	1742 – 1761: John Palmer
	1761 – 1777: Charles Bishop

'The King's School retained the confidence of the leading Gloucestershire families, who sent generation after generation of their sons to school there in the eighteenth century'.[2] This judgement by two 20th-century historians seems to have been based on the legacy of Maurice Wheeler, the broad curriculum he established and the healthy pupil roll that he had achieved by the time of his retirement.[3] In other respects, however, the school appears to have drifted into a period of stagnation following the departure of its great innovative headmaster, leaving the first part of the 18th century as a rather lacklustre period.

Wheeler's immediate successor, Benjamin Newton, who was headmaster from 1712 to 1718, was in some respects a promising choice. By chance he has become the first headmaster whose portrait survives, an engraving included as a frontispiece in a book of sermons which he published in retirement. Growing up as a child in Leicester, it is said that he showed 'a very early and remarkable genius for learning'.[4] For some years before he left school, he had developed such a retentive memory that he was able to read the morning newspapers and then recite the articles word for word to all and sundry later in the day. It is also claimed that as an adult he was so devoted to the pursuit of learning that he was scarcely ever seen without a book in his hands.[5] Despite these abilities, Newton also had a reputation

---

2   A. Platts and G. H. Hainton, *Education in Gloucestershire: A Short History* (1954), Gloucestershire County Council (1953), p. 13.

3   See Chapter Thirteen.

4   J. N. Langston, 'Headmasters and Ushers of the King's (College) School, Gloucester', *Records of Gloucester Cathedral,* volume III, H. Osborne Gloucester (1928), p. 221.

5   D. Robertson, *The King's School Gloucester*, Phillimore (1974), p. 73.

Figure 84: **Two pages from the King's School copy book of 1715; they transcribe prayers and the text of one of Headmaster Benjamin Newton's sermons, which referred to 'deliverance from the great and apparent dangers' of the Jacobite Rebellion of that year.**

for 'finding teaching rather irksome'.[6] Alongside his duties at King's, he took on other responsibilities in the church as Vicar of St Nicholas in Gloucester and as Rector of Taynton seven miles away. The real focus of his energies, however, went into becoming a burgess and freeman of the city and into writing articles for the increasing number of newspapers that sprang up at this time. The school register, which Maurice Wheeler had commenced with scrupulous care in 1685, seems to have been entirely neglected and no names at all were added for the years 1714 – 18.[7] The school was left to drift into a gradual decline and by 1739 the Dean and Chapter were reporting that 'parents and others are become generally prejudiced against the said school'.[8]

---

6   J. R. S. Whiting, *King's School Gloucester*, Orchard & Ind Gloucester (1990), p. 41.
7   Copy of the 'Scholae Regiae Glocestriensis Liber Censualis' in the King's School Museum.
8   W. Page, *The Victoria History of the Counties of England: Gloucestershire*, volume 2, London (1907), p. 332.

One of the problems the school faced, albeit not quite to the extent we have seen at the Crypt,[9] was the low salaries available for the master and usher. Their rate of pay had been specified in the Cathedral statutes of 1544 and was fairly typical for its day. The master's £13 a year plus other benefits initially ranked him considerably above the canons of the new Cathedral and the usher's £7 put him on a par with the lay clerks.[10] By the 18th century many office holders had received increments to take into account decades of inflation and in Gloucester even the minor canons got £150 a year. The salaries of the master and usher, however, remained very low and the Dean and Chapter cited the figures specified in the statutes as justification for resisting an increase. The results were

Figure 85: The earliest existing portrait of a Gloucester headmaster, an engraving by Gerard Vandergucht of Bloomsbury for a book Benjamin Newton published in 1736.

twofold: first, high-ranking educationalists failed to consider King's as a worthy headship; and second, those who did take on the job were forced to treat it as a part-time occupation that needed to be supplemented by other sources of revenue, usually other positions in the church held in plurality. As late as the 1830s investigations by the Ecclesiastical Commissioners found that the master and usher were paid only £20 and £10 respectively, forcing them to undertake other roles, which inevitably resulted in conflicting calls on their time and attention.[11]

---

9   See Chapter Fifteen.
10 See Chapter Seven.
11 W. Page, *The Victoria History of the Counties of England: Gloucestershire*, volume 2, pp. 326 & 334.

Another problem facing the school that lasted for more than a decade was the ambitious personality of one of its ushers, Joseph Gegg, and the long-running clash this caused with the collegiate nature of the school. After becoming usher in 1727, Gegg generally neglected his duties and set about enriching himself with the pluralism for which the 18th century became notorious. Throughout his time as usher, he was also Vicar of Ashleworth and Corse, and he held the chaplaincy of Gloucester Gaol.[12] All of this made him a man of independent means, enabling him to vanish for weeks on end without permission, sometimes travelling to France, disregarding his responsibilities and making himself absent from both lessons and Cathedral services.[13] The headmaster charged with disciplining this ambitious character was William Alexander, who has been described as 'a gentleman of great learning and candour and of extensive charity to the poor'.[14] Sadly, these were not qualities that equipped him to deal with Gegg and it was left to the Dean, Daniel Newcombe, eventually to use the clauses in Henry VIII's statutes to secure his removal. Gegg was given a warning from the Dean in 1736 'for not attending Divine service on holy days and holy day eves and lying out of the precincts of the college without asking leave of the Dean'.[15] Three years later he was dismissed from his post entirely on the grounds that 'it appears that the school has for some time been declining, chiefly through Mr Gegg's negligence of the proper school hours in the morning, for many years together, whereby the lower boys have not been duly forwarded in their learning'.[16] Specifically, Gegg was accused of 'taking the extravagant liberty of leaving the school at two of the clock in the afternoon and absenting himself from the scholars several days in the week until the last bell has been rung for evening prayers in the Cathedral'.[17] It was alleged that on numerous occasions classes were left unattended and copying had become rife among the boys. Gegg fought back by using the summer assizes of 1741 to sue the Dean and Chapter for unfair dismissal and a loss of income up to £300; at one point he even secured the assistance of a local blacksmith to barricade himself inside the

---

12 D. Robertson, *The King's School Gloucester*, p. 76.
13 J. R. S. Whiting, *King's School Gloucester*, p. 41.
14 *Gloucester Journal*, 4th May 1742.
15 J. N. Langston, *Headmasters and Ushers of the King's (College) School, Gloucester*, p. 227.
16 W. Page, *The Victoria History of the Counties of England: Gloucestershire*, volume 2, p. 332.
17 D. Robertson, *The King's School Gloucester*, p. 78.

Figure 86: The judgement of Bishop Martin Benson that confirmed the dismissal of the controversial King's School usher, Joseph Gegg.

schoolroom, causing such a disturbance that the rest of the school had to be moved to another room in the Cathedral from Michaelmas until Christmas.[18]

Some famous names associated with the school

After the drama of the Gegg case, life at King's quietened down into a period of welcome, though unremarkable, stability. William Alexander died in post in 1742 and the school was then presided over by its longest-serving 18th-century headmaster, Edward Sparkes. He was an Eton boy who graduated from King's College, Cambridge; he began his teaching

---

[18]   J. R. S. Whiting, *King's School Gloucester*, p. 42.

career as usher at King's and married his predecessor's daughter, Mary Alexander.[19] As with previous masters, the demands of holding more than one post in plurality once again meant that Sparkes failed to prioritise the needs of the school. His time was limited as he took on the parish of Hartpury and eventually added Churcham to his responsibilities. The lack of care he appeared to take in keeping up Wheeler's pupil register may be symptomatic of his whole approach. It suggests that little pride was taken in the way the school was run and that the standard of education Sparkes provided was likely to have had its limitations. No names of any new pupils at all were entered between 1743 and 1748, where there is a completely blank page in the register.[20] One of those thought to have attended but not to have had his name recorded was Button Gwinnett, who was born at Down Hatherley in 1735. In later life he went on to become Governor of the Colony of Georgia and one of the first signatories of the American Declaration of Independence. Another omission was the future headmaster, Thomas Stock, who is known to have entered the school in 1757, for which year the page in the register is badly torn.

Figure 87: Button Gwinnett, signatory to the US Declaration of Independence, who was probably at King's in the 1740s.

Despite the thirty-five years of Edward Sparkes's headship not being regarded as a period of great academic prowess, he does seem to have had a certain personal charisma that enabled him to recruit boys of high calibre. It was claimed of Sparkes that 'his goodness of heart and genuine erudition conciliated the love and respect of his scholars; and all must regard his memory with gratitude who consider that, under his tuition, were formed many who have been and still are shining ornaments of this county'.[21]

Among those who were educated at King's under Sparkes were a

---

19   D. Robertson, *The King's School Gloucester*, p. 100.
20   Copy of the 'Scholae Regiae Glocestriensis Liber Censualis' in the King's School Museum.
21   *Gloucester Journal*, 2nd May 1785.

Figure 88: John Stafford Smith, composer of the tune of the American national anthem, who was educated at King's in the 1760s.

Figure 89: Caricature of 'Jemmy' Wood, eccentric Gloucester banker, who enrolled at King's in 1768.

number who in adulthood were destined to take on leading roles in their city and their country. One of these was Robert Raikes, who joined the school in 1751 when he was already fourteen years of age; he would inevitably have attended other schools previously, leading to the suggestion that, like several others, he probably received some of his education at the Crypt.[22] In adult life Raikes would win national acclaim as a pioneer of prison reform and the Sunday school movement.[23] Another well-known King's pupil was James, Jacob or 'Jemmy' Wood, who enrolled in 1768; he eventually took over his grandfather's Gloucester Old Bank in Westgate Street and became such a well-known eccentric millionaire that Charles Dickens possibly had him in mind when creating the character of Ebenezer Scrooge. Other pupils from this time to win national acclaim included William Hawkins, Oxford Professor of Poetry, and John Stafford Smith,

---

[22] F. Booth, *Robert Raikes of Gloucester*, Redhill (1980), p. 36.
[23] See Chapter Seventeen.

who became organist at the Chapel Royal and composed the tune to which the words of the 'Star Spangled Banner' were later added and eventually adopted as the American national anthem.[24]

Famous 18th-century Old Boys of the King's School		
George Whitefield	Year of Admission 1726	Preacher and Methodist religious leader in Britain and the American colonies Completed his education at the Crypt
John Moore	1737	Archbishop of Canterbury responsible for the royal marriage of George IV to Caroline of Brunswick Completed his education at the Crypt
Button Gwinnett	c. 1744	Governor of Georgia and signatory to the US Declaration of Independence
Robert Raikes	1751	Prison reformer and founder of the Sunday school movement Possibly began his education at the Crypt before joining King's
John Henry Williams	1755	Leading churchman who opposed war against Revolutionary France
Thomas Stock	1757	Social reformer and scholarly Headmaster of the King's School
John Stafford Smith	1760	Organist at Chapel Royal and composer of the US national anthem tune, the 'Star Spangled Banner'
Joseph White	1764	Orientalist, theologian and Regius Professor of Hebrew at Oxford
Jemmy Wood	1768	Eccentric millionaire, owner of the Old Gloucester Bank and possible inspiration for Dickens's Scrooge
Joseph Parsons	1775	Classical and oriental scholar who edited the *Great Oxford Septuagint*
Henry Philpotts	1783	Bishop of Exeter and political figure involved in controversies over the Poor Law, Peterloo Massacre and the Great Reform Act
John Philpotts	1784	MP for Gloucester four times between 1830 and 1847

---

[24] J. R. S. Whiting, *King's School Gloucester*, p. 45.

Following the reforms made by Maurice Wheeler, many of the Cathedral choristers were educated at King's in the 18th century, although it did not become compulsory for them to join the school until the mid-19th century. Eight choristers continued to be maintained and their circumstances were probably as described by the antiquarian Thomas Fosbrooke in 1819: 'The choristers of the Cathedral have a right of admission and instruction in the King's grammar school, and very frequently are of the numbers included in it. The parents of some boys often find it suits their purposes best to request leave to have their children confined more to the learning of writing and arithmetic in other schools of the city, which permission is granted to them, provided their attendance at the Cathedral is regularly observed'.[25]

The revival of excellence at King's from the 1770s

The fortunes of the school were reinvigorated when Thomas Stock became headmaster in 1777. The son of a wealthy freeman and grocer who ran a business from premises near the Cross, Stock was himself a pupil at King's in the 1760s. He graduated as a B.A. at Pembroke College, Oxford, and secured his M.A. there three years later.[26] After a period as a curate in Berkshire, he was appointed headmaster at King's in 1777 along with a new usher, Thomas Evans. Unlike some of his predecessors, Stock was not a self-seeking pluralist and combined the headship with only minor posts, being curate at St John's Northgate and the adjoining parish of St Aldate, both of which were in close proximity to

Figure 90: Sketch of Thomas Stock, headmaster 1777 – 87, made by Robert Dowling.

---

25   T. D. Fosbrooke, *An Original History of the City of Gloucester*, London (1819), reprinted by Alan Sutton (1986), p. 116.

26   A. Morgan, *Reverend Thomas Stock: Man of Shadows*, St John's Northgate pamphlet (2015), p. 3.

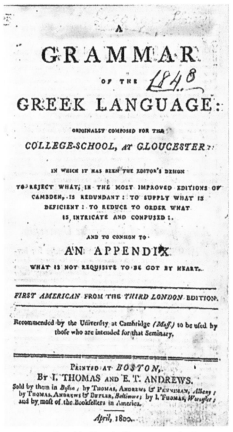

A

GRAMMAR

OF THE *1848*

GREEK LANGUAGE:

ORIGINALLY COMPOSED FOR THE

COLLEGE-SCHOOL, AT GLOUCESTER:

IN WHICH IT HAS BEEN THE EDITOR'S DESIGN

TO REJECT WHAT, IN THE MOST IMPROVED EDITIONS OF
CAMBDEN, IS REDUNDANT: TO SUPPLY WHAT IS
DEFICIENT: TO REDUCE TO ORDER WHAT
IS INTRICATE AND CONFUSED:.

AND TO CONSIGN TO

AN APPENDIX

WHAT IS NOT REQUISITE TO BE GOT BY HEART.

FIRST AMERICAN FROM THE THIRD LONDON EDITION.

Recommended by the University at Cambridge (Mass.) to be used by
those who are intended for that Seminary.

PRINTED AT BOSTON,

BY I. THOMAS AND E. T. ANDREWS.

Sold by them in Boston; by THOMAS, ANDREWS & PENNIMAN, Albany;
by THOMAS, ANDREWS & BUTLER, Baltimore; by I. THOMAS, Worcester;
and by most of the Booksellers in America.

April, 1800.

Figure 91: Stock's Greek Grammar, which circulated widely in the USA in the early 1800s.

the school, meaning that the duties he undertook there could be combined relatively easily with the many responsibilities he had at King's.[27]

In contrast to his immediate predecessors, Thomas Stock was a man of great vision, educational expertise and energy. He used his time at King's to revolutionise the teaching of Greek in the school, for which he gained a national reputation as one of the leading educationalists of his day.[28] In a distinct departure from all previous practice, he insisted that Greek could be learnt directly from English rather than through Latin. The novelty of this approach cannot be overemphasised, since it opened up the prospect for schoolboys all over the country to engage in the glories of Classical Greek literature without having to endure years of Latin drudgery. Stock's achievements were later reported in the national press along the following lines: 'That this taste for Greek in particular has been fostered by the old grammar schools none can doubt, and to no one of them are the public more indebted than to the Cathedral School at Gloucester, for perhaps it may be but partially known that this school was the first to break down the barbarous custom of teaching Greek through the Latin Language and first dared (for at that time it was a daring act) to assert in practice that, as the English was nearer the Greek in idiom, so it was the best medium for initiation into that language. One of the great reformers in this respect, whose name is well-known to

27 F. Booth, *Robert Raikes of Gloucester*, p. 79.
28 J. R. S. Whiting, *King's School Gloucester*, p. 43.

our literary readers, was the Rev Thomas Stock, late Headmaster of the College School at Gloucester'.[29]

Stock's reputation as an educational reformer spread far and wide. His textbook of 1780, *A Compendious Grammar of the Greek Language*, enjoyed a strong circulation and became one of the main texts used for teaching Greek declensions, adjectives, tenses and syntax across the country. In the preface Stock explained that 'the grammar is written in English because boys at their entrance upon Greek rudiments have seldom a competent knowledge of the Latin Language; that time therefore, which has been usually wasted in finding out the meaning of Latin rules, may be now employed in the immediate attainment and application of such as will be no sooner read than comprehended'.[30] Several editions of the book were brought out in the United States by John S. Popkin, who was Elliot Professor of Greek at Harvard, with the title *A Grammar of the Greek Language with an Appendix Originally Composed for the College School at Gloucester.* For several generations it was the only Greek Grammar permitted for use in New England and was known as the *Gloucester Greek Grammar.* A copy once used by Thomas Jefferson found its way into the Library of Congress.[31]

Stock's time as headmaster, although it amounted to no more than a decade, revived the standing of King's in all sorts of ways. With his encouragement, the year 1783 saw the creation of the first Old Boys' society and the first recorded reunion dinner for former pupils of the school. The society's first president, Joseph Chester, who had been a pupil in the 1750s at the same time as Stock, announced the meeting in the following terms: 'It having been proposed to establish an annual meeting of the gentlemen educated at the College School, the first meeting will be held on Friday the 3rd of October next at the Booth Hall Inn, where the company of any gentlemen there educated will be esteemed a favour'.[32] Thereafter reunions were held annually with the Bell Inn and the King's Head featuring as locations as well as the Booth Hall.

Stock had been a totally committed headmaster, and it was only in 1787 when he was promoted to Rector of St John's Northgate that he decided to

---

29   *London Illustrated News*, 30th November 1844.
30   T. Stock, *A Compendious Grammar of the Greek Language*, London (1780), p. iv.
31   G. E. Littlefield, *Early Schools and Schoolbooks of New England*, Boston (1904), p. 272.
32   *Gloucester Journal*, 20th September 1783.

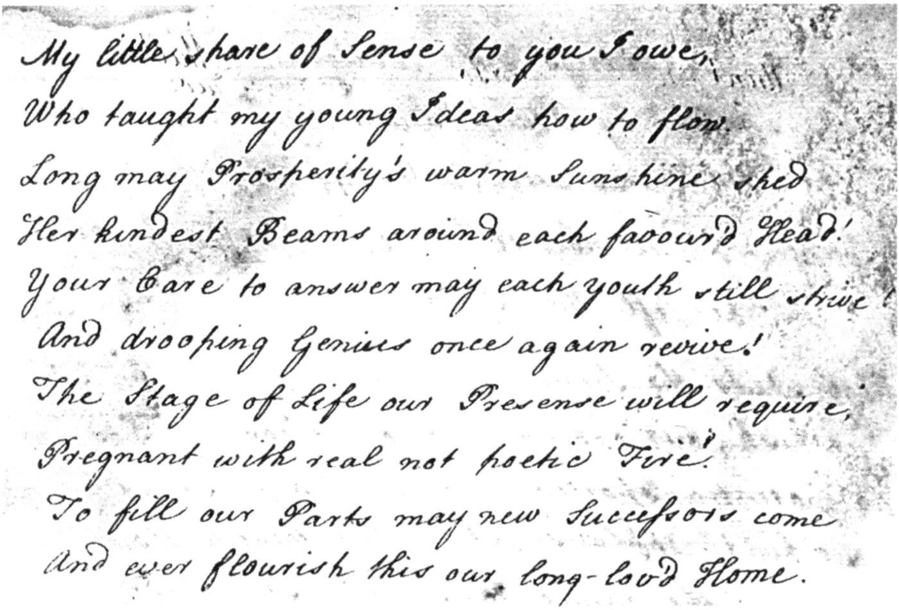
My little share of Sense to you I owe,
Who taught my young Ideas how to flow.
Long may Prosperity's warm Sunshine shed
Her kindest Beams around each favour'd Head!
Your Care to answer may each youth still strive
And drooping Genius once again revive!
The Stage of Life our Presense will require,
Pregnant with real not poetic Fire!
To fill our Parts may new Successors come
And ever flourish this our long-lov'd Home.

Figure 92: Poem penned to his teachers by Philip Dauncey, a boarder from Wotton-under-Edge, as part of an address delivered at Christmas 1776.

resign his post at the school. For the next sixteen years it is said that he devoted himself to parish life and 'gave self-effacing and devoted service'.[33] One of those taught at King's by Stock, the Gloucester solicitor and antiquarian George Counsel, described him as 'a man of great literary attainments and most exemplary conduct; and notwithstanding he made it the business and pleasure of his life to go about doing good by instruction in righteousness and works of charity, yet he never sought the applause of men'.[34] The impact of Stock's teaching on boys such as George Counsel was lifelong; in the early years of his career Counsel recalled how he was apprenticed in an ironmonger's shop, where 'he sat behind the counter and read Virgil and other Latin classics. He often served a customer with a pennyworth of tacks with his Latin author in his hand'.[35]

33 N. M. Herbert, *The Victoria History of the Counties of England: Gloucestershire*, volume 4, London (1988), p. 158.

34 G. W. Counsel, letter published in *The Evangelical Magazine and Missionary Chronicle*, London (1832), vol x, p. 488.

35 Note by H. Y. J. Taylor written in a copy of G. W. Counsel's *Some Account of the Life and Martyrdom of John Hooper* (1840).

When Thomas Stock died in 1803 the *Gloucester Journal* recorded that he was 'possessed with sincere and ardent piety' and was 'scrupulously just in all his dealings, inoffensive, kind and cheerful in domestic and social life'.[36] His monument in the south aisle of the Cathedral refers to him being 'diligent, learned and pious, successful in conveying instruction both to his pupils and parishioners'.

Late 18th-century Headmasters and Ushers of the College School	
Masters	Ushers
1777 – 1787: Thomas Stock	1777 – 1784: Thomas Evans
	1784 – 1788: Arthur Benoni Evans
1788 – 1841: Arthur Benoni Evans	1788 – 1794: Daniel Lewis
	1794 – 1815: William Hornidge

Arthur Benoni Evans, a graduate of Merton College, Oxford, was headmaster at King's from 1788 until 1841. As he had already done a four-year stint as usher, his career at the school stretched to a record of fifty-seven years. His period in office as the longest serving headmaster King's has ever had would have been enough to ensure his memory. In addition, however, Evans was another first-class Classical scholar who maintained the traditions and standards of Stock and the upward projection of the school. When Nicholas Carlisle produced his survey of grammar schools throughout England and Wales in 1818, he credited Evans's work by noting that 'the Cathedral School of Gloucester has been for many years in great repute and estimation'.[37] Another writer, Maria Hackett, a Birmingham philanthropist who conducted a national study of cathedral schools in the early 19th century, rated the boys at Gloucester among the best catered for anywhere in the country. 'Their duty is performed equally well with that of any Cathedral', she wrote, 'which stands the foremost of this praise. The choristers are always looked after by the Dean and prebendaries with all due care and kindness, making allowance for their youth'.[38]

---

36 J. Stratford, *Robert Raikes and Others: Founders of Sunday Schools*, London (1880), p. 109.
37 N. Carlisle, *A Concise Description of the Endowed Grammar Schools in England and Wales*, volume 1, London (1818), p. 451.
38 M. Hackett, *Brief Account of the Cathedral and Collegiate Schools*, London (1827), p. 32.

Figure 93: Colour version of a line drawing showing recreation at the King's School, c. 1840, by Art master Henry Brown; the schoolroom and Chapter House form the background.

In writing his history of Gloucester in 1829 George Counsel, who had been a pupil at King's in the 1750s, said 'the present very learned master, the Revd A. B. Evans, is justly esteemed for the extent of his Classical attainments as well as for his intimate acquaintance with most of the modern languages'.[39] Those who were taught by Evans seem to have held him in almost universal high regard. It is said that they nicknamed him 'Bold Arthur' and each year presented him with a silver leek as a jibe at his Welsh ancestry.[40] Joseph Ellis, who was a pupil at the school in the 1790s, used to reminisce about how Evans's teaching enabled him even in his old age to recite pages of Homer without fault. 'It is remarkable', said his son, 'how Arthur Benoni Evans drummed Greek repetition into the boys' heads, for to the very last my father, who was at the school, could repeat a good page of Homer's *Iliad* without a mistake'.[41] Another of his pupils, Edward Hawkins from Minsterworth, stated: 'I had ample opportunity for appreciating not only the repute in which he was held of being a thoroughly

---

[39] G. W. Counsel, *The History and Description of the City of Gloucester*, Gloucester (1829), p. 181.

[40] J. R. S. Whiting, *King's School Gloucester*, p. 48.

[41] F. Hannam-Clark, *Memories of the College School Gloucester*, Gloucester (1890), p. 19.

good Greek scholar, but of his aptitude and diligence in instilling into his pupils an accurate knowledge of that language.' Writing many years later when he was a canon at Llandaff Cathedral, he also commented that 'my recollection of the care and management of the boys while out of school leads me to think that the system he adopted was an easier and sterner one than would meet with approval in the present age'.

The pattern of life established at King's over the years continued with very little change until well into middle years of the 19th century, when Arthur Benoni Evans finally died. The schoolroom remained in its Tudor

Figure 94: The names of 18th-century schoolboys on the wall of the Cathedral's Lady Chapel: (upper) William Turner, who came from the hamlet of Througham, near Bisley; and (lower) William Butlin, a boarder from Buckingham.

location in the room now used as the Cathedral Library. It was to all appearances virtually the same as it had been more than a century earlier in Wheeler's day. 'During the greater part of the time I was at the school', wrote Canon Hawkins, 'we always did our work in the old schoolroom, to which we ascended from the playground, if I remember rightly, by some thirty or forty steps, and which was divided into two parts by a high railing, each arranged in classes for the upper and lower schools'.[42] Hawkins also described the 'very small and confined' old house, where Arthur Benoni Evans lived with a number of boarding pupils, perhaps as many as thirty. It was situated in the area now known at King's as the Gym Yard and was entered from Little Cloister through a doorway which can still be identified in the wall of the Dark Cloister passage. The house was demolished in the 1840s when Evans's successor relocated to new premises in St Lucy's Gardens at the corner of Hare Lane and Pitt Street.

As in Wheeler's day, the school playground extended beneath the old schoolroom from the north transept of the Cathedral as far as the end of the Lady Chapel. In the space between the headmaster's house and the Chapter House there was a fives court. The boys of this period developed a fad for inscribing their names on the walls of the Cathedral around this area, especially the north wall of the Lady Chapel and the wall of the north ambulatory. Whilst the majority of the names date from the early 19th century, some were cut in the 1790s, including those of William Turner, William Butlin, Thomas Croome, Samuel Fisher, George Price and Jacob Hammond. There has been a tendency for some members of the modern Cathedral community to blame King's School boys for graffiti of any kind appearing on the Cathedral site. Whilst there is no proof that the boys were responsible for anything scratched inside the Cathedral, on the walls that surrounded their playground it is a different story. The names here are carved deep into the stone and most of the letters are precise and accurate. They are quite unlike the casual graffiti plastered over some of the monuments inside the Cathedral. They must have taken a long time to complete and are therefore unlikely to have been done 'illegally' simply because a master's back was turned. One intriguing possibility is that it was a special privilege to be allowed to leave a name, perhaps as a rite of passage or a reward for good work, something akin to the honours boards that sprang up in most schools in the Victorian age.

---

42   Ibid, p. 20.

As the 18th century reached its end, a group of King's School boys met on 20th May 1800 to create a historical record of the key events of the beginning of the new century. Their names were Charles Morgan, Edmund Hopkinson, William Griffith and William Chavasse. Alongside an account of an attempted assassination of King George III in Hyde Park and news of campaigns against Napoleonic France, the boys recorded on the parchment they created that fresh lead had just been laid on the roof of the Lady Chapel. They noted that there were thirty-one boarders at the school and nearly the same number of day boys. Arthur Benoni Evans was acknowledged as uppermaster and William Hornidge (who is going to marry a Miss Snowden in June) as undermaster. Mr Hughes was recorded as writing master, Mr Duchemin as French teacher, Mr Sykes dancing master and Mrs Smith housekeeper.[43]

King's seemed to be in good form and to have a sense of the importance of recording its history, a reflection perhaps of the long tradition of study and scholarship already behind it and the important role the school had developed in shaping some of the leading figures of late 18th-century society.

---

[43] Transcript in *The King's School Magazine* (1971), pp. 17–18; the original parchment was said to have been in the keeping of Mr Clive of St Peter's School.

CHAPTER SEVENTEEN

Charity Schools and Sunday Schools:

Moves towards Mass Schooling

The majority of Britain's population did not attend a school of any kind in the 18th century, but signs of important changes were beginning to emerge. As developments in Gloucester demonstrate, the country was gradually starting to move towards the adoption of mass education right across the social spectrum.

The Gloucester Poor's School

One of the first developments in this process was the creation of schools accessible to the very poorest in society, the great majority of whom could never have aspired to attend even a petty school, let alone one of the grammar schools. Many of these boys and girls were required to work in the iron and pin-making workshops, for which Gloucester was well known in the 18th century, and the shifts they were required to put in could be up to fourteen hours long.

The inspiration for new kinds of school came largely from the London-based Society for the Promotion of Christian Knowledge (SPCK), which had been established in 1696 to spread Christianity among the godless poor. Funded by private subscriptions raised from the better off, it encouraged as many Church of England parishes as possible to establish schools for poor children of both sexes aged between seven and twelve. These charity schools were managed by committees of subscribers, each with a corresponding secretary to keep in touch with their national co-ordinating body.[1]

---

[1]   J. Lawson & H. Silver, *A Social History of Education in England*, Methuen (1973), p. 184.

A pamphlet of 1705 issued by the SPCK, *An Account of the Methods Whereby the Charity Schools have been Erected*, defined a charity school as one 'designed for the education of poor children in the knowledge and practice of the Christian religion, as professed and taught in the Church of England'.[2] It advocated that boys from the poorer classes should be taught reading, writing and arithmetic 'to fit them for services or as apprentices'; girls should learn to read and 'generally to knot their stockings and gloves, to mark, sew, make and mend their own clothes'.

The Bishop of Gloucester, Edward Fowler, was the first senior cleric in the country to join the SPCK and under his auspices the Gloucester Charity School was established in 1702. Known as the Poor's School, it was started under the initiative of Timothy Nourse and Francis Yate, who raised public subscriptions to fund it.[3] Located in part of the old Eastgate,[4] it set out to clothe and provide a basic education for poor orphan children, teaching them reading and religious instruction based on the catechism and prayer book. Boys also learnt writing and some simple arithmetic, aiming to give them the best possible chances of eventually securing an apprenticeship, whilst girls specialised in knitting, spinning and needlework.[5] The aim behind such schools was primarily social and religious, the desire to improve the manners of the poorer classes and reduce crime through teaching the poor to accept their inferior position in life.[6] They were also designed to provide an ever-increasing number of clerks to maintain the extensive record-keeping required by the world of commerce.[7]

One of the most prolific of early SPCK corresponding secretaries anywhere in the country was Maurice Wheeler, Headmaster of King's School. For more than a decade after 1704 he proposed far-reaching ideas to promote the extension of charitable education.[8] They included designs

---

2   M. Seaborne, *The English School: its Architecture and Organisation 1370 – 1870*, Routledge & Kegan Paul (1971), p. 105.

3   G. W. Counsel, *The History and Description of the City of Gloucester*, Gloucester (1829), p. 172.

4   S. Rudder, *A New History of Gloucestershire*, Cirencester (1779), republished by Alan Sutton in 2006, p. 129.

5   H. M. Jewell, *Education in Early Modern England*, Macmillan (1998), p. 41.

6   D. W. Sylvester, *Educational Documents 800 – 1816*, Methuen (1970), p. 170.

7   J. H. Plumb, *England in the Eighteenth Century*, Pelican (1950), p. 31.

8   A. Platts and G. H. Hainton, *Education in Gloucestershire: A Short History* (1954), p. 28.

for a horn-book which would teach writing as well as reading, a simplified spelling system for biblical words, plans for an annual conference of SPCK correspondents, schemes for financing new parish schools by enclosing part of a village's common land, and a proposal that literacy should become a basic requirement for anyone moving outside the parish of their birth. Perhaps his most enduring contribution was the idea of holding an annual public service in London for those who attended charity schools.

The Poor's School at Gloucester was recorded as having sixty children in attendance in 1707 and eighty-five in 1711.[9] Alderman John Hyett, who died in 1711, left the school legacies to the value of £1,500, which enabled the schoolroom to be completely rebuilt.[10] In the years that followed, the school was further enhanced by benefactions from John Powell, William Allen and Dorothy Cocks.[11] When Abel Wantner, the innkeeper at the White Hart at Minchinhampton, wrote his manuscript *History of Gloucestershire* in 1714, the existence of the Poor's School in Gloucester was clearly a mark of great pride. He recorded the satisfaction of local clergymen who 'promoted the setting up of a charity school for the education of the poor children of the city of both sexes, the boys to read and write and the girls to spin and sew, allowing the master twenty pounds a year and the mistress ten pounds a year, which is continued with great encouragement and good success to the everlasting praise and honour of those who were and are the promoters thereof'.[12]

The expansion of charity schools, which was a marked feature of the early years of the 18th century, seems to have come to an abrupt halt in most parts of the country about 1730.[13] The school in the Eastgate was taken over by the Poor Law guardians in 1727.[14] It was then transferred to the new workhouse, which was opened in 'large and commodious' premises known as the New Bear Inn to provide 'indoor relief', setting the

9   R. Furney, 'Manuscript of the History of the City of Gloucester' (1743), Gloucestershire Record Office D327/1, p. 136.
10 W. Page, *The Victoria History of the Counties of England: Gloucestershire*, volume 2, London (1907), p. 444.
11 S. Rudder, *A New History of Gloucestershire*, p. 129.
12 J. Fendley, 'Abel Wantner and his History of the City and County of Gloucester', *Transactions of the Bristol and Gloucestershire Archaeological Society* (2010), volume 128, pp. 174–175.
13 C. P. Hill, *British Economic and Social History*, Edward Arnold (1957), p. 202.
14 N. M. Herbert, *The Victoria History of the Counties of England: Gloucestershire*, volume 4, p. 341.

destitute to work, usually on pin-making.[15] Now known as the Workhouse School, it remained in existence throughout the 18th century, employing a schoolmaster and a schoolmistress to teach reading, writing and arithmetic. In the 1740s Thomas Launder, in receipt of an annual salary of £20, was recorded as the master of this school.[16] Starved of public funds, however, the main emphasis seems to have degenerated into simply teaching pauper children the necessity to work hard and to live in the fear of God and their social superiors.[17] The education the children were given became very hit-and-miss and, as soon as they were old enough, the workhouse officials were keen to get them off their hands in order to reduce costs to the ratepayers, farming the children out to domestic service or any employer who would take them.

Under such circumstances, the fortunes of the charity school declined and by the end of the 18th century it was described as 'the mere shadow of a school existing in the workhouse, with an illiterate pauper for its master'.[18] It was not until well into the following century that a new enlarged Poor's School with accommodation for up to 200 pupils would be opened in 1813 in a building in Lower Northgate Street on the initiative of Robert Raikes's brother, the Revd Richard Raikes, and leased by him to the Poor Law guardians.[19]

The beginning of Sunday schools

A much more successful enterprise that touched the lives of a far greater number of poor children was the Sunday school movement, which was begun on an ambitious scale in Gloucester by Robert Raikes and Thomas Stock.

Robert Raikes was born in 1736 in Ladybellegate House.[20] By all accounts he grew up to become a good-looking trend-setter, cutting a dashing figure around the city, wearing the latest designs of wigs and

15 T. Rudge, *The History and Antiquities of Gloucester*, J. Wood Gloucester (1811), p. 148.
16 J. Fendley, *Bishop Benson's Survey of the Diocese of Gloucester*, The Bristol and Gloucestershire Archaeological Society (2000), p. 89.
17 L. W. Cowie, *Hanoverian England*, Bell & Hyman (1967), pp. 36–37.
18 *The Evangelical Magazine and Missionary Chronicle*, volume XI (1833), p. 48.
19 T. D. Fosbrooke, *An Original History of the City of Gloucester*, London (1819), reprinted by Alan Sutton (1986), p. 218.
20 C. Heighway, *Gloucester: A History and Guide*, Alan Sutton (1985), p. 135.

Figure 95: Oil painting of Robert Raikes by the 18th-century portrait artist George Romney (1785).

Figure 96: Memorial to Raikes in the Church of St Mary de Crypt, which he attended.

three-cornered hats that were fashionable in this period.[21] The future headmaster of King's, Arthur Benoni Evans, who knew Raikes well, was of the opinion that 'excessive vanity was a prominent feature of Mr Raikes's character'.[22] The diarist Fanny Burney wrote, following a visit to his house, that Raikes was 'somewhat too flourishing, somewhat too forward, somewhat too voluble, but he is witty, benevolent, good-natured and good-hearted'.[23] Despite his flamboyance, Raikes was also a philanthropist of great generosity, someone with a strong sense of right and wrong. Gradually he came to the conclusion that the root cause of poverty and crime lay in the fact that the majority of the 18th-century population were illiterate and lacked access to any education.

Raikes used the *Gloucester Journal,* a newspaper that had been set up by his father in 1722, as a weapon to publicise the injustices he saw, beginning with the need for prison reform that was being promoted in Gloucestershire by Sir George Onesiphorous Paul.[24] Without any education, he came to

---

[21]   P. Moss, *Historic Gloucester,* Windrush Press (1997), p. 23.
[22]   A. B. Evans, letter published in *The Gentleman's Magazine* (1831), vol 101, part 2, p. 295.
[23]   C. Aslet, *Villages of Britain,* Bloomsbury (2010), p. 344.
[24]   C. Heighway, *Gloucester: A History and Guide,* p. 139.

realise that the children of the poor would be unable to make progress in life, leaving them trapped in desperate poverty and likely to end up in prison through law-breaking.[25] In spite of the huge social gulf that separated him from the lower orders, Raikes developed a genuine sympathy for the poor children, who most people at that time referred to as street urchins or ragamuffins. Those who attended his funeral in St Mary de Crypt Church in 1811 were each given plum cake and a shilling because it is said that Raikes would not have wanted them to be sad. As a mark of respect to his memory, one of the most quoted phrases attributed to Raikes has become: 'The world marches on the feet of little children. To change the world, reach its children.'[26]

Raikes told the story of how his conscience was spurred into action by a complaint he received from a woman living in St Catherine Street in the northern suburbs of Gloucester. He explained how he had gone there in search of his gardener and came across a group of poor children acting rowdily. 'I was struck with concern', he wrote, 'at seeing a group of children, wretchedly ragged, at play in the street. I asked an inhabitant whether those children belonged to that part of the town. "Ah! Sir", said the woman to whom I was speaking, "could you take a view of this part of the town on a Sunday, you would be shocked indeed; for then the street is filled with multitudes of these wretches who, released on that day from employment, spend their time in noise and riot, playing at chuck and cursing and swearing in a manner so horrid as to convey to any serious mind an idea of hell rather than any other place".'[27]

From experiences such as this Raikes realised the potential that Sunday schools could provide. Sunday was the one day in the week when poor children might be able to receive an education as they were not required in the factory workshops. Raikes corresponded with people who had already set up small-scale Sunday schools elsewhere, such as John Moffatt, who had opened a school in Nailsworth in 1772, and William King, a clothier who had established a school at Dursley Tabernacle in 1778.[28] He also visited a Sunday school in Sheepscombe that met in the house of a weaver named

---

25   F. Booth, *Robert Raikes of Gloucester*, Redhill (1980), p. 65.
26   E. L. Towns & V. M. Whaley, *Worship through the Ages*, Tennessee (2012), p. 162.
27   R. Raikes, letter to Richard Townley of Sheffield published in the *Manchester Mercury*, 6th January 1784.
28   J. H. Harris, *Robert Raikes: The Man and His Work*, Bristol (1899), p. 59.

Figure 97: Raikes's statue in Gloucester Park, a replica of one on the Thames Embankment in London.

John Twining.[29] The most influential person in shaping his ideas, however, was Thomas Stock, the highly regarded headmaster of King's School and curate of St John's, Northgate. Stock had already been responsible for a Sunday school in the chancel of his previous church, St Mary the Virgin in Ashbury (Oxfordshire), where his venture was so successful that it had to move into a nearby cottage.[30] Stock was a good influence on Raikes and made a hugely important contribution to the development of the new Sunday schools. In the view of Raikes's modern biographer, Stock had 'a more intimate knowledge of the parish and the needs of his parishioners than Raikes. He had a considerable degree of sympathy for the poor, which was reflected in their regard for him. Stock also had scholarship, teaching experience and a knowledge of children, teachers and school organisation, which must have proved invaluable.'[31]

Between 1780 and 1782 a whole network of Sunday schools came into being in Gloucester sponsored by Raikes and Stock acting in partnership. A heated controversy raged among Victorian historians about the respective credit that should be given to these two men, but it is likely that Stock provided the teaching expertise, while Raikes supplied the publicity

---

[29] J. Stratford, *Robert Raikes and Others: Founders of Sunday Schools*, London (1880), pp. 64–67.

[30] A. Morgan, *Reverend Thomas Stock: Man of Shadows*, St John's Northgate pamphlet (2015), p. 3.

[31] F. Booth, *Robert Raikes of Gloucester*, pp. 78–79.

through his newspaper.[32] Both men shared the financial outlay. Reacting against a growing tendency to emphasise the role of Raikes alone, a letter written in 1831 by Arthur Benoni Evans sought to set the record straight: 'All the senior inhabitants of Gloucester, of whom I am one, know the contrary to be the fact and I can produce to you several names of contemporary persons still living to confirm what I say. We, the contemporaries, know that the Rev Thomas Stock had an equal share in the establishment of those schools in Gloucester; nay, more than an equal share, for it was he that arranged the plan of the schools, drew up the rules for their management and had the sole superintendence of the three first schools of this kind'.[33]

Gloucester's first Sunday schools

The first of the Gloucester Sunday schools, and one of the first anywhere in the country to be formally referred to as a Sunday school, was opened in July 1780 in St Catherine Street in a cottage belonging to James King, who was steward to John Pitt, the City's MP.[34] It is said that over ninety boys were taught in this first school, the principal teacher being Mrs King. Her salary of 1s 6d per Sunday was funded jointly by Raikes and Stock.[35] Mrs King unfortunately died after three years in the role, but her husband carried on her work for several more years.[36] Despite being one of Gloucester's important historic sites, the cottage was regrettably demolished during the modernisation programme of the 1950s.

A significant number of other schools were established across the city in the months that followed. These were smaller than the original school in St Catherine Street, with classes of twenty being the norm, but the list is both long and impressive. They all took in children aged between five and fourteen, attending both in the morning and in the afternoon, when they were taken to church.[37] The first Sunday school for girls was also in St

---

[32] J. N. Langston, 'Headmasters and Ushers of the King's (College) School, Gloucester', *Records of Gloucester Cathedral*, volume III, H. Osborne Gloucester (1928), p. 232.

[33] A. B. Evans, letter published in *The Gentleman's Magazine* (1831), vol 101, part 2, p. 294.

[34] D. Kirby, *The Gloucester Story*, Sutton (2007), p. 105.

[35] P. Moss, *Historic Gloucester*, p. 24.

[36] T. B. Walters, *Robert Raikes: Founder of Sunday Schools*, London (1930), p. 46.

[37] N. M. Herbert, *The Victoria History of the Counties of England: Gloucestershire*, volume 4, p. 339.

Figure 98: Gloucester's first Sunday school for boys in James King's cottage in St Catherine Street, established in 1780 and demolished in 1957.

Catherine Street, on the corner with Park Street. Mrs Roberts was the mistress of a Sunday school that met in premises behind Number 103 Northgate Street and Mrs Brabant taught in a similar school nearby in the Oxbode.[38] A Mr and Mrs Bretherton were employed to keep another Sunday school in Hare Lane. There was a school in St Aldate's Square in the home of Mr Trickey, the sexton of St Aldate's Church.[39] Another Sunday school was established at Pye Corner at the bottom of Southgate Street at its junction with Commercial Road. This was the work of a well-known

---

[38]   F. Booth, *Robert Raikes of Gloucester*, p. 79.
[39]   A. Morgan, *Reverend Thomas Stock: Man of Shadows*, p. 5.

Figure 99: The house on the corner of Park Street and St Catherine Street used as the first Sunday school for girls (also now demolished).

Methodist lady, Sophia Cooke, who was a personal friend of John Wesley, and there she taught children who worked in her uncle's pin factory.[40] Immediately opposite the south porch of his parish church at St Mary de Crypt Raikes had yet another Sunday school, which met on the corner of Greyfriars and Southgate Street in the house of Mrs Sarah Critchley, who had previous experience in running a petty school.[41] Initially, this school was a mixed one, but eventually Mrs Critchley taught only the girls, leaving her husband to take charge of the boys. Other Sunday schools that have been located in the early 1780s included one in a house in Archdeacon Street, then known as Leather Bottle Lane, and another run by a Mrs Meredith for the children of the chimney sweeps of Sooty Alley, a very poor area opposite the city prison.[42]

---

[40]   J. Stratford, *Robert Raikes and Others: Founders of Sunday Schools*, p. 67.
[41]   Ibid, p. 99.
[42]   F. Booth, *Robert Raikes of Gloucester*, p. 80.

Today, we tend to think of a Sunday school as something happening for an hour or so to occupy a few young children while their parents attend a church service. The Sunday schools that Raikes and Stock created were much more serious affairs. They took in children across the full age range and taught reading and spelling. Writing and arithmetic were not included as Raikes realised that the cost of the materials and apparatus required would be beyond practical limits; he also believed that through reading all other skills could be acquired later in life.[43] Lessons took place for most of the day and Raikes's own description of the regime was as follows: 'The children were to come after ten in the morning and stay to twelve; they were then to go home and return at once; and, after reading a lesson, they were to be conducted to church. After church, they were to be employed in repeating the catechism till after five, and then dismissed with an injunction to go home without making a noise.'[44] Discipline was strict and stern in the schools. Punishments were meted out for bad behaviour, especially telling lies. Rewards were also used as an incentive to learning and good appearance. Those who made the greatest progress received slices of plum cake provided by Anne Raikes, Robert's wife.

A good impression of how the Sunday school in Hare Lane operated under Mrs Bretherton comes in an interview given by Priscilla Kirby, who was a pupil there in the 1790s: 'The children used to go to school at ten o'clock on a Sunday morning. We used to go to school in the church in the afternoon, and after service in the afternoon Mr Stock used to come to us. He used to explain the Scriptures to us. We used to learn reading, Catechisms and Answers, Mann's Catechism and Lewis's, I think.'[45] Miss Kirby eventually became the mistress of the Hare Lane school herself, acknowledging her debt to Thomas Stock. 'Mr Stock was a great disciplinarian', she said. 'I profited very much under him. He did me good. He gave me kind instruction and sound advice.'[46]

Another description of Sunday school life was recorded by Esther Summerell, who attended the school on the corner of Greyfriars and Southgate Street. Looking back in her old age in the 1880s, she said: 'We

---

[43]   *Gloucester Citizen Supplement*, 2nd June 1980, p. iv.
[44]   R. Raikes, letter quoted in *The Christian Observer: The Year 1841*, London (1841), volume 40, p. 353.
[45]   J. H. Harris, *Robert Raikes: the Man and his Work*, pp. 26–27.
[46]   F. Booth, *Robert Raikes of Gloucester*, p. 86.

went to school at nine o'clock every Sunday morning. About fifty boys and fifty girls attended. Our bonnets and tippets were taken off when we went to school and others of white linen were given us. We had to wear those till the afternoon so that we were obliged to come to afternoon school to get back our own. After school we were taken to church, which was over about 12.30; we went to church again at three and after church had school till six'.[47] She also recalled the prominent role taken by Raikes himself: 'I remember Mr Raikes quite plainly. The children of the school attended the services at Crypt church. Mr Raikes used to come to us in the chancel after service and hear us repeat the collect for the day. To those who said it best he gave a penny, which I was never able to gain. I think Mr Raikes noticed the boys rather more than he did the girls'.[48]

The impact of Sunday schools

The principal aim of Raikes and Stock was one of philanthropy. Through the education they provided, they hoped to raise the life chances of the very poorest, teaching them the moral principles of their day and the practical skills of reading and writing. One historian has summed up their motives as follows: they 'saw the schools as a way to give poor children or children from immoral homes what middle class and wealthy children were obtaining from their home or school life. They did not see Sunday Schools in terms of social control, but of religious revival'.[49]

Raikes urged the children attending his schools: 'If you have no clean shirt, come in that you have on; if you can loiter about without shoes and in a ragged coat, you may as well come to school and learn what may tend to your good in that garb'.[50] Other contemporary reports confirm that the most neglected of children could be found among his scholars. Caroline Watkins, granddaughter of Mrs Critchley, said of Raikes's school in Southgate Street that 'the children who were brought there were the very lowest kind that could be found'.[51] William Brick, who had attended the Southgate Street school in 1807, stated many years later that 'some terrible

---

47   *Gloucester Journal*, 3rd July 1880.
48   J. Stratford, *Robert Raikes and Others: Founders of Sunday Schools*, p. 182.
49   R. O'Day, *Education and Society 1500 – 1800*, Longman (1982), p. 256.
50   R. Raikes, letter published in *The Belfast Monthly Magazine* (1811), volume VII, p. 461.
51   J. H. Harris, *Robert Raikes: the Man and his Work*, p. 22.

chaps went to the school when I first went and there were always bad 'uns coming in.'[52] Another former pupil by the name of Bourne remembered an incident that took place in 1800. 'In the first Sunday School I went to a boy called Winkin' Jim brought a young badger with him and turned it loose. You should have seen old Mother Critchley jump!'[53]

A eulogy on the Sunday school movement published in 1788 underlined the important social role that these first schools were thought to provide. It recalled that the children who attended the Sunday schools used to meet Raikes at the Cathedral at the end of the early morning service. They were attracted by 'the gentleness of his behaviour towards them, the allowance they found him disposed to make for their former misbehaviour, which was merely from a want of better information, and the amiable picture which he drew for them when he represented kindness and benevolence to each other as the source of real happiness. The interest which they soon discovered him to have in their welfare, which appeared in his minute enquiries into their conduct, their attainment, their situation and every particular of their lives, all these circumstances soon induced them to fly with eagerness to receive the commands and be edified by the instruction of their best friend'.[54]

Not everyone, however, initially approved of the Sunday school venture and the schools were sometimes derisively referred to as 'Ragged Schools'. Critics argued that the schools were a desecration of the Sabbath as Christians should not be made to work on a Sunday; others believed that they would weaken home-based religious education. Some prominent church leaders, among them Samuel Horsley, the Bishop of Rochester, feared that the Sunday schools might be infiltrated by radical politicians keen to incite the poor to read their revolutionary tracts.[55]

Such fears were quickly allayed as from the very start the philanthropy of Raikes and Stock was tempered by their conservative and authoritarian instincts. Whatever sympathy they felt for the poor, they were also keen supporters of law and order. Those who attended Sunday schools were taught to obey their social superiors and to fit in with the expectations of society. Raikes recalled that his interest in Sunday schools had originated as

---

[52]   Ibid, p. 38.
[53]   Ibid, p. 40.
[54]   *The Gentleman's Friend*, London (1788), volume 58, part 1, p. 14.
[55]   N. Aston, *Christianity and Revolutionary Europe*, Cambridge (2002), p. 249.

Figure 100: Cox's Court in Hare Lane, demolished under a slum clearance scheme in 1933, but typical of the crowded alleyways of 18th-century Gloucester.

a result of 'a complaint which he had heard from a person respecting the disorderly behaviour of poor children on the Lord's Day'.[56] In publicising the virtues of his schools, he was keen to promote the effect they had on public law and order as well as on private morality. In a letter of 1786 he reflected that 'it occurred to me that an attempt to divert the attention of the vulgar from their formal brutal prostitution of the Lord's Day, by exhibiting to their view a striking picture of the superior enjoyment to be derived from quietness, good order and the exercise of that benevolence which Christianity particularly recommends, was an experiment worth hazarding. It was immediately determined to invite the gentlemen and people of the adjacent parishes to view the children of the Sunday Schools to mark their improvement in cleanliness and behaviour and to observe the practicability of reducing to a quiet peaceable demeanour the most neglected part of the community'.[57]

---

[56] J. Nichols, *Literary Anecdotes of the Eighteenth Century*, London (1815), volume 9, p. 540.
[57] R. Raikes in a letter of 7 October 1786 published in J. Nichols, *Literary Anecdotes of the Eighteenth Century*, London (1815), volume 9, p. 541.

In the *Gloucester Journal* Raikes wrote in 1784: 'The good effects of the Sunday Schools established in this city are instanced in the account given by the principal persons in the pin and sack manufactories. Great reformation has taken place among the multitudes whom they employ. From being idle, ungovernable, profligate and filthy in the extreme, they say the boys and girls are become not only more clean and decent in their appearance, but are greatly humanised in their manners, more orderly, tractable and attentive to business, and of course more serviceable than they ever expected to find them.'[58] The Gloucester magistrates responded at the Easter Quarter Session of 1788 by passing a unanimous vote to the effect that 'the benefit of Sunday Schools to the morals of the rising generation is too evident not to merit the recognition of this Bench and the thanks of the community to the gentlemen instrumental in providing them.'[59] It is for this reason that some modern historians have regarded Raikes's work with great suspicion, viewing the Sunday schools as essentially repressive organisations designed to persuade the lower orders meekly to accept their earthly lot.

'The growth of Sunday Schools throughout the kingdom', wrote one 20th-century historian, 'was a phenomenon in the history of education which is without parallel.'[60] Its success relied heavily on the publicity Raikes gave to his schools in Gloucester and the way it reached far and wide. His newspaper, the *Gloucester Journal*, was used to create a national Sunday school movement with many of the articles he wrote being reprinted in the London newspapers.[61] John Wesley spoke of the impact of the movement in 1784 when he remarked: 'I find these schools springing up wherever I go.'[62] Raikes received many visitors and in 1787 was invited to Windsor to tell Queen Charlotte about his work.[63]

Within Gloucester, Sunday schools became commonplace. The antiquarian George Counsel commented in 1829 that 'every parish in this city has its Sunday School; indeed they are now generally adopted

---

[58] *Gloucester Journal*, 24th May 1784.
[59] *Gloucester Journal*, 4th February 1788.
[60] F. Smith, *A History of English Elementary Education*, London (1931), p. 65.
[61] N. M. Herbert, *The Victoria History of the Counties of England: Gloucestershire*, volume 4, p. 157.
[62] *The Works of the Rev John Wesley*, London (1829), volume 4, p. 284.
[63] *The British Magazine and Monthly Register of Religious and Ecclesiastical Information*, London (1833), volume 13, p. 222.

throughout the kingdom, and Gloucester has the honour of having originated the design, the beneficial effects of which are evidently seen in the morals of the rising generation.'[64] Those who pioneered even more ambitious schemes for church-based elementary education right across the country in the early years of the 19th century were able to draw on the experiment initiated in Gloucester by Raikes and Stock. Thanks to their efforts, Gloucester and the whole country were now on the brink of the great expansion of elementary education that was to come.

---

[64] G. W. Counsel, *The History and Description of the City of Gloucester*, Gloucester (1829), p. 180.

The Dawn of the Modern Age

As the 19th century dawned, it was still true that the modern system of high-quality state-funded education for all, which nowadays we take for granted, remained some years in the future. Things were, however, beginning to develop quite rapidly as within thirty years church-based elementary schooling backed by grants of government money would widen access to a much larger extent than ever before. This makes the year 1800 a watershed of sorts, after which a whole new epoch opens in the history of education.

The Sunday school movement, which originated in Gloucester, led directly to the founding of two voluntary religious bodies that pioneered the way forward towards this new era of mass education. Joseph Lancaster, who in 1808 founded the first of these, the Nonconformist-led British and Foreign School Society, travelled to Gloucester to meet Robert Raikes and see his Sunday schools in action. The other rival body was the Church of England's National Society founded three years later by Andrew Bell. These two organisations drew on church funds and locally raised subscriptions, but crucially from 1833 they also became eligible for lucrative grants from central government coffers. It was under the aegis of these two societies that the number of church schools catering for those of poor and modest backgrounds began to multiply, gradually making a reality of the vision of a national system of elementary education.

In Gloucester it was the National Society that took the lead, establishing a network of its schools in the city's suburbs in the earlier half of the 19th century. The first of these catered for 300 boys and girls and was opened in 1817 in London Road, just beyond where St Peter's Church now stands. Its foundation stone was laid the previous year by none other than the Duke of Wellington. Over the next three decades another seven National Schools followed in various parts of the city, providing the origins for many of the primary schools we have today. Employing the monitorial system, by which the oldest pupils were used to teach lessons to the youngest, these schools were able to provide a cost-effective and sustainable approach to mass education.

It is for this reason that this study of Gloucester's ancient schools reaches its terminal point in 1800. From this moment on, a new era was clearly in progress, which promised to extend schooling far beyond the male-dominated elite who had been educated in previous centuries. That said, all three of the 'ancient schools of Gloucester' that were in existence in 1800 continued throughout the 19th century, although with varying fortunes. All three have gone on not only to survive but to flourish in the 20th and early 21st centuries; and all three now open their doors to girls as well as boys.

The Crypt remained a small school in the first half of the 19th century and, after closing for four years between 1857 and 1861, moved to new premises first in Barton Street and then in Friars Orchard. The school's modern trajectory began in the 1880s when a new scheme of the Board of Education brought it under the aegis of the governors of the Gloucester United Endowed Schools. In 1943 the Crypt finally moved to another new site at Podsmead on the outskirts of the city, where it remains to this day on land originally bought by Dame Joan Cooke at the time of the school's foundation in 1539.

The Bluecoat Hospital School benefited from an extensive rebuild on its original location in Eastgate Street in 1807. In the years that followed the scope of its curriculum gradually broadened beyond the apprenticeship training instituted by its founder in the 1660s. The school transformed itself into a grammar school in 1882, when it joined the Gloucester United Endowed Schools scheme and in the same decade moved to the premises in Barton Street that had been used briefly by the Crypt. A new site was established for the modern Sir Thomas Rich's School in Elmbridge in 1964.

Of the three schools, only King's has remained close to its original site nestling beneath Gloucester Cathedral, just like the medieval schools of St Peter's Abbey that preceded it. King's flourished for much of the 19th century, but went into a steep decline from the 1870s during which its education focused almost exclusively on the needs of the Cathedral choristers. The school was spectacularly rescued in the 1950s and gradually strengthened in the decades that followed to provide an important independent voice to add to the educational mix in the city.

A thousand years ago, the Benedictine monks of St Peter's Abbey and the Augustinian canons of St Oswald's and Llanthony Priories vied for control over the education of a small number of privileged boys in our city. Little could they have envisaged how their efforts, piecemeal though they seem to us, would eventually blossom into the rich and varied provision that is available to the youngsters of today.

The Schools of Gloucester prior to 1800

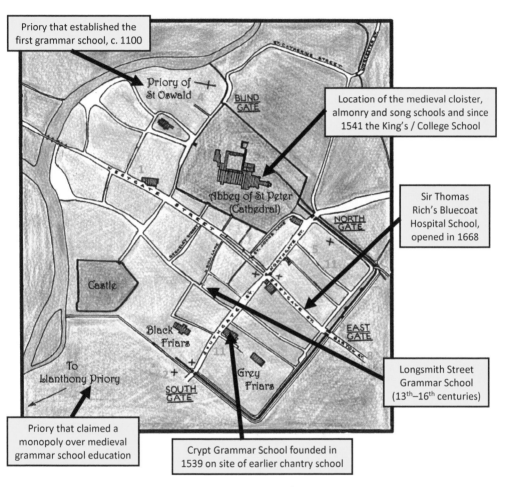

Priory that established the first grammar school, c. 1100

Location of the medieval cloister, almonry and song schools and since 1541 the King's / College School

Sir Thomas Rich's Bluecoat Hospital School, opened in 1668

Longsmith Street Grammar School (13th–16th centuries)

Priory that claimed a monopoly over medieval grammar school education

Crypt Grammar School founded in 1539 on site of earlier chantry school

Priory of St Oswald

BLIND GATE

Abbey of St Peter (Cathedral)

NORTH GATE

Castle

Black Friars

To Llanthony Priory

Grey Friars

SOUTH GATE

EAST GATE

Key to Numbers

1 Charity School of St Nicholas, 1446
2 St Owen's Petty School, 1580s
3 Thomas Rudge's Bookkeeping School in St Mary's Square, 1748
4 Priory House Private School, 1791
5 John Cooke's Private School in the Oxbode, 1779
6 Mrs Mutlow's Girls' School in Lower Northgate, 1780

7 Mrs Counsel's Private School for Girls in College Green, 1743
8 Barton Street Dissenting Academy, 1696
9 Gloucester Poor's School, 1702
10 First two Sunday schools, 1780
11 Other Sunday schools, 1780s

Select Bibliography

The most informative works which devote some detail to the history of education in the Gloucester area are:

N. M. Herbert, *The Victoria History of the Counties of England: Gloucestershire*, volume 4, London (1988)

N. Orme, *Education in the West of England, 1066 – 1548*, University of Exeter (1976)

N. Orme, 'Education in Medieval Bristol and Gloucestershire', *Transactions of the Bristol and Gloucestershire Archaeological Society*, volume 112 (2004)

W. Page, *The Victoria History of the Counties of England: Gloucestershire*, volume 2, London (1907)

A. C. Percival, 'Gloucestershire Grammar Schools from the 16th to the 19th Centuries', *Transactions of the Bristol and Gloucestershire Archaeological Society* (1970), volume 89

A. Platts and G. H. Hainton, *Education in Gloucestershire: A Short History*, Gloucestershire County Council (1953).

For the history of specific schools, the following are substantive and essential texts:

R. Austin, *The Crypt School Gloucester*, John Bellows Gloucester (1939)

F. Booth, *Robert Raikes of Gloucester*, Redhill (1980)

F. Hannam-Clark, *Memories of the College School*, Packer Gloucester (1890)

J. N. Langston, 'Headmasters and Ushers of the King's (College) School, Gloucester', *Records of Gloucester Cathedral*, volume III, H. Osborne Gloucester (1928)

C. Lepper, *The Crypt School Gloucester*, Alan Sutton (1989)

D. Robertson, *The King's School Gloucester*, Phillimore (1974)

D. J. Watkins, T*he History of Sir Thomas Rich's School*, Gloucester (1966)

J. R. S. Whiting, *The King's School Gloucester*, Orchard & Ind (1990).

Also of importance are a number of general Gloucester histories written by antiquarians of the past. These include:

G. W. Counsel, The *History and Description of the City of Gloucester*, Gloucester (1829)

T. D. Fosbrooke, *An Original History of the City of Gloucester*, London (1819) republished by Alan Sutton in 1986

S. Rudder, *A New History of Gloucestershire*, Cirencester (1779), republished by Alan Sutton in 2006

T. Rudge, *The History and Antiquities of Glouceste*r, J. Wood Gloucester (1811).

More modern histories covering aspects of the City's past and containing references to schools amongst other topics are:

S. M. Eward, *No Fine But A Glass of Wine: Cathedral Life at Gloucester in Stuart Times*, Lymington (1985)

S. M. Eward, *Gloucester Cathedral Chapter Act Book 1616 – 1687*, The Bristol and Gloucestershire Archaeological Society Record Series, volume 21 (2007)

C. Heighway, S. Hamilton et alii, *Gloucester Cathedral: Faith, Art and Architecture*, Scala (2011)

C. Heighway, *Gloucester: A History and Guide*, Alan Sutton (1985)

F. A. Hyett, *Gloucester in National History*, John Bellows Gloucester (1906)

J. Johnson, *Tudor Gloucestershire*, Alan Sutton (1985)

B. Lowe, *Commonwealth and the English Reformation: Protestantism and the Politics of Religious Change in the Gloucester Vale*, Routledge (2010)

P. Moss, *Historic Glouceste*r, Windrush Press (1993)

G. Waters, *King Richard's Gloucester: Life in a Mediaeval Town*, Alan Sutton (1983)

D. Welander, *The History, Art and Architecture of Gloucester Cathedral*, Alan Sutton (1991).

For setting our schools in their national context, the following are invaluable summaries:

K. Charlton, *Education in Renaissance England*, Routledge & Kegan Paul (1965)

C. Dainton, 'Medieval Schools of England' in *History Today*, volume XXIX (1979)

J. Lawson, *Medieval Education and the Reformation*, Routledge & Kegan Paul (1967)

J. Lawson & H. Silver, *A Social History of Education in England*, Methuen (1973)

A. F. Leach, *The Schools of Medieval England*, Methuen (1915)

A. F. Leach, *Educational Charters and Documents*, Cambridge (1911)

H. M. Jewell, *Education in Early Modern England*, Macmillan (1998)

N. Orme, *Medieval Schools from Roman Britain to Renaissance England*, Yale University Press (2006)

M. Seaborne, *The English School: its Architecture and Organisation 1370 – 1870*, Routledge & Kegan Paul (1971)

J. Simon, *Education and Society in Tudor England*, Cambridge University Press (1966)

D. W. Sylvester, *Educational Documents, 800 – 1816*, Methuen (1970)

W. A. L. Vincent, *The Grammar Schools: Their Continuing Tradition, 1660 – 1714*, John Murray (1969)

F. Watson, *The English Grammar Schools to 1660*, Cambridge (1908).

Photographs and Figures

The majority of the photographs of buildings and monuments featured in this book were taken by the author himself. Thanks are also due to the following for the figures specified: Richard Auckland for figures 21 and 47; Peter Cresswell for figure 31; Jessica Gordon for figure 28; Lyndon Hills for figures 10 and 58; Kevin Lewis for figures 38 and 50; Rebecca Phillips for figure 57; and Robert and Joan Tucker for figure 70. Figures 33, 36 and 52 were taken by Phil Boorman for Purcell Architects.

A large number of the photographs relating to buildings and monuments are reproduced with permission from the Chapter of Gloucester Cathedral; these are figures 3, 4, 5, 7, 9, 10, 13, 19, 20, 21, 23, 24, 26, 34, 38, 43, 44, 47, 50, 58, 59, 70 and 94. Figures 28, 29, 33, 36, 37, 52, 54 and 83 are incorporated with the permission of Discover DeCrypt. Figures 39, 41 and 49 are included with the approval of the King's School and figure 31 with the approval of the Crypt School. Permission to use figures 2, 16 and 97 has been granted by Gloucester City Council. Thanks are also due to the Rectors of Headbourne Worthy and Wappenham for permission to use figures 22 and 74 and to the Master, Fellows and Scholars of Pembroke College, Oxford, for figure 61.

The originals of many of the documents featured can be seen in the Library at Gloucester Cathedral; the use of figures 1, 40, 42, 48, 57, 60, 65, 66, 67, 69, 72, 73, 76, 84, 86 and 92 has been authorised by the Cathedral Archivist with permission from the Chapter of Gloucester Cathedral. Thanks are due to Gloucestershire Archives for permission to reproduce figure 30 (reference GBR/J5/1), figure 32 (reference D3270/4), figure 35 (reference Clifford/28) and figure 100 (reference GBR/L12/acc.3258). The use of figures 55, 77, 78, 82, 85, 88 and 95 has been authorised from the National Portrait Gallery collections. Figures 6 and 25 are included with permission from the British Library in London. The artist responsible for figure 56 is Wayne Laughlin, who shared it with the author as part of the 1993 commemorations of the Siege of Gloucester.

Other figures have been included on the understanding that they are in the public domain, originating well before the 20th century and created by individuals who have been deceased for at least 70 years. Permission to use figure 64 has specifically been granted by the Bridgeman Art Library and to use figure 68 by the Harry Ransom Center, University of Texas at Austin. Figures 14, 15, 27, 63, 71, 79 and 89 have been taken from Ancestry Figures (antiqueprints.com). Figures 8, 62, 80, 81 and 87 have been placed in the public domain by Wikipedia. Figures 18, 45 and 46 are derived from Pinterest, figure 11 from Robert Freidus (Victorianweb.org), figure 12 from Picryl and figure 17 from Research Gate (researchgate.net).

The author wishes to express his gratitude for each of the above individuals and organisations that have so generously supported the ability to create this book.

Index of People, Places and Topics

About the Author

David Evans, a Cambridge-educated historian, spent most of his teaching career at the King's School in Gloucester, where he was Deputy Head for many years. He is currently a trustee at Discover DeCrypt, the charity that administers the original Crypt schoolroom, and he has family connections with Sir Thomas Rich's School. David has been involved with Gloucester's Heritage Open Days for more than a decade and is a Cathedral guide.

The front cover illustration features the Bluecoat Boys of Sir Thomas Rich's Hospital School and the illustration on the rear cover the pupils of the King's School at play outside Gloucester Cathedral (both by 19th century local artists).

Lightning Source UK Ltd.
Milton Keynes UK
UKHW020250181122
412368UK00001B/5